«Without a vision, the people perish» (Proverbs 29:18)

Reflections on Latin American Ecofeminist Theology

Mary Judith Ress

The Con-spirando Collective
Santiago, Chile
2003

**Without a vision, the people perish
Reflections on Latin American Ecofeminist Theology
Mary Judith Ress**

Copyright 2003 by Mary Judith Ress

Published by:
Sociedad Con-spirando, Ltda.
Casilla 371-11, Correo Nuñoa
Santiago, Chile
Fono/fax: (562) 222-3001
E-Mail: conspira@emol.com
Web Page: www.conspirando.cl

All rights reserved.

Members of the Con-spirando Collective:
  Elena Aguila
  Andrea Gálvez
  Josefina Hurtado
  Mary Judith Ress
  Ute Seibert
  Luz María Villarroel

Photo: Claire Fulcher

Graphic design and layout:
  Ariel Corbalán

Printing: Art

**Santiago de Chile
Mayo, 2003**

*People do not change
because of intellectual convictions
or ethical inclinations,
but rather through transformed imaginations.*

In memory of Madonna Kolbenschlag
(1935-2000)

Table of Contents

Chapter I: The Context: Reflecting on Experience   9

   Introduction 9
   Latin American feminist theology: Three stages 14
   Elsa Tamez' schema 15
   Ivone Gebara's schema 20
   My own journey 25
        First stage: 1970s 29
        Second stage: 1980s 34
        Third stage: 1990s to the present 36
   Current status of liberation theology 38
   Third Stage feminist and ecofeminist critique 45

Chapter II: Ecofeminism: A genealogy   53

   Introduction 53
   Sources of Ecofeminism (Chart) 55
   Ancient wisdom traditions 56
   Activist women's role 58

   I. Deep Ecology   **60**
        The New Science 65
        Cybernetics 70
        The New Cosmology 74
        Indigenous Cosmology 84
        Economic sustainability/bioregionalism 89

   II. Radical/Cultural Feminism **91**
        Stages in the development of patriarchy: 96
            Paleolithic or Hunter-Gatherer Stage 96
            Neolithic Revolution: The Age of Agriculture 97
            Classical Civilizations 99
            Modern Period 99
        Feminist anthropology: Goddess images 100
        Jungian psychology 107
        Body as Source of Wisdom 116
        Attempts at forming post-patriarchal communities 121

Chapter III: Ecofeminist Theology — 135

    Latin American ecofeminist theology 145
        Ivone Gebara 145
            Con-spirando's Ecofeminist contribution to ecofeminism 158
                Unmasking theological violence toward women 161
                Renaming and celebrating the Sacred 162
                Embodied theology 165
                Ecofeminist perspective 166

Chapter IV: Charting the change: 12 women's reflections — 179

    Summary of the interviews — 182
        Definition of the human: who am I at this juncture of my history 191
        Images/names to describe Ultimate Mystery 199
        Beliefs about death and afterlife 207
        Ethics and ethical practices 214
        Spiritual practice/discipline that nourish belief 223
        Understanding of Jesus 228
        Reflections on liberation theology 232
        Commitment to ecofeminism 235
    Summary of Workshop 242
        Impact of the interviews on those interviewed 243

Chapter V: Clues for Transformation: — 253
Reflections, Conclusions and Challenges for the Future

    Shifting anthropology 254
    Shifting cosmology 256
    Shifting epistemology 260
    Ethical implications 262
    Emerging spiritual practice 264
    Relationship with liberation theology 267
    Challenges to ministry 268
    Surprise without end 271

Bibliography 277

The spiritual quest meets us at the borders of our soul, in our encounters and experiences, in the struggles and surprises within and without.
–Madonna Kolbenschlag[1]

Chapter I

The Context: Reflecting on experience

Introduction

Like many of my fellow humans, I have searched for relevant images of the godhead all my life in order to guide my way of being and acting in the world. And at each stage, I have found images that satisfied me—for a time at least, until I was prodded to seek out more authentic images that reflected both a new stage of personal growth and a changing historical landscape.

While feminist theology over the years has provided me with the analytical tools to "suspect" the patriarchal underpinnings of our god images, it has not yet satisfactorily offered me more authentic images of Ultimate Mystery that incorporate the insights coming from the scientific discoveries of this post-Einsteinian era. Yet we humans need **constructs of meaning** upon which to build our lives and nurture our spirits. "Without a vision, the people perish" (Proverbs, 29: 18). This becomes urgent in my own case: as I head into the later years of my life, I want images that makes sense to me—and not only make sense, but that urge me, like Miriam of old, to lead the people in song and dance in praise and thanksgiving for the marvels that come with conscious awareness, or in Carl

Sagan's words, to celebrate "the local embodiment of a Cosmos grown to self-awareness."[3]

As each day passes, I become more convinced that humanity is "groaning" for a new definition of ourselves that perceives us as part of the Earth community, rather than somehow apart from it. This is a major conviction of ecofeminism, as I will attempt to illustrate. While I am a North American and still claim the United States as "home," since 1990 I have been deeply involved in the development of Latin American ecofeminist thought and its theological, ethical and spiritual perspectives as a founding member of the Con-spirando Collective, a team of women working in the areas of ecofeminist theology and spirituality in Santiago, Chile. As a passionate ecofeminist, my hunch is that there is a growing awareness that an emerging ecofeminist worldview can offer us, at this juncture in our history, a new cosmovisión, a workable utopia with which to meet the future. It was with that hunch in mind that I designed this research, which was part of my dissertation work for my doctorate in feminist theology. The doctoral program, in which I had the privilege to study, was designed specifically for Third World women by noted US feminist theologian, Dr. Letty Russell. Entitled "Feminist theologies in context," Dr. Russell has been nurturing a whole generation of new feminist theologians from Africa, Asia and Latin America through this innovative program which takes her students to a Third World country during every three-year cycle, while at the same time allowing us to study "in context" in our own countries.

I also want to gratefully acknowledge the guidance of Dr. Ivone Gebara, Latin America's foremost ecofeminist theologian. Dr. Gebara was my dissertation advisor and is also a friend and mentor. Much of this work reflects her influence on my thought and practice.

My "hunch," which developed into a working hypothesis, as I conceived it in July, 2000 was:

> In Latin America during the 1990s, a growing number of activist, faith-based women who had historically aligned themselves

with liberation theology and its practice are now describing themselves as "ecofeminist". This is evident in the way they perceive themselves in relation to the rest of the Earth community and to the Universe as a whole; in the way they are re-imaging/re-naming Ultimate Mystery; in their beliefs about death and rebirth; and in their spiritual and ethical practice. On the whole, the region's liberation theologians are not acknowledging this shift. I propose to document the process that is bringing about this change by interviewing—in depth—a representative sample of women throughout Latin America who now call themselves ecofeminist. I will then publish these interviews with the hope of engaging liberation theology and ecofeminist theology, as they have arisen in context, in a new dialogue.

I hope to show, on the one hand, why liberation theology and its practice is no longer as appealing to faith-based women activists as it once was during the 1970s and 1980s and, on the other hand, demonstrate why these same women are frequently attracted to ecofeminist theology and spirituality. This shift, for the most part unnoticed or ignored by progressive Latin American male theologians, must be documented and then (hopefully) dialogically engaged among both women and men.

To test this hunch, I set three objectives for myself. First, I conducted in-depth interviews with 12 women who have been active in the liberation theology movements in Latin America. All 12 are currently working in feminist theology. They are: Agamedilza Sales de Oliveira (Brazil), Marcia Moya (Ecuador), Coca Trillini (Argentina), Sandra Duarte (Brazil), Fanny Geymonat-Pantelís (Bolivia), Sandra Raquew (Brazil), Graciela Pujol (Uruguay), Alcira Agreda (Bolivia), Clara Luz Ajo (Cuba), Doris Muñoz (Chile), Gladys Parentelli (Venezuela) and Silvia Regina de Lima (Costa Rica). My goal was to elicit from them their theological/spiritual journey toward ecofeminism. These interviews attempted to focus on the evolution in their worldview: their understanding of themselves, of Ultimate Mystery, and of their spiritual and ethical practices.

Second, I brought these women together for a 4-day workshop in Santiago, Chile in April 2002 so that together they could draw conclusions from their histories and raise questions/set directions for Latin

American ecofeminist theology as well as challenge liberation theologians to incorporate these insights into their thought.

Third, I published these interviews (which included more "right-brain" contributions from each woman, such as poetry, photographs, drawings and in some cases excerpts from their own research; an Introduction by myself contextualizing the interviews and a Prologue by Ivone Gebara describing the workshop in Santiago and its significance for the evolution of eco/feminist thought here in Latin America). The book's title, in Spanish, is *Lluvia para florecer: Entrevistas sobre el ecofeminismo en América Latina* (Santiago, Chile: Colectivo Con-spirando, Julio, 2002).

With regard to the parameters of these reflections, I limit my exploration into liberation theology only as it relates to the development of feminist theology in Latin America. I concentrate on the "third stage" of feminist theology, where ecofeminist theology and spirituality come to center stage. I chart the theological concerns arising from an ecofeminist analysis in the context of Latin America, specifically concentrating on the work of Ivone Gebara. I also show how this ecofeminist thought, although situated in the Latin American context, is influenced by ecofeminist theology coming from other parts of the world. However, my dialogue with ecofeminism and ecofeminist theology is highly influenced by U.S. authors. This reflects my double heritage: I was born and raised "theologically" within the United States, but for the last 30 years have been living and working theologically in Latin America. Beyond Latin American contributions, I limit my research to U.S. authors while recognizing the great contribution European and Canadian ecofeminists are making to the field.

I have no doubt that I am qualified to engage in this research—if for no other reason than my longevity/immersion in the Latin American Catholic liberation milieu of the last quarter century. Indeed, it is high time that I systematized my reflections. I have been living and working in Latin America as a missionary, human rights advocate, journalist/editor and feminist since 1970. Throughout the 1980s, I was managing editor of *Latinamerica Press/Noticias Aliadas,* a weekly newsletter committed to reporting peoples' struggles through the lens of liberation theology. In those years, I interviewed many of Latin America's leading liberation theologians and count Gustavo Gutierrez, the "father" of liberation theology, as an old friend. At the same time, I have been involved with Christian feminism in Latin America from its beginnings and have participated in its development. Indeed, I am one of those "activist faith-based women" who, in the company of many others, is shifting from a faith rooted in the tenets of liberation theology to an ecofeminist perspective. I will be consulting two of Latin America's foremost feminist theologians—Elsa Tamez and Ivone Gebara—both of whom have charted this development. I then situate my research within the third stage of Latin American feminist theology, which is marked by an ecofeminist, anti-patriarchal hermeneutical approach in its attempt to propose a new, inclusive, non-patriarchal theology. I rely on those ecological, feminist and ecofeminist scholars who are saying that, in general, the biblical myths are no longer adequate in telling us "who we are" and that we are in need of a "new story" to reinterpret our origins as well as our destiny. These myths are human productions that have given great meaning to our lives in the past, but it is now time that they be re-situated and reinterpreted at this point in our evolution as a species. I review the works of Christian scholars such as "geologian" Thomas Berry, physicist Brian Swimme, theologians Diarmud O'Murchu, Rosemary Radford Ruether, and Ivone Gebara, among others, to help me frame my research.

My motivation for putting energy into this research at the ripe old age of 60 is quite simple: I am committed to this research because I firmly believe in the need to lift up the voices of a dozen Latin American women whose faith-inspired commitment to the poor and oppressed is undisputed, but who are now forging a new theology, which is best described as "ecofeminist". I am convinced that a number of Latin American "worlds" will be enriched by having these women's stories available to them: first and foremost, grassroots women's groups who may easily relate their own lives to these narratives; second, the region's theological world, especially those engaged in liberation theologies who hopefully will delight in the expansion of theology the interviewees propose; third, religious women, pastors and pastoral workers who will see these women as their companions on the journey and take heart; fourth, young people, including my own sons, Peter, 25, and Benjamin, 24, who are looking for some "anchors" for understanding the older generation's commitments. Perhaps other "worlds" will also be taken by surprise by these testimonies and experience a certain homecoming. That would be like "oil running down the beard, the beard of Aaron" (Ps. 133:2). .

Latin American feminist theology: Three stages

Latin American feminist theology was born and matured within liberation theology, but today would be in critical dialogue with that theology. The evolution of Latin American feminist theology spans more than thirty years, which can be divided into three stages paralleling the decades of the 1970s, 1980s and 1990s. Feminist consciousness within Latin American theology evolved from women theologians' and biblicists' total identification with liberation theology (first stage), to a growing awareness of—and discomfort with—liberation theology's patriarchal mindset (second stage), to challenging the patriarchal anthropology and cosmology present in liberation theology itself and calling for a total reconstruction of theology from a feminist perspective (third stage).

Scholarship on this evolution continues to grow. However, three Latin American feminist theologians have detailed this historical development more systematically: Mexican feminist theologian María Pilar Aquino,[4] Costa Rican feminist theologian Elsa Tamez[5] and Brazilian ecofeminist theologian Ivone Gebara[6]. Aquino describes the first two stages in rich detail, using women's testimonies and women's groups' reflections throughout Latin America to substantiate her research. Tamez' periodization is the most systematic and succinct of the three: she describes each stage by setting it in the context of three congresses that gathered together Latin American women theologians in 1979 (Mexico),

1985 (Argentina) and 1993 (Brazil). In each stage, she describes the political, economic, ecclesial and theological context, the development of feminist consciousness, feminist hermeneutics and the use of inclusive language. Gebara, while also describing the first two stages, concentrates on the third stage. Indeed, Tamez places Gebara's work on holistic ecofeminism at the center of third stage Latin American feminist theology.[7]

Because of my focus on ecofeminism, which comes to the fore at the third stage in the 1990s, I will limit my summary of Latin American feminist theology to Tamez' and Gebara's schemas.

Elsa Tamez' schema

Tamez first presented her description of the stages of feminist theology in Latin America in a lecture at the ecumenical congress of women theologians and biblicists held in Rio de Janeiro in December 1993. She continues to reflect upon and update her schema with rigor.[8]

For Tamez, while three fairly clear stages are observable in the evolution of feminist consciousness among women working in theology and biblical hermeneutics, she stresses that: "it is important to recognize that the hermeneutical experiences of one decade do not cancel out those of another. Very often different, even conflicting experiences coexist, sometimes within the same person (...). Nor is one phase to be treated as more important than another."[9]

Tamez describes the **first phase** of Latin American feminist theology (the decade of the seventies), as an exciting period that saw the emergence of left-wing political parties and grassroots movements of campesinos, workers, neighborhood and solidarity groups. In this same time period, however, the region's revolutionary struggles, which coalesced a decade earlier, were severely repressed by military dictatorships (Argentina, Bolivia, Brazil, Chile, Peru, Uruguay in South America; military governments were already in place in Nicaragua, Guatemala, El Salvador and Honduras in Central America). These dictatorships were infamous for their use of torture, assassination and disappearances of activists. However, in the midst of this repression, there was an amazing growth in the number and strength of Christian Base Communities (CEBs), whose members were mostly urban slum dwellers, gathered together in their CEBs to reflect on biblical texts from their own experiences as militants. (Exodus, the Babylonian captivity and liberation texts from the Gospels were favorites.)

During this decade, women theologians and biblicists were enthusiastically committed to liberation theology's method and practice. They saw women as historical subjects in their own right, capable of being protagonists of liberation. They also lifted up the double oppression women suffer, that is, both as women and as members of the oppressed class. Tamez notes, however, that there was practically no dialogue with either Latin American feminist organizations or with first world feminist theologians. In those years, most women working in theology saw feminism as simply another imperialistic invasion from the North, which could be even dangerous in that it diverted poor women from the primary contradiction of their economic and political oppression as a **class.** Women were seen as implicitly part of the category of the poor; therefore, the option for the poor meant the option for poor women. Time was spent on studying those Old and New Testament stories where women were leaders (Deborah, Judith, the mother of the Maccabees) or renown for their subversive acts (the midwives of Egypt), or women like Hagar, triply oppressed because of her class, race and sex and yet whom God blesses by allowing her son to found a new people. Tamez underlines that reflections on these selected texts of liberation nourished hope in a new society based on socialist ideals where it was assumed that egalitarian relations between the sexes would fall into place. However, in this period, there was no awareness of inclusive language and God was addressed as masculine.

In the **second phase** (the decade of the eighties), Tamez notes that an uneasiness was beginning to be felt by women theologians and biblicists about the affirmation that women were implicitly included in the category of the poor and they began to see the need to read the Bible from the standpoint of women.

In this decade, the political context shifted to Central America, where the Sandinistas came to power in Nicaragua and left-wing revolutionary struggles made headway in El Salvador and Guatemala. At the same time, most of the dictatorships in South America were replaced with restricted democracies where the Armed Forces remained vigilant watchdogs. In these years it became more and more evident that the foreign indebtedness of Latin American governments was sucking the lifeblood out of their peoples—so much so that the 1980s is seen as "the lost decade" in terms of the region's development.

This decade saw a right-wing backlash to liberation theology, especially from Rome. The Vatican's Congregation for the Doctrine of the Faith published a document warning against the dangers of liberation theology. Leonardo Boff, one of Latin America's best known liberation theologians, was summoned to Rome and subsequently silenced for a two-year period.

Theological reflection grappled with these realities by centering on themes of the kingdom of God and human history, theology of life and theology of death, idolatry of the market, discipleship of Christ, martyrdom and a spirituality of liberation. At last, a dialogue began between male liberation theologians and their female counterparts on the oppression as women, as women. Also, by the mid-80s gatherings were taking place to reflect on black and indigenous theologies.

In these years, more and more activist Christian women became involved in theological and biblical reflection. They gradually realized that liberation theology's discourse was tainted with androcentrism and patriarchal constructs and insisted that theology done from the viewpoint of women's experience would reflect different cultural, biological and historical experiences than that of men. Especially challenged was liberation theology's emphasis on economic oppression when holding up the option for the poor at the expense of cultural oppression and domestic violence. These were years of much creative theological production by women in liturgy, art and poetry. Also, first attempts at outreach to the region's feminist movements and to First World feminist theologians were initiated.

With regard to hermeneutics, women began to search for female images of God and to refer to God as both mother and father. The Holy Spirit was seen as feminine. They called for not only the practice of justice, but also for the need for tenderness, loving solidarity and comfort toward those who suffer unjustly. Tamez, herself a biblicist, calls attention to three aspects of women's biblical work in these years: First, the search for greater freedom in speaking about God, especially in the area of daily life's joys and sorrows. Second, a critical analysis of those biblical texts that were clearly patriarchal and discriminated against women. When a text did not allow for a more inclusive re-interpretation, it was dismissed as non-normative. This posture raised the question of the authority and inspiration of the Bible as the Word of God. Third, an affirmation of womanly virtues such as motherliness, unselfishness and tenderness—virtues that, historically, society did not consider important. The virtues of commitment, resistance and sacrifice were also seen as liberating in this context.

God-language began to change in some circles because of the influence of some Christian feminists who began to address God as both father and mother. However, the word "feminist," although more widely accepted, was still shunned by many as an import from the North. "Doing theology from the standpoint of women" and reading the Bible "through women's eyes" were more acceptable.

In the **third phase** (the decade of the nineties to the present), is characterized by a radical, anti-patriarchal hermeneutical approach to propose a new, inclusive and non-patriarchal theology, indeed, a total reconstruction of theology itself. Ivone Gebara calls this phase one of holistic ecofeminism.

In this decade, progressive forces in Latin America have been deeply marked by the collapse of the communist governments of Eastern

Europe and the demise of historical socialism. The defeat of the Sandinistas in Nicaragua has also dampened the region's hope for an alternative to the capitalist order. Economically, the current neo-liberal economic model, which gives supremacy to the demands of world markets, is seen as the only viable alternative. Socially, once effervescent grassroots movements have stagnated, including the Christian Base Communities (CEBs), which have gone into steep decline. On the other hand, the inroads being made by Pentecostalism throughout Latin America is indeed remarkable. (A common phrase heard among Latin American pastoral agents these days is: "liberation theology may have opted for the poor, but the poor have opted for Pentecostalism.") All this has affected the vibrancy of liberation theology (a subject that will be treated more thoroughly below).

One bright spot in an otherwise dismal political landscape is the rise of the indigenous movement as a result of the 500th anniversary of the European invasion of the Americas in 1992. Indigenous theologians are calling for liberation theology´s "option for the poor" to be expanded to include an "option for the impoverished other" because the "otherness" of the continent's diversity needs to be taken into account along with economic disparities.

For a growing number of women in these years, it has not been enough to speak of the feminine face of God. They find current theological discourse androcentric and patriarchal to the core and see their task as the reconstruction of the whole of theology from a feminist perspective. A major influence on these women has been the introduction of gender analysis to their theological and biblical work, along with new insights coming from feminist anthropology. In this research, there is a much more open, welcoming attitude toward both Latin American feminism and to colleagues in the First World.

One of the most forceful new hermeneutical categories feminist theological and biblical scholarship is using is that of the body. Concrete bodies of women and men are becoming a new locus for doing theology. Efforts are also being made to offer a non-sacrificial reading of redemption to free many poor women from accepting violence, especially domestic violence, as somehow "the will of God". New non-gender-specific names are emerging for the divine such as grace, compassion and energy. As Tamez concludes about this phase: "We are aware of the radical nature of this challenge, which means reworking, or rather reinventing, the whole of Christian theology. There is difficulty in re-reading the great theological themes such as Christology, the Trinity and ecclesiology because of their androcentrism. It is recognized that the implications of reconstruction take us beyond orthodoxy."[10] She ends her overview by emphasizing that the priority for feminist theologians and biblicists in Latin America is to always link their work to the basic concerns of the poor.[11]

Ivone Gebara's schema

While Gebara's systematization is not as detailed as Tamez', she also sees three stages in the development of Latin American feminist theology but points out that they are not necessarily chronological and often overlap, depending on historical circumstance and the level of feminist consciousness in a specific country or group. Gebara elaborated on this development in a course she gave in Chile in April 1993, which I attended. At the end of her time in Chile, I interviewed her on these stages, especially focusing on the third stage, which she calls "holistic ecofeminism".[12]

For Gebara, the **first stage** of feminist theology is characterized by women's discovery of their oppression as historical subjects—an oppression present in theology, the Bible, in the churches. She credits the secular feminist movement—not the churches—with nurturing this insight among Christian women. In this stage, women rediscovered many women in the Bible (such as Sarah, Hagar, Miriam, Ruth, Esther, Judith, Mary, Magdalene, the women at the empty tomb) and reclaimed them as key actors in the history of liberation. But for Gebara, while important, this was not enough. She says that women tended to overvalue the feminine in this stage and to fall into the patriarchal trap of lifting up those domestic qualities historically associated with women, such as motherhood and the double-duty workday. Gebara also challenges work done in those years to hold up women liberators such as Judith as models, without questioning the violent patriarchal framework in which the Book of Judith is situated. She also feels that during this stage (which she also situates in the seventies), women tended to think that they were the "good" gender and somehow spiritually superior to poor, weak men. There was also a certain desire to "even the score" with male counterparts.

Gebara calls the **second stage** the "feminization of theological concepts." This was a time when women theologians worked to rediscover the feminine, maternal face of God in biblical texts. She also notes that in those years (the decade of the eighties), women were given a voice within the churches and within liberation theology to present "the women's perspective". This pleased progressive male theologians and pastors and it particularly pleased male liberation theologians who had always insisted that they were open to including women theologians in their ranks. However, according to Tamez, Gebara has pointed out that what women had been doing was "patriarchal feminist theology".[13]

Gebara finds that liberation theology in general has not challenged the underlying patriarchal structure of Christianity itself. While she acknowledges that liberation theology offers a more collective understanding of God and stresses the social nature of sin and that God is a God of life and of justice who has a preferential option for the poor, she finds that its anthropology and cosmology remains riddled with patriarchy.

Gebara situates the **third stage** of Latin American feminist theology in the post-modern paradigm and invites us to consider what she calls holistic ecofeminism. I will be dealing with Gebara's understanding of, and contribution to ecofeminism in Chapter II.

I have relied heavily on the schemas elaborated by Tamez and Gebara to describe the development of Latin American feminist theology for my own theological work. I have devised the following chart, which combines the insights of both.

The Three Phases of Latin American Feminist Theology

First phase: (1970-80)

Political/economic context:
Effervescence of left political parties and popular movements (union, barrio, etc.)
Revolutionary struggles, which provoked military coups, followed by dictatorship
Repression: massacres, disappearances, torture, generalized human rights abuse.

Ecclesiastical/theological context:
Christian base communities spring up all over Latin America
Grassroots reading and interpretation of the Bible *"lectura popular"*.
Option for the poor; texts read with the "eyes of the poor"
Medellin and Puebla documents
Ecumenism based on option for the poor, which cuts through denominational lines
Theology of Liberation comes into its own with its methodology of reflection based on *praxis*.
The poor become the theological *locus*.
Key themes: the Exodus, "valley of tears", the historical Jesus

Construction of feminist consciousness:
Women theologians and Biblicists identified totally with liberation theology.
Women were seen as oppressed historical subjects in the Bible, in theology and in the churches.
Women began to reclaim a more equal space within society in general.
Theological point of departure became the double oppression of women: because of both sex and class.
In this stage there was a tendency to overvalue the feminine, there was a certain wanting to "even the score" and make women into the "good gender".
There was almost no dialogue between feminist theologians from Latin America or with those from the North (instead, there was a good deal of suspicion).

Hermeneutics:
Biblical interpretation was both militant and grassroots-based.

Liberation texts were emphasized over other texts.
Task: to rediscover biblical women as key players in the history of liberation (Sarah, Miriam, Ruth, Ester, Deborah, Judith, Magdalene, Mary, the Egyptian midwives, Hagar)—this took place without seeing the patriarchal context of the text itself (for example, the history of Judith).

Inclusive language:
There is no awareness of sexist language.
The divinity is masculine.
The world "feminist" is rejected as a foreign concept, imposed from the North.

Second phase (1980-90):

Political/economic context:
Central America: Sandinista triumph; revolutionary movements in El Salvador, Guatemala.
Southern Cone: Dictatorships give way to restricted democracies.
Bush-Reagan era; Santa Fe documents.
The foreign debt becomes a crushing weight levied against the poor.

Ecclesiastical/theological context:
Ideological polarization becomes acute: CLAI v. CONELA:
Vatican documents condemning liberation theology.
Liberation theologians become interested in the "women's perspective".
Liberation theology becomes more receptive to the topic of "women" *per se*.
Key themes: theology of life v. theology of death; idolatry: martyrdom; spirituality of liberation.

Construction of feminist consciousness:
Commitment to see "women's perspective" at every turn.
Growing critique of all theology for its anthropocentrism and patriarchal mindset.
Starting point: women's experience, which *de facto* brought to the theological scene a different discourse because of biological, cultural and historical influences.
Efforts to rescue discourse related to God; i.e. the "maternal face" of God.
Efforts toward the feminization of theological concepts.
Praxis of love and caring.
Lots of innovation in liturgy.
Openness to feminist contributions from both Latin American and northern feminists.

Hermeneutics:

Biblical interpretation: see every text from women's perspective
Search for feminine images of God (mother/father; Holy Spirit as feminine).
Commitment to feminize theology, to combine justice with tenderness.
Biblical work centers on: valuing the ordinary, pleasure, play. Reinterpreting virtues traditionally linked to   women: maternity, tenderness, sacrifice, commitment.
Confrontation with patriarchal texts: Insistence that they are not normative.
Reconstruction of texts: questioning of biblical authority.begins.

Inclusive language:
God as "mother/father", as "he/she"
Identification with the word "feminist" becomes more common.

Third phase (1990 and onward)

Political/economic context:
Fall of the Berlin Wall—and with it, socialism as a model.
Gulf War, invasion of Panama, Defeat of the Sandinistas
Neo-liberal economic model firmly entrenched; market ideology reigns supreme.
State as benefactor is dismantled.
Popular movements in general are weakened, lack-luster interest in "reform".

Ecclesiastical/theological context:
CEBs stagnate.
Ecclesial crisis within both Protestantism and Catholicism.
Santo Domingo document (Catholic) weak.
CLAI III document (Protestant) weak.
Amazing growth of Pentecostalism.
New energies coming from indigenous movement (anniversary of 500 years)
Chiapas: rallying cry, "a society where all fit!"
Women's movement gains strength, as well as Black movement.
Key themes: the market and the gods of sacrifice; the new evangelization; ecology and the land; dialogue with other religions.
Option for the poor evolves into option for the impoverished other.

Construction of feminist consciousness:
Feeling of being "boxed in"—no more room to expand.
Need to reconstruct all theology from a feminist perspective.
Use of gender theory to analyze situation of oppression.

Growth of contributions coming from Black and indigenous women;
New theories coming from anthropology of symbolism.
Challenge to confront the patriarchal structures latent in Christianity itself.
Challenge to confront the patriarchal anthropology and cosmovision present in liberation theology.
Calls for redefinition of both the human and the divine.
Openness to "holistic ecofeminism" (Ivone Gebara is key here).

Hermeneutics:
Body/the ordinary is considered a hermeneutic category.
Call for a non-sacrificial reading of redemption.
Key themes: the fiesta, joy, embodiness, sexuality.
Gender theory applied to biblical texts.
Creative reconstruction of texts to hear the lost voices of women.
Major challenge: To re-invent all Christian theology in relation to the concepts of God, Jesus, Trinity, sin, redemption: This reconstruction goes beyond what is currently considered "orthodox".
Key question being raised in this phase: How can a feminist hermeneutic be articulated that takes into account the basic problems of our impoverished peoples?

Inclusive language:
Non-sexist names for the divinity (energy, mercy, infinite compassion, grace).
Terms "feminist" and "ecofeminist" now commonly accepted.

(*Both Gebara and Tamez insist that these are not fixed periods; often two phases can overlap in the same country or area or church.)

My own journey

In 1996, when I discovered Elsa Tamez' systematization, I was inspired to review my own life journey, which closely parallels the "three stages" of feminist theology in the region as she and Ivone Gebara lay out.[15] Since the key starting point for doing feminist theology is one's own experience, I thought it only right to share something of my own comings and goings here.

A few preliminaries: I was born on a May morning in 1942 to a close-knit tribe in a small U.S. mid-western town, famous for its high school football team. My grandparents and all their children and grandchildren lived on the same short street. We all went to the same parish, which also provided most of our social life. I went to Catholic grade and high schools, where I found myself incredibly attracted to the sisters who taught me.

I entered the convent after high school and spent three years as a novice at the Motherhouse farm in western Pennsylvania. During those years, my prayer was "Dear God, let me just keep up with this dedicated bunch." My fellow novices (40 of us!) were a healthy, happy crowd and the sisters in charge of our formation were warm and caring. I will always link my continual searching for community to my experience among the Sisters of the Humility of Mary. I was a member of this community for 14 years.

After the novitiate, I was sent to college, destined to become a high school teacher. Many of us were put into an academic track to major or minor in Spanish at this time, because the community, responding to Pope John XXIII's call to re-christianize our "sister continent" of Latin America, had just opened a mission in Temuco, Chile to work with Mapuche women.

After graduation from college, I taught Spanish and Social Studies for the next four years at one of the community's flagship schools for wealthy young women. I wore lots of hats in those very busy years, but two things stand out in particular: Taking a bus load of students across the country on a school bus to live with Cesar Chavez and the migrant farm workers for a month; and taking a handful of girls to Mexico for summers (and one summer to Spain) to study Spanish. However, by my third year as a high school teacher, I found myself getting a bit restless. One could not be with high school kids forever! In 1969 I applied for and was awarded a 15-month East-West grant to study at the University of Hawaii, with three months of field work in India. BUT as the fates would have it, about a month after receiving the grant, the Mother Superior of the community called me and told me that one of the sisters was leaving the school and asked me to postpone my grant and reapply the following year. Which I did, but I wasn't given the grant again. On the rebound, I decided to join the Cleveland Mission Team to El Salvador. Throughout the ensuing years, I've mulled over this "fate" of being denied the chance to study in India and how I went to El Salvador instead. That "rebound" decision has so shaped my life: I've been living and working in Latin America—with some short intermissions—since 1970.

Before going on to life in Latin America, I want to track the development of my images of the divine, because they will bear comparison with the women I interviewed as part of my research. Having grown up in the pre-Vatican II Catholic tradition of the 1950s, my earliest image of the Divine was Mary, Mother of God and Mother of Christ. Mary was truly my mother: I went to her to be comforted when I was hurt or confused. All my prayers of petition were to her, because—as the popular theology of the times taught—"to Jesus through Mary." She was the mediatrix *par excellence*, because how could Christ refuse anything asked in his dear Mother's name? As a young girl, God the Father was some remote being (I supposed he looked like the infamous old man with the beard, Michelangelo fashion, but I can't say I had a very vivid vision or interest in this faraway force.) Jesus, of course, was Jesus, and I trotted faithfully behind him through the liturgical cycle of his birth, boyhood, public life, suffering, death, and resurrection. But if the truth be known, although God's Son and somehow then also God, he was, in the end, just Mary's kid.

I cannot stress enough the importance of Mary as my **root image** of the Divine. My childhood was marked by May crownings, May altars and Novenas to Mary—all in the context of the liturgical cycle of my parish, "St Mary's," which was known for celebrating all the Marian feasts with great pomp and circumstance. As a teenager, I joined the Sodality, an organization whose members consecrate themselves in a special way to Mary, and became one of its leaders. Through the Sodality, I felt called to serve the poor and less fortunate—in the spirit of Mary (and her son) and engaged in a variety of apostolic services. All through these years, there were strong female models in my life whose devotion to Mary—

and love of life—continually inspired me: these of course were the religious sisters who taught me throughout my Catholic girlhood. I was very attracted to their way of life and as you now know, I eventually entered religious life myself.

Again, the congregation I entered had a special devotion to Mary. For several months during my Novitiate years I even consecrated myself secretly as a "slave of Mary" (a rather macabre series of observances taught by the French saint, Louis De Monfort) until my Novice Mistress found out and forbade my "slavery."

Now, with the wealth of feminist research into the patriarchal repression of the goddess image in our history as a species, I am much better able to put my Marian devotion into perspective.

However, with my religious training in the convent, I was more rigorously introduced to the Jesus of the Gospels, as well as to a more enlightened understanding of Trinitarian theology. Jesus became more pivotal: it was he who introduced us to his Father as "abba," it was he who left us his Spirit to be with us always. But not only did Jesus become an attractive historical figure; he became my "spouse". (My convent formation is right on the cusped that divides a more scripture-based Vatican II theology from a more pietistic theology where religious became "brides of Christ".) I remember clearly that on the day of my first vows, I had a mystical experience of being wed forever to this god-bridegroom who, because he loved me in such a special way, would be most demanding of me ("to much is given, much will be asked"). And so, at the age of 21, wearing His betrothal ring, I set out to save the world for Christ.

At the same time, the Second Vatican Council was taking place, along with an eruption of Catholic social encyclicals from Popes John XXIII and Paul VI calling the church to "open the windows" to let in the Spirit of justice and compassion. Key to those times was the conviction that the church was not a structure or institution but the "people of God" on a journey. Ever a product of my times, I became an enthusiastic Vatican II Catholic, preaching, teaching and trying to put into practice the new social doctrine of the church. Nourished by a simpler, more understandable liturgical cycle where the Mass really became a meal shared among friends, I found myself involved in the civil rights movement, in the anti-war movement, and, as mentioned above, in the grape boycott to give the migrant farm workers a more just wage. Radical to the core, the habit and veil gradually changed to jeans and sweatshirt and by 1970, (not entirely altruistically, having just lost the chance to go to Hawaii and India) I decided that the most authentic way to live out my gospel commitment was to become a missionary in Latin America.

First stage: The 1970s

Need I say that living in El Salvador in 1970 was a major change from teaching at an upper-class girls' school? The tremendous poverty, the heat, the government corruption and violence, the growing political restlessness of the people overwhelmed me. I was 28 years old and my only qualifications as a missionary was that I was a high school Spanish teacher and had been deeply "converted" to establishing peace and justice in the world by taking to heart the social doctrine of the church!

I still remember the evening I arrived in El Salvador. Some of my future teammates met me at the airport in a jeep and after what seemed like hours bouncing over dark mountain roads in a downpour, we arrived at what appeared to be the end of the world, where I promptly descended from the jeep only to find myself knee-deep in mud and crud. (No wonder that there are so many gentle jokes aimed at new missioners. Dressed as I was in my Sunday best "cool nun digs," I could not have been more the oxymoron to those villagers in that tiny hamlet of Chirrilagua. Truly a creature from another planet.) I was so relieved to have finally arrived that I didn't cry over my mud bath. However, when folks amiably conversing outside my window awakened me the next morning at 4:30 am, I did indeed weep. I quickly learned that because of the heat, the best hours for socializing are those of the wee dawn and even I, who all my life has hated to get up early, found myself rising in those cool pre-dawn hours to stroll in the refreshing breeze and visit with folks—all of whom are up and ready for a new day.

I came to El Salvador as an idealistic young nun ready to serve the poor. Since I had been a popular high school teacher in the United States, I assumed I would be equally successful working with teenagers in the barrios. Very quickly, however, I realized I was now in a different world where poverty was so acute that children really did die of hunger and disease. I quickly learned that here in El Salvador I was being faced with unjust structures so imbedded in the very air we breathed that only something like a revolution could change the stifling status quo.

I only lasted two years in El Salvador. During that time, I worked with youth and formed a youth center in La Union that brought together most of the town's young people, until the local bishop—who was also the chaplain of the local military barracks—shut it down for being "subversive." After that major setback, I began working to solidify the several Christian base communities that the mission team was forming both in La Union and in the outlying *cantones*. Another sister and myself developed a group dynamics program for rural women because it soon became evident that women needed to be able to express what they were feeling, but were so timid about speaking out in a group.

I so clearly remember the campesinos with whom I worked. As they discovered their dignity and their power through a militant reading of the scriptures they would often tell us that they would rather "die on their feet than live on their knees". Engraved in my memory forever is the moment during those first CEB meetings in El Salvador when we pastoral agents would ask: "Brothers and sisters, is there injustice in our world?" A long pause, and then, finally, *Si, madre, hay mucha injusticia en nuestro mundo*. And then the process of what Brazilian educator Paulo Frerie called *concientización* would begin. It was in these CEB meetings that I too discovered a new way of reading the scripture texts. I discovered a Jesus who in his day took sides with the oppressed and downtrodden in their struggles for a more just society. However, I couldn't see a role for myself in this struggle, a naïve *gringa* who couldn't even play the guitar! I also realized that the same injustices and class divisions in society that cried out for vengeance also existed within the church, which was in turn polarized around the causes of the extreme poverty of El Salvador's majority. I had the honor of meeting Archbishop Oscar Romero when he was known for being a conservative (this was before his conversion). I remember how he came out to a course I was attending for campesina girls. The most vivid recollection I have of him was his frayed cassock and his kindness and real interest in the girls.

A word about my pastoral team experience in El Salvador: The mixed team of priests and sisters was a whole new experience for me in that I had been used to living with only women for the past 10 years. I think I fell in love with each of my male teammates at least once—which made quite clear what I had known for a long time: I was not made to live a celibate life.

I left El Salvador in 1972, quite disillusioned about the possibility that the kingdom of God might come to this long-suffering people—at least during my lifetime. I left convinced that I had seen what liberation theologians called "social sin"—the exploitation, torture, hatred and utter disrespect that the wealthy and powerful had toward the poor. I felt that I had been confronted with the almost invisible "powers and principalities" of a dominant class so entrenched in its position of privilege that it would never willingly relinquish anything that would compromise that position. I became more sympathetic to armed struggle—I saw no other way out than some sort of violent revolution.

Most significant for my life's meaning has been the fact that the woman who replaced me on the mission team in El Salvador was Ursuline Sister Dorothy Kazel who was murdered along with three other religious women by the Salvadoran security forces in 1980. "There but for you, go I."

I returned to the States with a real crisis of both faith and identity. I left religious life and felt pretty much a failure as a missionary. I went to Chicago where I roomed with a good friend who had left the community a year before. Almost immediately, I fell madly in love with a theology professor at Loyola—an ex-Jesuit seminarian. This relationship did not really develop, however, and I spent a rather dreary year as a "swinging single."

Then one day I saw an ad in the *National Catholic Reporter* inviting folks to be a part of a missionary team to a small village in the Andes of Peru. After several letters back and forth, I met David, the priest coordinating the effort, in Washington and agreed to be a part of his team. We both admit, with hindsight, that it was "love at first sight".

I spent three years (1973-1976) in Huarochiri (pop. 2,000; altitude, 10,000 feet) working as a pastoral agent. I taught school, worked with a women's group, and helped form a consumer's co-op. (Although I worked closely with women's groups in both El Salvador and in Huarochiri, my commitment to a feminist analysis was only implicit while my overriding commitment to the class struggle was all-important.) I also got to know first hand the "church of the poor" and those working in liberation theology. We were committed to Freire's method of *concientization* and to the "see, judge, act" method of praxis to be able to delve into the roots of oppression with our people. In those years, I came to know Gustavo Gutiérrez and his circle of Christians who were developing liberation theology and its practice. David was deeply involved in the progressive priests' movement, ONIS, and we were both committed to what we all called "a new way of being church." I call my years in Huarochiri my "contemplative time" because of the absolutely breathtaking beauty of the Andes—and because the villagers all went to their fields around six in the morning and came home around six in the evening. It was hard to do much organizing, so I would walk the hills and valleys of this majestic part of the planet. Little by little I also drew close to a people and a culture so rich in history and tradition that has marked me for a lifetime.

With hindsight, I admit that I was quite dogmatic in those years. My letters home to my family and friends were filled with revolutionary zeal and condemnations of capitalism. I stubbornly wore my "revolutionary uniform" everywhere—jeans, poncho and boots. I felt most identified with my biblical namesake, Judith of the Old Testament, who killed the oppressor Holofernes to save her people.

David's and my relationship also deepened, but he was very much committed to the priesthood, as the liberation theologians understood priesthood in those days. (The Colombian guerrilla priest, Camilo Torres was still a heroic figure to many.) In 1976, however, the bishop of our area, an Opus Dei man, dismissed all the priests, sisters and pastoral agents working in the six parishes up and down the valley and replaced us with his own missionaries from Spain. This caused a major crisis, not only for those of us involved, but also in the Peruvian church. In the end, I went back to the States (with a bad case of hepatitis) and David, although he left his community, continued as a priest and went to work in the mining camps in southern Peru.

Back in the States, I was at the lowest ebb I've ever been in my whole life. I made a retreat with a good friend, tried to let go of David and pull my life together. In the fall of 1976, I went to New York where I enrolled in the Graduate School of Social Research and earned a Masters in Economics. In order to live, I looked up friends at Maryknoll and found out that Sergio Torres, a Chilean priest and liberation theologian in exile, was trying to organize groups who were doing liberation theology around the USA. So I worked as Sergio's "bi-lingual secretary" and networker at the Theology in the Americas office (which would eventually also become the office for EATWOT, the Ecumenical Association of Third World Theologians) during the day and studied at night—until one fine day in October when David called to propose!

Marriage for us who had been brought up on liberation theology was always frowned upon. Such a step would lead to "abandoning the struggle." Inevitably, so the logic went, one became bourgeoisie and forgot the option for the poor. But love is love, and so we married in 1977. The songs at our wedding reflected our determination to continue accompanying the oppressed "as long as we both shall live." On our honeymoon, we went to Appalachia where we thought we might find meaningful work. Midway through our trip, however, we received word from the

American Friends Service Committee (Quakers) that they would like to interview us to see if we would qualify to be their representatives in Chile.

We arrived in Chile in October 1977. I was seven months pregnant and our first son, Peter, was born on Christmas Day of that year. Our second son, Benjamin, was also born in Chile in June 1979. Motherhood caught me by surprise. Always considered the quintessential "bachelor girl", I found I loved being a mother! These maternal sentiments also awakened a surprising link to the struggle against the dictatorship because I felt a deep connection to the mothers who had their loved ones "disappeared". I became more aware of the role that women—as women—were playing in the resistance movement. Although I still was firmly within the liberation framework of class analysis, in my last year in Chile I began to read more about feminism. I discovered that I had always been a feminist! But it would only be in the next decade that I would begin to use feminist intuitions to dialogue critically with liberation theology.

The four years we spent in Chile (1977-81) were most intense: it was at the height of the Pinochet dictatorship and our work involved supporting human rights groups, soup kitchens, artisan groups, Mapuche groups, as well as sending reports back to headquarters monitoring the human rights situation. We worked closely with the Catholic Church's Vicariate of Solidarity and also participated actively in a CEB located in a shantytown on Santiago's west side. In June 1981 David was arrested and interrogated by Chile's secret intelligence service for 24 hours. After some negotiation, he was allowed to stay in Chile until October when we agreed to leave the country.

Second stage: The 1980s

In some real sense, I spent much of this decade trying to make sense of all that happened to me in the previous decade. The experiences of El Salvador, Huarochiri, Peru and Chile under the Pinochet dictatorship are enough to keep me journaling for the rest of my life!

But life did not stand still. In early 1982, we found ourselves in

Lima as director (David) and managing editor (myself) of the weekly "Latinamerica Press/Noticias Aliadas". We spent seven years at LP covering the church and the world of the poor in Latin America—always, of course, from the perspective of liberation theology.

Thinking about those years in retrospect, I realize how privileged we were. We were able to come into contact with the key actors who were struggling for structural change in the 1980s, a viable socialism that would take into account the idiosyncrasies of Latin America. It was during those years that I discovered how much I loved to write and edit. I also had a chance to interview many of the key liberation theologians in those years: Gustavo Gutierrez, the Boff brothers—Leonardo and Clodovis, Jon Sobrino, Sergio Torres, Diego Irrarazaval, Ronaldo Muñoz, and others. But I also interviewed *comandantes* in the liberated areas of El Salvador, women who were searching for their disappeared loved ones, pastoral workers, religious sisters and priests who were committed to "a new way of being church" among poor communities. Our journalism tried to show the region's "other face" that the mainline media ignored.

With regard to the evolution of my feminist consciousness, in 1983 I joined several women who had participated in a workshop on *Patriarchy and the Church* at the Second Encounter of Latin American Feminists held outside Lima, to form what would become the Circle of Christian feminists, *Talitha Cumi*, a collective of women committed to reflecting from a feminist perspective on issues of faith and society. This group of women became my community during the years I lived in Lima. Two of Talitha's founders, Maryknoll Sisters Rose Timothy Gavin and Rose Dominic Trapasso, (the famous "Roses of Lima") have been key mentors for me over the years. It was with these women that I began to see the implications of patriarchy—especially as it exists within the Catholic Church and even within liberation theology. It was also with the Talithas that I began to search for more relevant images of the Sacred that would water my spirituality. Little by little, I started to question the obvious absence of women among liberation theologians as well as the absence of themes taken up by liberation theology that directly related to the lives of poor women (for instance, sexual ethics and domestic violence). By the end of the decade, I was deeply engaged in the proposals coming from feminist theology and its challenges to liberation theology. If the truth be known, I had become tired of seeing so much martyrdom, so many calls for sacrifice to bring about a revolution that never seemed to come.

We left Lima in 1989 and went to Rome where David became Executive Secretary of IDOC and I was named editor of the bi-monthly magazine *IDOC Internazionale*. We were supposed to turn a dying organization around—which in the end, couldn't be done. However, my work was exciting because I was to give the magazine a new focus: ecology and theology, within a Third World perspective. One of the unexpected synchronicities of my life has been that job: because of that mandate, I began to rearrange my worldview and my place within the larger story of the universe. But the repercussions of this switch would only show up in the next decade.

Third stage: The 1990s to the present

In 1990 David and I gave up on IDOC and decided to return to Latin America by joining the Maryknoll lay mission program. This was not a surprise move since we had been close to the Maryknoll missionaries—priests, sisters and lay people—for many years. Now as Catholic missionaries, we found ourselves back in Chile in early 1991. Our two teenage sons rediscovered their Chilean roots.

I returned to Chile now as a convinced feminist and as a budding ecologist. In Rome I had devoured books and articles dealing with the discoveries coming from what has come to be called the "New Science". Most basic to this conversion was Thomas Berry's *The Dream of the Earth*. Berry, along with authors such as Brian Swimme, Charlene Spretnak and Starhawk, among others, began to captivate me with their new understanding of the universe as an ever more complex, transformational *cosmogenesis*. I began to realize that that everything is interconnected—and always has been—but that somewhere during our development as a species we managed to forget that basic fact (our current patriarchal mentality). My feminism evolved toward' ecofeminism and my theological questions veered toward more cosmological quests. Today I am more comfortable with describing the developing Mystery in which we live as "the call of the future" because it is closer to my understanding of cosmogenesis.

In Chile I began to search for a community like I had experienced in Lima among the Talithas. A Christian feminist organization such as Talitha Cumi did not yet exist in Santiago, but there was interest among several women in forming a group where we could gather to celebrate our lives and our spiritualities according to our own lights, without fear of being criticized. Thus the Con-spirando Collective was born.

In 1993, Ivone Gebara came to Chile and gave her now famous course on "holistic ecofeminism". Her insights were like rain on dry land for me—I felt she was able to name and contextualize my questions and doubts about definitions of God, the place of Jesus in my life today, how to be faithful to the option for the poor and to the struggle for a better world when I no longer have the same revolutionary fervor of yesteryear.

Compared with the decades of the 1970s and 1980s, I now find I have no Great Project to struggle for, although I admit being drawn to wanting to be part of a bioregion, an "ecological village" a "shared garden". I continue to search for a sustainable economic and cultural model that can be an alternative to current neo-liberal capitalism. I try to eat lower on the food chain; I am committed to recycling, composting, organic gardening, to using the bus more and the car less. However, I must admit that it is David who prods me to actually do these things and more frequently than not, I am a total failure as a practicing ecologist. I still love to plan and celebrate rituals that try to capture where we are on our journey—these rituals over the years have become less wordy and more embodied through using dance and movement more freely.

I also recognize that, more than anything, I am a woman in search of ever more authentic answers to the meaning of life. I now am tremendously uncomfortable with the androcentrism and anthropocentrism I find in the central doctrines of Christianity. But I do not consider myself post-Christian. I am a pilgrim who, along with a growing number of other wayfarers, is searching for post-patriarchal theological/cosmological answers that will give us energy and pleasure to be alive at this time in history in this small corner of the planet.

Beloved: we are earthlings and our history as well as our future is radically connected to the fate of this fragile green planet we call home. We are entering a strange new epoch, where hopefully we humans will engage in a profound listening. A listening to voices long forgotten: that of the sea, the rivers, the mountains, the forest, the stars, the moon; those arising from our genetic memory—our ancestors, both human and otherwise; that of our own bodies—mine, yours, the friend who has been abused, the new baby, the youngster, the old woman now wrinkled and worn, the Earth itself. A broader sense of kinship is key here. In a very real way, there is no other—the other is myself because we all come from the same source; we are all, in the end, earthlings.

I have the feeling that my sense of who I am is expanding. I am not only this individual named Judy, this current marvelous conglomeration of energy; I am also memory and possibility. Sometimes I experience flashes of this expanded self and then I realize that I am my grandmother, I am a Paleolithic woman sharing her dream to the tribe around the fire at night. At those times I also realize that I will be present in my grandchildren and great grandchildren. My sense of com-munion is becoming more physical, more real. "We are what we eat," said old Feuerbach. I must face the fact that, just as every other species, we humans live and die, eat and are eaten. All members of the Earth's community of life eat of one another and the death of one brings life and nourishment to another, which in the end creates a deeply intimate reciprocity. That, somehow, is enough.

Current status of liberation theology

Because Latin American feminist and ecofeminist theology grows out of liberation theology but is now taking a more critical view of several of its key tenets, it is important to review the current status of liberation theology.

A heated debate is taking place within liberation theology as to whether or not it is "in crisis," given what appears to be the collapse of historical socialism. Some, like Gustavo Gutierrez, continue to insist that the end of the communist world does not affect liberation theology since its commitment was never to Marxism but to the poor. He argues that liberation theology is more urgent than ever in the face of neo-liberal capitalism, which has aggravated the disparities between rich and poor.[16] Gutierrez affirms the preferential option for the poor and reminds us that poverty has human and socio-economic causes. While he acknowledges that liberation theology may have overemphasized economic factors, he insists that in its description of the poor as the "insignificant ones of history" women, especially poor women, as well as ethnic minorities were always implicitly included. He especially welcomes the current biblical reinterpretation from a women's perspective.[17]

Juan-José Tamayo, a Spanish liberation theologian who has written and taught extensively on Latin American liberation theology for more than 30 years, is perhaps one of the most enthusiastic protagonists of including emerging Latin American theologies under the general heading of liberation theology. Asking, "who are the poor?" Tamayo answers that at first liberation theology emphasized the socio-economic aspects of poverty and class conflict, but that now, conscious of its own reductionism, it has opened itself to the new faces of the poor—marginal races and ethnic groups, cultures that have been overlooked, religions that have been outlawed, doubly- and in many cases triply-oppressed women, oppressed Nature, abandoned street children, entirely excluded peoples and countries, etc.[18] Convinced that liberation theology simply has to grapple with the major changes of the 21st century, he welcomes the challenges coming from these "new faces". Tamayo is up to date on the discomfort feminist theologians feel regarding the androcentrism in much of liberation theology. He lauds feminist theologians' use of the "hermeneutics of suspicion" to deconstruct those categories that exclude women not only from theological discussion but from the Christian experience itself. He underlines the work feminist theologians are doing in initiating a post-patriarchal reconstruction of Christianity. Familiar with the work of Conspirando and its ecofeminist posture, he also sees ecofeminism as a logical development in the search to discover the root causes of women's oppression and the destruction of the Earth. For Tamayo, these are exciting, viable themes that an expanding liberation theology must address. Thus he speaks of both feminist and ecofeminist liberation theology.[19]

However, some leading Latin American liberation theologians would not be so enthusiastically open to these "new faces". No where was this tension more evident than in the Theological Congress, sponsored by the *Sociedad de Teología y Ciencias de la Religión* (SOTER), held in Brazil in July 2000 where many of the "fathers" of liberation were present. It became evident during the congress that humanity is not only facing a major change in epoch, but an end to a theological era, "characterized by fragmentation and a search for new theological spaces, an enormously complex time in its pluralism, but at the same time promising and fruitful in its resources".[20]

At the Congress, it was not feminist or ecofeminist theology that produced a heated debate, but rather Leonardo Boff's work in the area of ecological theology. In his presentation, Boff expanded his definition of the option for the poor. In the 1960s, he said, liberation theology emphasized the economically and politically poor; in the 1970s, the definition was extended to the culturally poor and included indigenous, blacks and other discriminated minorities; in the 1980s, emphasis was given to the question of gender and the oppression of women, and now in the 1990s liberation theology has begun to hear the cry of the earth, "also impoverished because it is unjustly despoiled and exploited systematically. For each concrete oppression, we responded by developing a corresponding strategy and liberating pedagogy. Never has the Theology of Liberation fallen victim to an impoverished concept of the poor. It always tried to deepen its understanding of the complex reality of any poverty imposed unjustly."[21] The great "poor" at this time, then, is the Earth itself which humanity can collectively destroy. We must change or we will perish, Boff warns, using the metaphor of the space ship with both its first class passengers and with its many poor confined to the baggage department. All share the same destiny for the welfare of the ship. There is no Noah's ark this time round to save a few while the rest perish.[22]

Boff calls upon liberation theology to situate its reflection in the context of the new cosmology emerging from the latest scientific discoveries that contemplates a broader understanding of evolution. He argues that all of us are being held hostage by a way of living, a way of production and by relations with the environment that imply systematic violence against persons, social classes, countries, ecosystems and the Earth itself. He concludes: "The option for the poor—the hallmark of Theology of Liberation—must be integral: all the poor with all their many faces, and the great poor one, the Earth, known as Gaia, Pachamama and Great Mother. It is important to free all. But there are priorities. First, is the urgent need to liberate the Earth through a real revolution in our paradigm of relationality with her. (...) This suggests a holistic paradigm based on reverence, respect and care for her biodiversity, integrity and beauty."[23]

Boff's expansion of the "option for the poor" to include the Earth itself caused a major altercation between himself and his brother Clodovis at the one of the Congress' plenary sessions. Clodovis Boff represents those liberation theologians that find Leonardo Boff's embracing of the new cosmology dangerous to liberation theology's traditional commitment to poor and downtrodden *people*. In Gustavo Gutiérrez' words, *¿dónde dormirán los pobres?* (Where will the poor sleep?). It is the poor majorities of Latin America who have always been liberation theology's central focus. There is a growing fear among some liberation theologians that the concrete lives of the poor will no longer be the locus of their theology, or will be watered down by new "paradigms" such as the cosmological one, where the issue of the poor seems to be losing its theological and ethical prominence.[24] It seems likely that the debate on how broadly liberation theologians can interpret the option for the poor and still be considered doing theology of liberation is destined to continue.

José Comblin, another of liberation theology's pioneers, is more blunt in his assessment of liberation theology's future: "Liberation theology is at a standstill," he says, "because Catholic theology and Christian theology in general are at a standstill; nothing new is coming out...there is no more interest in theology."[25] Comblin is pessimistic about liberation theology's accomplishments. At 80, he is now quite free to be blunt. He says that the major reason why there has been stagnation in people's willingness to participate in CEBs is the arrival of television. Even more pointedly, he says that the CEB movement arose not from the people but from pastoral agents who saw in them a new form of church and the promise of a new society. When such hopes were frustrated, pastoral agents often gave up on them.[26] He finds the CEBs riddled with clericalism and therefore condemned to wither on the vine. He notes that Catholics, along with everyone else, are consulting other wisdom traditions and constructing their own belief syntheses.

He believes that if liberation theology had been grounded in a strong autonomous culture, it too could have been autonomous. But given the current state of Latin American culture, such a situation is still a dream. He asks: "Where is Latin American liberation theology taught today? Who reads it? In Latin America, a tiny minority of the educated religious public. Rejection has produced an isolation, the upshot of which is that liberation theology is better known and more read in Europe and the United States than in Latin America itself."[26] For Comblin, the value of liberation theology is that it questions theology as a whole. It directs Christian thinking beyond traditional scholastic theology and the church's traditional social teaching inspired by that theology.[27] However, he challenges some of liberation theology's most prized affirmations. For instance, he says that the "irruption of the poor" only happened in the sense that the church became aware of the poor. He also argues that while liberation theologians and pastoral workers were proposing radical change, most of the poor simply wanted to improve their lives. He says that the real revolution that took place in the second half of the 20th century was the migration of millions of campesinos to the cities. That migration meant moving from one civilization to another.[28] He also blasts consciousness-raising as "injecting ideology into the mind of the popular classes: a task of instilling doctrine so that the people would learn to feel what the theory said that they ought to feel and to want what the theory said that they should want."[29]

Comblin notes that the last stronghold of Christianity was the family. But with the sexual revolution, and the discovery of effective means of birth control, women were able to cut the cords of economic dependency on their male partners. He marks other effects of the sexual revolution: the manifestation of those "repressions, fantasies, and taboos—an unconscious or semiconscious world that had never been brought to awareness... For many women, the sexual revolution was—and still is—experienced as the most visible and most vital manifestation of personal freedom."[30]

Comblin concludes that women, indigenous people and blacks have been unwilling to be assimilated into liberation theology, and rightly so. He says that the starting point for feminist theology is a questioning of almost the entire history of humanity from the perspective of patriarchy. "For women, it is not enough to return to early Christianity: the solution will not be found there. And it is not very likely that the issue of women will be resolved through a theology, because it has much deeper roots which go beyond the domain of Christianity."[31] He says that the problem of liberation theology is internal to Christianity: what was early Christianity, why did it change, how can we return to its roots?

Comblin's frank evaluation concurs with what other analyses have been pointing out. Although the problems of poverty, marginality and inequitable income distribution have exacerbated, there is a growing shift in consciousness: the current situation of oppression is not a result of capitalism alone, but of a system that goes back more than 5000 years which today we name "patriarchy". Although liberation theology has been persecuted by an ever more conservative papacy, this is not the major cause for its apparent demise. The collapse of historical socialism has meant a loss of a utopian horizon, without which it becomes difficult for liberation theology activists to focus, mobilize and sustain a struggle for a different, more just, world. That world must be able to be imagined, and at this juncture of history, it cannot be. No revolution can survive without a utopian vision. And today, the old words and symbols that once energized a generation of liberation theology activists simply no longer evoke the revolutionary energy they once did. It appears that our dreams our changing, and that there is a deep historical shift taking place.

Some would see this shift as a call to go deeper and address issues that liberation theology did not address, seek new paradigms and new sources of inspiration for action. Many liberation theologians would see this an enriching experience, while others would say questions coming from feminist and cosmological perspectives go beyond the basic commitment of liberation theology to the poor. These new perspectives include not only an analysis of neo-liberal capitalism as the cause of oppression, but also the older oppression of patriarchy; questioning traditional theism with an omnipotent, anthropomorphic Creator; addressing the lingering dualism that separates mind from matter, natural from supernatural, the human from the rest of the life community. At the same time it is important to stress that liberation theology was key for those who have gone on to newer theological perspectives—indeed, it opened the possibility to dream in new ways. It is also necessary to acknowledge that the realities of poverty, injustice and oppression that liberation theology addressed in the 1970s and 1980s have not gone away and the blood of the martyrs still cries out. But there are also urgent new challenges and questions to be addressed.[32] Among them are:

- Can we speak of the poor and their children inheriting the Earth that is devastated and poisoned, bereft of so many soulful presences?
- Can we live out an option for the poor without rediscovering our deep kinship with all living beings, our spiritual belonging to the wildly creative, deeply spiritual, unfathomably interdependent

network we call the Cosmos?
- Can we be of service to the Latin American poor, most of whom are *mestizos*, without more deeply imbibing the religious wisdom of their largely forgotten indigenous heritage?
- Can love for the people be sustained without a profound rediscovery of our bodies, of the healing and animating power of tenderness and sensuality?
- Can we expect the poor to be empowered while failing to deal with our gender issues, our hierarchical habits, our Western craving for control?
- Can our solidarity bear fruit if our allegiance is to an immutable anthropomorphic deity with a ready-made plan for the human future?
- Can the god-images of traditional theism fill us with the energy, the burning passion required to face these historic challenges?[33]

Third Stage Feminist and Ecofeminist Critique

While Latin American feminist and ecofeminist theologians do not dispute their origins in liberation theology, they are now experiencing varying degrees of ambiguity about whether they are still doing liberation theology, or if their criticisms of patriarchal theology place them outside this theological playing field altogether. There are no conclusions as yet in this matter. While most feminist theologians are increasingly critical of liberation theology's engrained masculinist bias, in actual fact these liberation theologians also have faces. Most first generation liberation theologians are clerics and have been the teachers of today's eco/feminist theologians. Thus there is a long history of friendship and a certain reluctance to criticize one's mentors. But besides strong personal relationships, eco/feminists still agree with much of liberation theology's analysis, especially regarding the devastating effects of the current neo-liberal economic model on the region's poor. They ask, "what can feminist theology from Latin America and the Caribbean contribute to the knowledge, criticism and defeat of this globalized, neo-liberal economy?"[25] They would also engage in theology from the locus of the poor, focusing on poor women and continually deepening their analysis regarding the feminization of poverty in a globalized world.[26]

One of the severest criticisms eco/feminist theologians level against historical liberation theology is its avoidance of taking up the issues of sexual and reproductive rights, especially as they affect poor women. Finnish feminist scholar Elina Vuola has examined this gap in her book, *Limits of Liberation*, where she charges that Latin American liberation theologians' stances on sexual ethics have not moved from traditional Catholic teaching, which reflects the church's misogynist view of women. And yet, she notes: "one of the first causes of death for women of reproductive age all over the Third World, including Latin America, is the complications after an illegal abortion, (but) preventing the death of poor women has not been an explicit part of liberation theologians' 'agenda' of defending the poor."[27]

For Vuola, the concept of "the poor" in liberation theology is a vague and homogenized concept. Until recently the poor were defined principally in economic terms and as productive and political subjects.[28] She points out that: "there has been a yawning gap in LT which has to do with human corporality, sexuality and sexual ethics. The right of a female subject to her body and "bodiliness" has been absent."[29] There seems to be an inability to see "domestic" problems as "real" problems, given the supposedly more pressing survival struggles of the poor majorities. Furthermore, the unequal power struggles existing between men and women have been largely ignored. This, Vuola charges, underlines liberation theology's disconnection between theory and practice: "Nothing is said of the reality of illegal abortions and the high rates of domestic violence and households headed by women, which are some of the most burning problems for Latin American women."[30] She concludes that sexual ethics is an area where liberation theologians are far from their stated ideals and method as a praxis-oriented theology that considers ethical reasoning and action key. "Preventing the death of poor women has not been an explicit part of liberation theologians' agenda for defending the life of the poor. The reason is that 'the poor' are seen mainly as productive subjects, understood in the framework of Marxist class analysis, and not as bodily, gendered, and reproductive subjects as well."[31]

Mexican feminist theologian Pilar Aquino argues the same point: "The masculine theological focus has covered up the oppressive relations lived in the private area, and concealed relationships of domination exercised in the domestic sphere, where it is women who always endure the worse part. Ordinary daily life for an androcentric vision does not have epistemological value, nor does it form part of its attempts to understand the horizon of reality, that is, it does not influence the doing of theology. What, in effect, happens here is that the masculine theological focus grants a character of **naturality** to private, everyday life."[32]

Criticism of liberation theology's androcentric vision has come to the fore in the third phase of eco/feminist theology. Ecofeminist theologian Ivone Gebara argues that while feminist theology embraces liberation theology's critique of Euro-centered universalism, she points out that liberation theology is guilty of a similar masculine and androcentric universalism—the result of the formation in Aristotelian and Thomistic philosophy and theology in which most male liberation theologians (who are also clerics, she stresses) have been educated. This, she says, is where the two perspectives are most in conflict. Ecofeminist theology relies on different philosophical sources and conducts its research outside clerical circles and at the margin of ecclesial centers of power.[33] Liberation theology's frame of reference continues to be one of underlining the discontinuity between God's life and human life. Gebara argues that: "the fundamentally anthropocentric and androcentric character of liberation theology appears unquestionable. It speaks of God in human history, a God who in the end remains the Creator and Lord. (…) It senses no need to reexamine the cosmological and anthropological foundations of the Christian faith. It reaffirms the goodness and justice of God's being without raising questions about the repercussions, throughout human history, of traditional or historically conditioned images of God."[34] (I will take these arguments up again in Chapter III when I review Gebara's understanding of ecofeminism.)

There are two very clear currents within the third stage of Latin American feminist theology: Holistic ecofeminism and feminist biblical hermeneutics. The two are not exclusive, and can indeed compliment one another. But those feminist scholars working to re-interpret biblical texts from the standpoint of feminist hermeneutics are, perhaps, more committed than their ecofeminist counterparts to redeem the biblical tradition from its patriarchal interpretations.[35] According to Colombian feminist biblicist, Carmiña Navia, feminist biblical scholarship is alive and well in Latin America. She reports that today it is not just a question of re-reading texts with a critical feminist eye, but searching for and examining the scriptures on topics that range from themes such as the body, to violence and peace. She mentions feminist biblicists such as Alicia Winters, Tania Sampaio, Elsa Tamez, Irene Foulkes and herself, among others, as protagonists here and cites the biblical journal *Ribla*, published in Costa Rica, as a major source of publication for these scholars' work.[36] Another feminist biblicist, Brazilian Methodist scholar Nancy Cardoso, should also be mentioned here.

For Navia, ecofeminism in Latin America is especially rich in offering a more vibrant spirituality to the region where there is "a full reconciliation with one's being born a woman; a rediscovery of one's female genealogy and the role played by mothers, grandmothers, aunts, etc. in transmitting the faith; a joyful and full reconciliation with our bodies; a search for alternative forms of tenderness; and above all, a recovery and reworking of traditional symbols of the sacred."[37] Here she mentions the contributions being made by Ivone Gebara and the Con-spirando Collective.

This second current, ecofeminism, with its implications for theology, ethics and spirituality, will be the subject of the following chapters.

1 Madonna Kolbenschlag,. *Eastward Toward Eve: A Geography of Soul.* New York: Crossroad Publishing Company, 1996, p. 135. While a good number of wise women have mentored me, no one more than Madonna opened the paths of spiritual journeying for me. She died suddenly in January, 2000 here in Santiago, Chile where she had come to lecture on goddesses, myths and archetypes at the first School of Ecofeminist Spirituality and Ethics, sponsored by the Con-spirando Collective. She continues to be my spirit-guide; I dedicate these reflections to her memory.

3 Carl Sagan, *Cosmos.* New York: Ballantine Books, 1980. p. 286.

4 María Pilar Aquino, *Our Cry for Life: Feminist Theology from Latin America.* Maryknoll: Orbis, 1993. Aquino's work is especially insightful on the first two stages of Latin American feminist theology.

5 Elsa Tamez,. "Latin American Feminist Hermeneutics: A Retrospective," *Women's Visions: Theological Reflection, Celebration, Action,* Ofelia Ortega, ed. Geneva: WCC Publications, 1995.

6 Mary Judith Ress, "Ecofeminism and Panentheism: Interview with Ivone Gebara," *Readings in Ecology and Feminist Theology,* Mary Heather MacKinnon and Moni McIntyre, eds. Kansas City: Sheed & Ward, 1995.

7 Tamez, "Latin American Feminist Hermeneutics," p. 89.

8 Elsa Tamez, "Descubriendo rostros distintos de Dios", *Panorama de la Teología Latinoamericana,* Juan-José Tamayo y Juan Bosch, eds. Navarra, España: Editorial Verbo Divino, 2001. pp. 647-660.

9 Tamez, "Latin American Feminist Hermeneutics," p. 78.

10 Ibid., p. 86.

11 Ibid., pp. 77-89. I have basically summarized Tamez' article, adding my own reflections from my experience of the development of feminist theology in the region. As managing editor of the Lima weekly, *Noticias Aliadas/Latinamerica Press* throughout the 1980s, I followed and reported on its development closely. I am also a founding member of the Christian feminist collective, Talitha Cumi, founded in Lima in 1983 where I lived through much of the evolution in feminist theology and biblical interpretation that Tamez describes.

12 This interview was originally published in Spanish in *Con-spirando; Revista latinoamericana de ecofeminismo, espiritualidad y teología,* No. 4 (junio, 1993) under the title, "Entrevista con Ivone Gebara: Ecofeminismo holístico", pp. 44-49. It has since been translated into English and reproduced in several feminist anthologies.

13 Tamez, "Latin American feminist hermeneutics," p. 85.

15 Mary Judith Ress, ed. "Elsa Tamez: tres fases de la teología en América Latina," *Revista Con-spirando,* No. 18 (Diciembre, 1996). Pp. 2-12. After presenting the description of each stage, I reflect on "where was I" at each stage. I also included this reflection in the introduction to *Lluvia para florecer: Entrevistas sobre el ecofeminismo en América Latina.*

16 Gustavo Gutiérrez, "Situación y Tareas de la Teología de la Liberación" *Teología Latinoamericana: Evaluación, Retos y Perspectivas. Alternativas, No 18/19.* Managua: Editorial Lascasiana, 2001. p. 54.

17 Ibid., pp. 62-66.

18 Tamayo, *Panorama de la Teología Latinoamericana,* pp. 18-19.

19 Ibid., pp. 30-35.

20 "Presentación," *Alternativas, No 18/19,* p. 7. This issue of *Alternativas* contains many of the papers given at the Congress.

21 Leonardo Boff, "El Pobre, la nueva cosmología y liberación: Cómo enriquecer la Teología de la Liberación", Alternativas No. 18/19, p. 76.

22 Ibid., pp. 79-80.
23 Ibid., p. 86.
24 Márcio Fabri Dos Anjos, "Teología en América Latina: Cambios y Alternativas," *Alternativas, No. 18/19*. p. 40. Another telling example of this tension is present in the following quotation from the same documents: "But there were resistances and questioning, among them: the revelation in our thought of a universe of millions of light years—won't this be a form of making us fly away from the grounding of an economic and political reality in which the poor suffer? In this paradigm, eminently holistic, won't complexity and fluidity become so enlarged to the point of giving us over to a type of "panthcratic fixation with the cosmos", congealing our commitments and responsibilities?", cited in Luiz Carlos Susin, "Teologia y nuevos paradigmas" in *Alternativas No.18/19*, p.28. This issue of Alternativas contains the papers presented at the SOTER meeting in Brazil in 2000.
25 José Comblin, *Called for Freedom: The Changing Context of Liberation Theology*. Maryknoll: Orbis, 1998. p. 203.
26 Ibid., p. ix.
26 Ibid., p. 55.
27 Ibid., p. 57.
28 Ibid., p. 78.
29 Ibid., p. 80.
30 Ibid., p. 181-182.
31 Ibid., pp. 214-215.
32 David Molineaux, Notes on the Current Status of Latin American Liberation Theology. Talk given at the Call to Action Conference, Los Angeles, July 2002. pp. 2-4.
33 Ibid., p. 5
25 Elsa Tamez, ed. *La sociedad que las mujeres soñamos*. San José, Costa Rica: DEI, 2001, p. 13. This work contains lectures and the final document from the EATWOT meeting of women theologians from Latin America and the Caribbean in Bogota, Colombia in August, 1999.
26 María Arcelia González Butrón, "Efectos de la globalización neoliberal en algunos aspectos de la vida de las mujeres: Una mirada desde América Latina y el Caribe", Ibid., pp. 17-38.
27 Elina Vuola, *Limits of Liberation: Praxis as Method in Latin American Liberation Theology and Feminist Theology*. Helsinki: Suomalainen Tiedeakatemia, 1997, p18.
28 This development can be traced in *Mysterium Liberationis: Fundamental Concepts in Liberation Theology*. Ignacio Ellacuría, S.J. and Jon Sobrino, S.J, eds. Maryknoll: Orbis, 1993.
29 Vuola, p. 88.
30 Ibid., p. 183.
31 Ibid., p. 218
32 Ibid., p. 146.
33 Ivone Gebara, "Ecofeminismo: Algunos desafíos teológicos," *Teología con rostro de mujer, Alternativas, No. 16/17*. Managua: Editorial Lascasina, 2000. pp. 174 -175.
34 Ivone Gebara, *Longing for Running Water: Ecofeminism and Liberation*. Minneapolis: Fortress Press, 1999, pp. 46-47.
35 Carmiña Navia Velasco, "Teología desde la mujer, un paradigma fértil, " *Alternativas No. 16/17*, p. 134.
36 Ibid., p. 134.
37 Ibid., p. 135.

All beings at some time have been my mother

—Buddhist teaching[20]

Chapter II

Ecofeminism: A genealogy

Introduction

There is the story—both ancient and new—that we are earthlings, that our history as well as our future is radically connected to the fate of this fragile green planet we call home. And it is from there that I would attempt to allure you toward the insights coming from ecofeminism, a "remembering of who we are" that does, indeed, offer a new utopian vision.

Ecofeminism insists that the interdependence of all things is the *constitutive reality* of the Universe. Poised as we are on the threshold of a new millennium, there appears to be a new urgency to refashion ourselves as a species. Being "masters of the universe" leaves us with a bitter taste of being orphaned from the matrix from which we have evolved. Indeed, it is slowly dawning on us that while we are part of a greater whole, the greater whole is also part of us and it is precisely because of the evolution of the greater whole that we now realize how related we are to everything else.

Discoveries made during the last 20 years in quantum physics and in biology are radically changing our definitions of the origin and scope of our universe as well as who we are as a species. A major paradigm shift is occurring that challenges our current mechanistic way of understanding the universe and entices us toward the idea of an emerging cosmology where the material universe is seen as a dynamic web of interrelated events.

For me, ecofeminism is a new term for an ancient wisdom—a wisdom that still lies dormant deep within our genetic memories. Ecofeminism's greatest insight is the dawning conviction that everything is connected—and therefore everything is sacred. Ecofeminists make the connection that the oppression of women and of people of color by a system controlled by ruling class males and the devastation of the planet are two forms of violence that reinforce and feed upon each other. Furthermore, they both come from a terribly misguided sense of the need to control, to dominate the other, that which is different (in short, the patriarchal mindset). From being the **source** of life, both women and the earth have become **resources** to be used—and abused—as the power structures see fit.

Ecofeminists join with all those searching for a more holistic worldview that recognizes and celebrates the web of all life. This ecofeminist posture places those embracing it firmly in the postmodern debate as well as in the post-patriarchal quest for a more relevant and passionate understanding of who we are in relation to the entire cosmos. This posture has engaged us in the struggle to redefine the divinity as well as the human enterprise. We search for a more adequate cosmology, ethics and spirituality. Ecofeminism ignites a good deal of passion and purpose, which I hope to convey below.

I have been working in the areas of ecofeminist thought, especially as it applies to theology, ethics and spirituality in the context of Latin America, for the past 12 years. Over this time, I have developed the following chart as a sort of genealogy to help our understanding of the spectrum of influences that coalesce in ecofeminism:[21]

Sources of Ecofeminism

```
                    Ancient
                    wisdom
                    traditions

                              Women activists
                              against ecological
                              destruction
                                    ↓ ↓ ↓
    Radical/Cultural    ←→   Ecofeminism   →   Deep Ecology
       Feminism                  ↕                  ↓              Cybernetics
          ↓                  Ecofeminist           New Science
    Feminist Anthropology:    Theology                ↕
      Goddess images                                                Indigenous
          ↓    ↘                                    New             Cosmovisions
     Jungian  → Body as source                   Cosmology
    Psychology    of wisdom
                     ↓
                 Attempts at        Sustainable
                 forming Post- ←→   economies/
                  patriarchal       Bioregionalism
                  communities
```

Using this chart as a guide, in this Chapter, I will develop the foundational influences of ecofeminism and how it is related to ecofeminist theology. In the next Chapter, I will then concentrate on Latin American ecofeminist theology as it is being developed by Brazilian ecofeminist theologian Ivone Gebara and by the Con-spirando Collective.

Ecofeminism combines insights coming from deep ecology and radical or cultural feminism. Deep ecology, in turn, has been influenced by discoveries coming from what is being called "the New Science" and by new thinking in cybernetics. This has evolved into a new way of viewing the universe, a new cosmology. While new, this cosmology finds that it shares much in common with the forgotten wisdom of the earth's original peoples (indigenous cosmologies). Deep ecologists call us toward new ways of organizing ourselves that are more sustainable and reflect the caring capacity of the earth's bioregions.

Radical/cultural feminism looks at the patterns of culture and consciousness that sustain patriarchy. These feminist researchers have found major insights into the development of patriarchy through work being done in feminist anthropology, especially in re-examining early goddess myths and culture. They have also been influenced by concepts such as the collective unconsciousness and the archetypes as developed by psychiatrist Carl Jung. Radical/cultural feminists are rediscovering the wisdom that dwells within the body. They urge us to work toward a postpatriarchal world where equalitarian relationships exist between the sexes and between humans and the earth community.

Ancient wisdom traditions

Before examining each of these sources more in depth, I would like to reaffirm my conviction that ecofeminism is a new term to describe a deep intuition that is present in the wisdom traditions of the medieval Christian mystics, as well as in Buddhism and Shamanism, to name only three. These traditions teach communion with nature and describe the divine in terms other than masculine or heaven-centered. While it is beyond the scope of this work to examine these more ancient roots, it is worth mentioning the renewed interest among ecofeminist theologians in the life and work of Hildegard of Bingen, a 12th century German mystic. Hildegard's reflection on God's "greening" as that vital energy present in all creation is closely linked to deep ecology's belief that all matter is bio-spiritual.

Turning to more contemporary influences, I would like to acknowledge four "precursors" who have influenced current ecofeminist thought, especially my own. In 1962, Thomas Kuhn, in his now classic *The Structure of Scientific Revolutions*, described the concept of paradigm shift as "a constellation of achievements—concepts, values, techniques, etc.—shared by the scientific community and used by that community to define legitimate problems and solutions."[22] According to Kuhn, shifts in paradigms occur in rapid, discontinuous and revolutionary breaks. Now, 40 years after he described the paradigm shift taking place within the scientific world in quantum physics, we are aware that this was part of a much larger shift in cultural transformation, as we shall see below.

Another precursor is none other than Albert Einstein, that great human being of the last century who discovered the theory of relativity—as a result, we now know that the universe is expanding and therefore had a beginning. This discovery opened the doors for other scientists to begin to question our Cartesian mindset; in the second half of the 20th century, quantum physicists began to see that within the sub-atomic world, there was no such thing as an "essential building block of life" because "matter" at the subatomic level dissolved into wave patterns that had an infinite number of probabilities in terms of behavior. Nature, it seems, is made up of a complex web of relationships which comprise, in the end, a unified whole. This has caused a revolution in the scientific world, changing the definitions of what is the material basis for life.

A third precursor is marine biologist Rachel Carson, whom many have dubbed the first "ecofeminist". In 1962, she wrote *Silent Spring*, now considered the first voice to alert the industrialized world about the interconnectedness of all the planet's life. She was a leading voice against the use of DDT, one of the "dirty dozen" pesticides. DDT was sprayed on some of the richest agricultural lands in California to rid crops of insects. Carson said that you cannot kill the insects without killing the songbirds, and you can't kill the songbirds without poisoning the children. Carson argued that pesticides would accumulate through the food chain, seeping into the water supply and into the soil so that chemicals spread on crops would poison the birds and animals and humans, and thus create a "silent spring." The chemical industry's response to Carson was to mock her as a "spinster in galoshes who worried about birds."[23]

A final precursor is the French Jesuit paleontologist Pierre Teilhard de Chardin who first raised the possibility that the cosmos was conscious (the noosphere) and therefore sacred. It was he who first told us that we lived in a self-transforming universe or "cosmogenesis". His books *Phenomenon of Man* and the *Divine Milieu* nourished a whole generation of seekers within the Catholic world and beyond.

Activist women's role

Ecofeminism in Latin America is quite new; indeed its philosophy and theology is only in the initial stages of becoming known and accepted and women's environmental activism has not been seen necessarily as ecofeminist practice. However, in other parts of the Third World—especially in India—ecofeminist activists have been raising their voices since the 1970s.

Credit for coining the world "ecofeminism" is given to French feminist Francoise d'Eaubonne, who in 1974 argued that male control of production and of women's sexuality brought the twin horsemen of environmental destruction and overpopulation. She called for "a planet in the female gender".[24]

During the late 1970s and early 1980s, the term ecofeminist was used to describe activist women who organized to protect themselves and their families from environmental disasters. Classic examples often cited include:
- the Chipko movement in India, a movement of poor women who protected large swatches of forest in the Himalayan mountains against clear cutting by "hugging trees" (*chipko* in the native language) in defiance of the loggers' advance, causing them to retreat. (The Chipko movement has been documented by Indian ecofeminist Vandana Shiva in her book *Staying Alive*, where she shows how poor rural women's link with the natural world is the reality of

their daily lives. She argues that "maldevelopent" has been created by the North to impose its model of development, which is synonymous with the violation of nature and women.)[25]
- the Green Belt movement in Kenya, led by anatomy teacher Wangari Maathai, which has galvanized hundreds of rural women to engage in extensive tree-planting to resolve firewood shortages as well as to prevent desertification and soil erosion by surrounding their villages with a "green belt".
- the Love Canal protest in Niagara Falls, New York, led by housewife Lois Gibbs, who exposed the fact that for many years government officials had been using an abandoned canal trench as a chemical dump, but it had been covered over and a school had been built on the site. The chemicals were also seeping into the town's water supplies. Gibbs began documenting the relationship between the town's inordinately high number of birth defects and miscarriages and the chemical dump. No one believed this "hysterical housewife" until Gibbs found a scientist to translate her "housewife data" into legitimate scientific jargon.[26]

In Latin America, one of the most dynamic movements is the ecology movement. The majority of its members are women and young people. Worldwide, women form 60-80 per cent of the membership in grassroots environmental organizations, although the leadership profile does not reflect this phenomenon.[27]

Before proceeding with the theoretical underpinnings of ecofeminism, I want to call attention to the fact that ecofeminist practice emerges from the critical demands of life, those imperatives of a particular historical setting —and not from any prefabricated theory. When women protest against the destruction of their environment, they automatically make the connection between what is happening to their surroundings and the fact that they are women: they experience two kinds of violence—that waged against the environment and that (which perhaps they had not really noticed before) leveled against them because they are poor women (rural women in the case of India and Kenya, or "hysterical housewives" in the case of the United States). What many are documenting in the last 15 years is the growing number of women—most of whom have not been politically active before—who are either indignant or terrified at what is happening to their environment and its effects on the health and well being of their families. They recognize their own as well as their families' vulnerability to increasing environmental disaster and their lack of access to those centers of power causing the disasters. This has led many women to search for a coherent critique of the present model of development.

It is from this activism and this search that ecofeminist theory is evolving. Women sense that there is a more systemic way of understanding what is happening to the planet—and, in many cases, they also are looking for a spirituality that will water present and future struggles. At this point in history, ecofeminism provides this theoretical framework.

I. Deep ecology

Deep ecology does not separate humans from the natural environment but conceives the planet as a network of phenomena that are fundamentally interconnected and interdependent. Deep ecology recognizes the intrinsic value of all living beings and views humans as just one particular strand in the web of life.[28]

Deep ecology is both a philosophical school and a global grassroots movement that was founded by Norwegian philosopher Arne Naess in the early 1970s. Naess distinguished between "shallow" and "deep" ecology, characterizing shallow ecology as anthropocentric in that it views humans as above or outside nature, as the source of all value. Only by recognizing that humanity is no more, but also no less important that the rest of the Earth community can humans learn to dwell within their own environmental niche and allow other species to flourish. For deep ecologists, anthropocentric hierarchies would be replaced by biocentric or ecocentric egalitarianism. This perspective sees the world as an intrinsically dynamic web of relations in which there are no absolute dividing lines between the living and the nonliving, the animate and the inanimate, or the human and the non-human.[29] Deep ecology is passionately committed to overturning those mindsets such as anthropocentrism, dualism, atomism, hierarchalism, rigid autonomy and abstract nationalism that are apparently responsible for humanity's destruction of the biosphere.[30] A mature humanity, deep ecologists agree, would understand its interrelationship with everything else.

For physicist Fritjof Capra, one of today's leading deep ecologists, deep ecology is ultimately committed to a deepening spiritual awareness: "When the concept of the human spirit is understood as the mode of consciousness in which the individual feels a sense of belonging, of connectedness to the cosmos as a whole, it becomes clear that ecological awareness is spiritual in its deepest essence."[31] Capra and others underline the paradigm shift in values taking place within a deep ecology perspective. They note the spiritual, psychological experience (as opposed to a more logical approach) that nature and the self are one. They point to a change in the perception of the self that gradually widens to identify with other beings. As deep ecologist Michael Dowd summarizes:

> The message of deep ecology is timely news for humanity, and for the planet as a whole. It offers reconnection to our genetic memory and billions of years of evolutionary wisdom. Its application can empower us to live in synergistic cooperation and harmony with the rest of the body of Life. We can begin to experience a harmonious connection alien to us when we thought of ourselves as separate from and superior to our larger body. We can begin to experience a consciousness of heavenly rapport with all of life. Timely as it may be, the message of deep ecology must be taught and integrated into our society on a massive scale if our grandchildren and theirs are to be saved from a toxic and literal hell on Earth. It must be put into fervent daily practice in every area of our lives. The planet is calling us to create communities that live and love ecologically. This is essential for the salvation of millions of species, especially our own.[32]

Deep ecologist Joanna Macy is a leading voice in this extended understanding of the self. I first "met" Macy through reading about the amazing ritual she and ecologist John Seed developed called "The Council of all Beings". (I later participated in this ritual in a workshop led by Seed here in Chile). Later, I heard about the "Despair Workshops" she was holding and felt a deep empathy with this woman. Macy, a Buddhist, is convinced that, at this time, we humans are feeling a deep despair that we try to keep at bay. Nevertheless, we are being bombarded by data that render questionable the survival of our culture, our species, and even our planet as a viable home for conscious life. Despair, in this context, is the loss of the assumption that the species will inevitably pull thorough. Macy's "despair work" deals with the willingness to acknowledge that inner pain and grief.

For Macy, until we can grieve for our planet and its future inhabitants, we cannot fully feel or enact our love for them. Such grief is frequently suppressed. At the root of this suppression lies a dysfunctional notion of the self as an isolated and fragile entity. So long as we see ourselves as essentially separate, competitive, and ego-identified beings, it is difficult to respect the validity of our social despair, deriving as it does from our interconnectedness. Macy believes that the acknowledgment of despair, like faith, is a letting go of the manipulative assumption that conscious ego can or should control all events.[33]

Macy calls us to take account of the inner resources we have for sustaining our action and our sanity—among which are the ways in which we view our world and our relationship to it. She sees four particular ways people on spiritual paths look at the world: First, the world as a *battlefield*, where good and evil are pitted against each other. Such a view is very good for arousing courage as well as for giving a sense of certainty. This view is very strong among monotheistic religions. Second, the world as *trap*. Here the spiritual path is to disentangle ourselves and escape for this messy world. This stance is based on a hierarchical view of reality, where mind is seen as higher than matter and spirit is set over and above nature. There is contempt for the material and a great emphasis on detachment from the tough work of social change. Third, the world as *lover:* Instead of a stage set for our moral battles or a prison to escape, the world is beheld as an intimate and gratifying partner. Desire plays a creative, world-manifesting role here: one feels embraced in the primal erotic play of life. When we see the world as lover, every being, every phenomenon, can become an expression of that ongoing, erotic impulse. Finally, the world as *self:* Hunger for this union springs from a deep knowing, to which mystics of all traditions give voice. For Macy, once the bonds of our limited egos snap, the individual heart becomes one with its world.[34]

To experience the world as an extended self and its story as our own extended story does not involve a surrender of our own individual self. Having gained distance and sophistication of perception, Macy says that we can now recognize who we have been all along. Now we can realize that we are "our world knowing itself"—and thus relinquish our separateness: "We have all gone that long journey, and now, richer for it, we come home to our mutual belonging. We return to experience, as we never could before, that we are both the self of our world and its cherished lover. We are not doomed to destroy it by the cravings of the separate ego and the technologies it fashioned. We can wake up to who we really are, and allow the waters of the Rhine to flow clean once more, and the trees to grow green along its banks."[35]

One of Macy's most compelling concepts is her notion of the "ecological self,' or the "greening of the self," which she describes as that wider construct of identity and self-interest that is coextensive with other beings and the life of the planet. Macy believes that what is taking place is a shift in identification. This arising of the ecological self is happening because of three converging developments: First, the conventional small self, or ego-self, is being impinged upon by the psychological and spiritual effects we are suffering from facing the dangers of mass annihilation. Second, a new way of dismantling the ego-self is arising out of science itself, which now calls for a systems approach to everything. From the perspective of the "new science," life is seen as dynamically composed of self-organizing systems, patterns that are sustained in and by their relationships. Third, the resurgence in our time of non-dualistic spiritualities. For Macy:

> The ecological self, like any notion of selfhood, is a metaphoric construct and a dynamic one. It involves choice: choices can be made to identify at different moments, with different dimensions or aspects of our systemically interrelated existence—be they hunted whales or homeless humans or the planet itself. In doing this, the extended self brings into play wider resources—courage, endurance, and ingenuity—like a nerve cell in a neural net opening to the charge of the other neurons. **There is the sense of being acted through and sustained by those very beings on whose behalf one acts. This is very close to the religious concept of grace. In systems language we can talk about it as synergy.** With this extension, this greening of the self, we can find a sense of buoyancy and resilience that comes form letting flow through us strengths and resources that come to us with continuous surprise and sense of blessing.[36]

Insights coming from deep ecology have led activists to put their own lives at risk in defense of the planet's forests, oceans, rivers, wildlife sanctuaries, etc. A recent example of this has been the case of Julie "Butterfly" Hill. Beginning in 1998 she spent two years living in a 200-foot old-growth redwood tree in northern California to stop loggers from cutting it down. I heard Hill speak of her experience living in "Luna" (her name for the tree) and her mystical description of how she and the tree became as one, and how in storms Luna actually protected her from thunder and lightening. I was very moved by this young woman's testimony of how the experience of living in Luna has changed her entire perspective of the relatedness of all things. (That evening she shared the stage with her friend and mentor, Joanna Macy.)

However, while ecofeminists and deep ecologists share much in common, and would agree that nature must be seen as alive and as having its own agenda and agency, there is a difference in emphasis. Ecofeminists' central criticism of deep ecology is that while it condemns anthropocentrism (human-centeredness) it ignores the role that androcentrism (male-centeredness) plays in ecological destruction. As ecofeminist Mary Mellor has pointed out, "the question of whether humanity as a whole should be held accountable for the ecological crisis, or some aspect of its internal organization such as patriarchy, has given rise to a prolonged debate between ecofeminists and deep ecologists."[37] Ecofeminists see many male deep ecologists remarkable sexist in their approach to saving the planet, with stress placed on male individualist values such as reclaiming the "wild man" or the "noble man confronting nature," or the "freedom to roam the forests as the perennial backpacker," etc.[38] They would call upon deep ecologists to embrace a "lived awareness that we experience in relation to particular beings as well as to the larger whole" and call for a more grounded approach to human-nature relations, which include the issue of sex/gender relations and the particularity of women's lives.[39] Ecofeminist Marti Kheel is especially clear on this point: "Whereas the anthropocentric worldview perceives humans as the center or apex of the natural world, the androcentric analysis suggests that this worldview is unique to men" and questions whether deep ecologists' search for an expanded self is "a way of transcending the concrete world of particularity".[40] She reminds us that under patriarchy, women's identities, unlike men's, have been identified with the devalued natural world. (This issue will be addressed more fully below.)

The New Science

Deep ecology owes much of its shift in worldview to the discoveries coming from science in the later part of the 20th century. While it is beyond the scope of this work to detail these discoveries, an overview to show the enormity of the change in perspective is in order. Excellent summaries of these discoveries can be found in the writings of Thomas Berry and Brian Swimme,[41] Fritjof Capra's *The Web of Life* and Diarmuid

O´Murchu´s *Quantum Theology*.[42] These authors point to a paradigm shift from a mechanistic and reductionist way of understanding the universe by concentrating on the parts that make up the whole, to an emphasis on the whole, or on what has been come to be called "systems thinking". As Capra explains: "A system has come to mean an integrated whole whose essential properties arise from the relationships between its parts and 'systems thinking' is the understanding of a phenomenon within the context of a larger whole."[43] Systems thinking began among organic biologists who observed that the essential properties of an organism are the essential properties of the whole, which none of the parts have unto themselves. These properties arise from the *relationships* among the parts and can only be understood within the context of the larger whole. This shift in perception created a profound revolution in the way scientists thought.

The next science to have its worldview shaken was physics. The reductionist view had been that all physical phenomena could be reduced to the smallest "building block" or particle. However, with quantum physics, at the sub-atomic level there are no building blocks, only wavelike patterns of probabilities of interconnections. The amazing discovery here was that "sub-atomic particles have no meaning as isolated entities but can be understood only as interconnections, or correlations…in other words, sub-atomic particles are not 'things' but interconnections among things and these, in turn, are interconnections among other things, and so on. In quantum theory we never end up with any 'things'; we always deal with interconnections."[44]

As Werner Heisenberg, one of the founders of quantum theory, put it, "The world thus appears as a complicated tissue of events, in which connections of different kinds alternate or overlap or combine and thereby determine the texture of the whole."[45]

Systems thinking uses the concept of a network to describe living systems. At each level, the parts of one network turn out to be smaller networks. Thus there are networks nesting within other networks.

Seen in another way, the new science would posit that our universe is a sphere of belonging—indeed, there are "horizons of belonging" which biologist Rupert Sheldrake calls "fields." Sheldrake believes we belong to something greater than ourselves, which is forever unfolding and evolving.[46]

Beginning with Einstein's discovery of the theory of relativity, then, the mechanistic worldview that had dominated scientific thought for the past 200 years started to unravel. This worldview began in the 16th and 17th centuries when the earlier notion of the universe as an organic, living being was replaced by the idea that the world was a machine. Names such as Rene Descartes and Isaac Newton and linked to the Enlightenment's Scientific Revolution are key here: Descartes was responsible for the method of analytic thinking, which consisted of breaking everything into pieces in order to understand the whole by understanding the properties of its parts. For Descartes, the world was a perfect machine governed by mathematical laws. Newton applied this same reasoning to the solar system, concluding that the universe was indeed a large mechanical system running to laws of motion that were entirely predictable and deterministic. The metaphor was that of a clock with God as the Great Time-keeper who wound the clock and then sat back and let the universe tick on its own.

However, with the paradigm switch to systems thinking, today's "scientific revolution" has once again returned to an earlier, more organic view of the universe. For instance, scientists have learned that time and space are not two separate entities, but that together they form a space-time continuum, and that energy and mass are, in fact, part of the same phenomenon. Thus, things can be understood only relative to each other, not independent of each other. This theory was extended to include gravity, the mutual attraction of all massive bodies, which has the effect of curving space and time. Thus our universe is not a flat plane, but a curved one—and it is this curvature that effectively holds everything in place and enables the universal life process to function as a great whole.

Following Einstein's lead, scientists began to question the determinist laws of nature as posited by Descartes, Newton and their followers and to posit—once again—an alive universe. They discovered that radiation (either light or heat) is not emitted continuously, but in the form of "quanta," energy packets that could be either particles or waves, depending on how and in what medium they were observed. Quantum physics has revolutionized the way scientists understand the subatomic world. It appears that there is no "basic building block" but only probabilities. As Irish priest and sociologist Diarmud O'Murchu summarizes:

> It is at a perceptual level that the theory evokes a new way of viewing and understanding our world. In essence, it states that everything we perceive and experience is a great deal more than the initial, external impression we may obtain, that we experience life, not in isolated segments, but in wholes (quanta); that these bundles of energy which impinge upon us are not inert, lifeless pieces of matter, but living energies; that our naming of the living reality we experience will at least be a probability-guess at what its real essence is (an essence best understood by interacting with it experientially rather than trying to conceptualize it at an "objective" distance).[47]

Basic to the paradigm shift from the mechanistic view (the whole equals the sum of its parts) is that the whole is *greater* than the sum of its parts; furthermore, the whole is also contained in each of the parts. Thus, the concept of *holon* (Greek for whole) is beginning to emerge as a new metaphor to name this shift, and we now speak of a "hologram" as that key feature whereby each part contains information about the whole object. Holograms were first discovered in the area of optics: a method of lens-less photography in which the wave field of light scattered by an object is recorded on a plate as an interference pattern. Through the hologram a three dimensional image appears, and any piece of the hologram will reconstruct the entire image. Thus, the form and structure of an entire object appears to be enfolded within each region of the photographic record.

David Bohm, a physicist who worked with Einstein, has proposed that the universe itself is a hologram. All that unfolds before our eyes is only an external, fragmentary manifestation of an underlying unbroken wholeness that he called an "implicit order." Bohm held that all matter could be discussed in terms of folding and unfolding. He called this the holomovement, an unbroken and undivided totality. Everything emerges by unfoldment from the holomovement, which then enfolds back into the implicate order. For Bohm, "the implicate and explicate together are a flowing, undivided wholeness. Every part of the universe is related to every other part but in different degrees."[48] Our primary reality, says Bohm, is the implicit order, which is the subtle, universal reservoir of all life, the wellspring of all possibility and the source of all meaning. The explicit order, which is visible and discernible, is the product of the former. For Bohm, the primary reality is not the external, visible sensory world, but the invisible, enfolded realm of potential and possibility. What we perceive, then, is not a landscape of facts or objects, but one of events, process, movement and energy. Bohm saw that in this creative flow, past, present and future were all one. Every creation of matter is a recapitulation of all past creation and carries an inherent propensity to become something more than it is at any present moment. Moreover, the universe seems to be knitted together by a type of memory network that builds matter around itself in various forms, ranging from molecules to plants, to galaxies and stars, to our own species. As O'Murchu, influenced by Bohm, concludes: "Wholeness, which is largely unmanifest and dynamic (not stable) in nature, is the wellspring of all possibility. In seeking to understand life, we begin with the whole, which is always greater than the sum of the parts: paradoxically, the whole is contained in each part, and yet no whole is complete in itself."[49]

    This change in perception of reality is affecting not only physics and biology but astronomy, geology, chemistry and mathematics as well. A new language for understanding the complex, highly integrative systems of life has emerged as well: dynamic systems theory, the theory of complexity, nonlinear dynamics, network dynamics, etc. Chaotic attractors, fractals, dissipative structures, self-organization, and *autopoesis* are some of its key concepts. The list of pioneers in the "new science" is growing everyday as they bring their expertise to bear on the conviction described by biologist Elisabet Sahtouris: "Our planet and its creatures constitute a single self-regulating system that is in fact a great living being, or organism."[50]

Cybernetics

Patterns of organization, a guiding principle in both organic biology and in quantum physics, became the explicit focus of cybernetics. Insights coming from cybernetics would break down former dualisms between mind and body and thus become a major factor contributing to the paradigm shift taking place in the scientific world.

The best-known cyberneticist is Gregory Bateson. Bateson thought of himself primarily as a biologist and saw the many fields he became involved with—anthropology, epistemology, psychiatry, cybernetics—as branches of biology. His lifelong aim was to discover common principles of organization in their diversity—or, as he put it "the pattern that connects." Bateson is hard for most of us laypersons to understand, but he is unquestionably a major seminal thinker of our times. He has made significant contributions in the area of family therapy by pioneering a systems approach, developed a cybernetic model of alcoholism, and authored the double-bind theory of schizophrenia.[51] However, Bateson's most important contribution to science and philosophy was the concept of Mind, which he developed based on cybernetic principles. His thinking opened the door to understanding the nature of Mind as a systems phenomenon and became the first successful attempt in science to overcome the Cartesian division between mind and body.

Batesonian holism posits that:
- fact and value are inseparable:
- nature is revealed in our relations with it and phenomena can be known only in context (participant observation);
- unconscious mind is primary;
- quality takes precedence over quantity;

- mind/body, subject/object are each two aspects of the same process;
- circuitry rather than infinite, linear progress is the norm
- single variables in the system cannot be maximized;
- we cannot know more than a fraction of reality;
- logic is both/and (dialectical);
- process, form and relationship are primary;
- wholes have properties that parts do not have;
- living systems, or Minds, are not reducible to their components.
- Nature is alive.[52]

Bateson was convinced that it was possible to find the same sort of laws at work in the structure of a crystal as in the structure of society. He believed that all phenomena, including individuals and societies, are organized entities that are "coded" in a way that is coherent. Immersed as he was in cybernetic theory, Bateson saw that we live in a world of circuit structures and that we know a thing only in context, in relation to other things. He developed an epistemology that holds that there are always Minds within Minds:

> A man himself is a Mind, but once he picks up an ax and starts to chop down a tree, he is part of a larger Mind. The forest around him is a larger Mind still, and so on. In this series of hierarchical levels, the homeostasis of the largest unit must be the issue. Thus "person" or "organism" has to be seen as a sub-Mind, not as an independent unit. Western individualism is based on a confusion between Sub-Mind and Mind. It regards the human mind as the only mind around, free to maximize any variables it chooses, free to ignore the homeostasis of the larger unit.[53]

For Bateson, there is no "self" cutting down a tree "out there." Rather, a relationship is taking place, a systemic circuit, a Mind. The whole situation is alive, not just the human being, and this aliveness is immanent in the circuit, not transcendent to it. And what is going around this circuit –tree-eyes-brains-muscles-ax-stroke-tree—is information. This circuit of information is the Mind, the self-corrective unit, now seen to be a network of pathways which is not bounded by the purposive consciousness of the man cutting down the tree, but extended to include the pathways of all unconscious thought, as well as all the pathways along which information can travel. Clearly, then, as we can see from this example, large parts of the thinking network lie outside the human body.

Another example Bateson uses is that of the pollution of Lake Erie. (I grew up along Lake Erie in the 1950s and can attest to its levels of pollution; in fact it was so contaminated with lead and other chemicals from the local industry that it was referred to as a "dead lake". However, in the late 1970s there was a major clean-up effort and today Lake Erie is once again "alive".) Since Mind is immanent in the ecosystem—and indeed in the total evolutionary structure of the universe—then if we pollute Lake Erie until "it loses its mind," we too will also go somewhat insane, because we are a Sub-Mind in a Larger Mind that we have driven a bit crazy. The resulting insanity becomes part of our thought and experience. Furthermore, says Bateson, there are clear limits to how many times we can create such situations before the planet, or Larger Mind, reacts and does something do save itself.[54]

For Bateson, a mental system, or Mind, can have two types of possible behavior: self-correction or runaway. In a self-corrective system, the results of past actions are fed back into the system and this new bit of information then travels around the circuit, enabling the system to maintain something near to its optimal state. A runaway system, on the other hand, becomes increasingly distorted over time because the feedback is positive, rather than negative or self-corrective. Bateson points to addiction as the perfect example of a runaway system: the addict needs an increasingly larger fix. Addiction, he says, characterizes every aspect of industrial society in is effort to control everything. Any system that maximizes certain variables (such as fossil fuels, for example) violates the natural steady-state conditions that would optimize those variables, and is by definition, in runaway. Bateson insists that there is no escaping self-corrective feedback, even if it takes the form of the total disintegration of the entire culture.

Batesonian wisdom is based in the recognition of circuitry, which implies the recognition of the limits of conscious control. He holds that the individual ego is only the visible arc to the larger Self. He insists that the part can never know the whole, but only—if wisdom prevails—put itself at its service. For Bateson, any lack of systemic wisdom is always punished. As he puts it, "if you fight the ecology of a system, you lose—especially when you win."[55]

Before concluding this section, I would like to mention briefly two parallel schools of thought which support and deepen Bateson's thinking: the research of Humberto Maturana here in Santiago, Chile and the Gaia Hypothesis as developed by James Lovelock and Lynn Margulis. Both schools point to what they see as the self-organizing principle at the heart of the universe.

Maturana, a biologist, has coined the term "autopoisis" as the ability of living systems to renew themselves continuously and to regulate this process in such a way that the integrity of their structure is maintained and continuously enhanced. This "will-to-life" stretches into infinity.[56]

Lovelock, an atmospheric chemist, and Margulis, a biologist, have posited the theory that the earth (Gaia, the Greek word for earth) creates the conditions for its own existence. They have identified a complex network of feedback loops that point to the self-regulation of our planetary system. They found that the earth's entire cycle—which links volcanoes to rock weathering, to soil bacteria, to oceanic algae, to limestone sediments, and back to volcanoes—acts as a giant feedback loop, which contributes to the regulation of the earth's temperature. As the sun gets hotter, bacterial action in the soil is stimulated, which increases the rate of rock weathering. This in turn pumps more carbon dioxide out of the atmosphere and thus cools the planet. According to Lovelock and Margulis, similar feedback cycles—interlinking plants and rocks, animals and atmospheric gases, microorganisms and the oceans—regulate the earth's climate, the salinity of its oceans, and other important planetary conditions.⁵⁷

The New Cosmology

This new perception of interconnectedness is also affecting theology—or as many would prefer to name what is happening—a new cosmology is being born.

As can be seen from our overview of the new science, in the quantum view, the reality of our universe does not need an external, supernatural *raison d'être* to uncover what is real. The laws governing the universe are such that matter and energy can organize themselves into the complex forms and systems that make up the ongoing evolutionary process. Indeed, opposite concepts such as beginning or end, inside or outside become outmoded.

According to physicist Paul Davies,

> The picture we obtain for the universe is a remarkable one. At some finite instant in the past, the universe of space, time and matter is bounded by a space-time singularity. The coming-into-being of the universe is therefore represented not only by the abrupt appearance of matter, but of space and time as well. The significance of this result cannot be overstressed. People often ask: Where did the Big Bang occur? The Bang did not occur at a point in space at all. Space itself came into existence with the Big Bang. There is a similar difficulty over the question: What happened before the Big Bang? The answer is: There was no "before".⁵⁸

O'Murchu, struggling to respond theologically to the quantum paradigm shift, develops a set of 12 principles of Quantum Theology. The first is: "Life is sustained by a creative energy, fundamentally benign in nature, with a tendency to manifest and express itself in movement, rhythm, and pattern. Creation is sustained by a superhuman, pulsating restlessness, a type of resonance vibrating throughout time and eternity."⁵⁹

He describes Ultimate Mystery (he shies away from using the word "God" or the "divinity") as a creative energy that is constantly changing, evolving and transforming itself into ever-greater complexity. This energy is the substance of life, the unrelenting wellspring of pure possibility, the symmetry within all.

"Geologian" Thomas Berry, a priest and cultural historian, and his disciple, physicist Brian Swimme have been two of the most influential interlocutors who have wrestled with the insights coming from deep ecology, the new science and cybernetics and confronted those findings with Christian thought. Although there are other voices calling humanity toward a new cosmology, I will concentrate on the insights of these two men.

For me, reading Thomas Berry's *The Dream of the Earth* in 1989 was one of "ah-ha, at last someone has given me a meaningful framework to describe what I had been vaguely intuiting but not able to express in any coherent way." Like Paul, it was a "falling off my horse" conversion experience, which I suspect I share with a growing number of men and women from the Christian tradition who have found that tradition more and more "stale" in light of the recent scientific paradigm shift described above.

Berry offers what he calls "a new story"—a functional cosmology—to guide us toward what he believes is a dawning ecological age. This involves a deeper understanding of the relationship between the human community and the earth. "A truly human intimacy with the earth and with the entire natural world is needed," he says. "We need to present ourselves to the planet as the planet presents itself to us. In an evocatory rather than a dominating relationship."[60] He points out that:

> This re-enchantment with the earth as a living reality is the condition for our rescue of the earth from the impending destruction that we are imposing upon it. To carry this out effectively, we must...reinvent the human as a species within the community of life species. Our sense of reality and of value must consciously shift from an anthropocentric to a biocentric norm of reference.[61]

Berry reminds us that we cannot live without a myth, a story that tells us who we are. He says that the deepest crisis experienced by any people is that moment when its story is no longer adequate for the times. The human species is at that moment in our history. Berry holds out hope, however, and believes that we are discovering a new origins story, which is the story of the universe as an emergent evolutionary process:

> The story of the universe is the story of the emergence of a galactic system in which each new level of expression emerges through the urgency of self-transcendence. Hydrogen in the presence of some millions of degrees of heat emerges into helium. After the stars take shape as oceans of fire in the heavens, they go through a sequence of transformations. Some eventually explode into the stardust out of which the solar system and the earth take shape. Earth gives unique expression of itself in its rock and crystalline structures and in the variety and splendor of living forms, until humans appear as the moment in which the unfolding universe becomes conscious of itself: The human emerges not only as an earthling, but also as a worldling. We bear the universe in our beings as the universe bears us in its being. The two have a total presence to each other and to that deeper mystery out of which both the universe and ourselves have emerged. (...) This might be considered a new revelatory experience; a new paradigm of what it is to be human emerges.[62]

For Berry, history is governed by those overarching movements that give shape and meaning to life by relating the human venture to the larger destinies of the universe. Creating such a movement might be called "the Great Work[63] of a people," the title of his latest book. The Great Work now, as we move into a new millennium, is to carry out the transition from a period of human devastation of the earth to a period when humans will be present to the planet in a mutually beneficial manner. Berry underlines over and over that the deepest cause of the earth's present devastation is to be found in a mode of consciousness that has established a radical *discontinuity* between the human and other modes of being—along with the bestowal of all rights on the human. He invites us to a new understanding of the earth, based on deep feelings of wonder at its magnificence and mystery. He calls us to move from our human-centeredness to an earth-centered understanding of who we are. He insists that the earth as a bio-spiritual planet must become for us the basic referent for identifying our own future. He reminds us that the human species is at a cultural impasse and as a way out of this impasse we must look beyond our cultural coding and discover our primary source of guidance in the inherent tendencies of our genetic coding. These tendencies identify with those psychic energy constellations (what psychologist Carl Jung calls primary archetypal forms) that take shape deep in our unconscious. For Berry, we are in desperate need of a new revelatory experience wherein human consciousness awakens to the grandeur of the earth:

> This awakening is our human participation in the dream of the Earth, the dream that is carried in its integrity not in any of the Earth's cultural expressions but in the depths of our genetic coding. Therein the Earth functions at a depth beyond our capacity for active thought. We can only be sensitized to what is being revealed to us. We probably have not had such participation in the dream of the Earth since earlier shamanic times, but therein lies our hope for the future for ourselves and for the entire Earth community.[64]

Berry believes that as the earth's physical resources become less available, psychic energy will be key to supporting the human project. The universe will be experienced as the Great Self. Each is fulfilled in the other: the Great Self is fulfilled in the individual self, the individual self is fulfilled in the Great Self—and new fields of energy will become available to support us as we go into the future.

He also reminds us that we have a four-fold wisdom to guide us into the future: the wisdom of indigenous peoples, the wisdom of women, the wisdom of the classical traditions and the wisdom of science. Berry's development of the classical wisdom of Judeo-Christian thought is especially provocative, seen as it is with his long view of the earth's history.

For Berry, the essential flaw in our Judeo-Christian heritage is the belief in a monotheistic, personal male deity, creator of a universe that is clearly distinct from himself. Supposedly we have direct communication from this supreme personal deity, who later appeared in human form as teacher and savior. The historical dynamism of this tradition has driven the course of the Western world down through the ages. This tradition holds that the entire human community is being led to fulfillment in a divine kingdom, a kingdom with a millennial fulfillment here on earth in historical time (a time when peace and justice reigns once and for all and the "lion lays down with the lamb") and a post-historical fulfillment in an eternal transcendental mode of being (heaven). Berry argues that because we see ourselves as a transcendent mode of being, we have a hard time believing that we really belong to the earth, that we are indeed "earthlings". This, he stresses over and over again, is a deeply ingrained pathology and has led to an understanding of ourselves as having a destiny beyond that of the earth's. This theological context has given us permission to use the earth as we see fit because "it is not our true home."

Berry also finds that Christianity's stress on redemption—that we are a "fallen race" in need of a Savior, who came and "saved" us so that we might return to some heavenly paradise—neglects the primary revelatory experience of the natural world:

> If this sense of the sacred character of the natural world as our primary revelation of the divine is our first need, our second need is to diminish our emphasis on redemption experience in favor of a greater emphasis on creation processes... We need to see ourselves as integral with this emergent process, as that being in whom the universe reflects on and celebrates itself.[65]

Yet Berry has always been an optimist. He tells us that we are experiencing a moment of grace as we enter the 21st century. He is convinced that a comprehensive change of consciousness is coming over the human community:

> We are now experiencing a moment of significance far beyond what any of us can imagine. What can be said is that the foun-

dations of a new historical period, the Ecozoic Era, have been established in every realm of human affairs. The mythic vision has been set into place. The distorted dream of an industrial technological paradise is being replaced by the more viable dream of a mutually enhancing human presence within an ever-renewing organic-based Earth community.[66]

Brian Swimme is Berry's foremost disciple. Together they have written *The Universe Story* (1994), now a classic. However, Swimme prefers to use the medium of video to transmit his development of the New Story (*The Canticle to the Cosmos*, 1988: *The Hidden Heart of the Cosmos*, 1996). Here in Chile, I belong to a study group that has watched and discussed the Swimme videos over several years.

Swimme's first video series, *The Canticle to the Cosmos*, is the attempt of a physicist to give flesh to and expand Berry's insights into the workings of the cosmos as the primary revelation. He resituates the scientific quest as a sacred journey and invites his fellow scientists to step away from an uninvolved rationalism and move toward a participatory consciousness in the scientific enterprise. This series develops each of Berry's 12 cosmological principles:

1. The Universe, the solar system and the planet Earth in themselves and in their evolutionary emergence constitute for the human community the primary revelation of that ultimate mystery whence all things emerge into being.

2. The Universe is a unity, an interacting and genetically related community of beings bound together in an inseparable relationship in space and time. The unity of the planet Earth is especially clear; each being of the planet is profoundly implicated in the existence and functioning of every other being of the planet.

3. From its beginning the Universe is a psychic as well as a physical reality.

4. The three basic laws of the Universe at all levels of reality are differentiation, subjectivity and communion. These laws identify the reality of the Universe, the values of the Universe and the direction in which the Universe is proceeding.

5. The Universe has a violent as well as a harmonious aspect, but it is consistently creative in the larger arc of its development.

6. The Earth, within the solar system, is a self-emergent, self-propagating, self-nourishing, self-educating, self-governing, self-healing, self-fulfilling community. All particular life forms must integrate their functioning with this larger complex of mutually dependent Earth systems.

7. The genetic coding process is the process through which the world of the living articulates itself in its being and its activities. The great wonder is the creative interaction of the multiple codings among themselves.

8. The human is that being in whom the Universe activates, reflects upon and celebrates itself in conscious self-awareness.

9. At the human level genetic coding mandates a further trans-genetic cultural coding by which specific human qualities find expression. Cultural coding is carried on by educational processes.

10. The emergent process of the Universe is irreversible and non-repeatable in the existing world order. The movement from non-life to life on the planet Earth is a one-time event. So, too, the movement from life to the human form of consciousness. So also the transition from the earlier to the later forms of human culture.

11. The historical sequence of cultural periods can be identified as the tribal-shamanistic period, the Neolithic-village period, the classical civilizational period, the scientific-technological period and the emerging Ecozoic era.

12. The main task of the immediate future is to assist in activating the intercommunion of all the living and non-living components of the Earth community in what can be considered the emerging Ecozoic era of Earth development.[67]

In his latest video series, *The Earth's Imagination*,[68] Swimme develops further Berry's conviction that we are at a decisive moment in the development of human consciousness and that we are, indeed, on the threshold of reinventing ourselves as a species. In this series, Swimme explores how the human mind developed.

For Swimme, the fundamental way to understand the human being — from *the context of the Universe as a whole* — is as a transformation of the dynamics of evolution. In other words, the human is a macrophase transformation of the very dynamics of evolution. He explains:

> If you went back a billion years and asked yourself, "How are the elemental forms evolving, and particularly: how is this carbon atom evolving?" You'd have to discuss the ways in which the hydrosphere, atmosphere and biosphere are involved with its movement. And it's a very complex and intricate movement: it's drawn up into a living body, it perishes, it goes into the soil, it goes down to the bottom of the oceans, it goes up into the atmosphere: an intricate process we call the **carbon cycle.**
>
> The carbon cycle, in this cybernetic system of the Earth, processes two billion tons of carbon a year. In our time, however, the human moves six billion tons a year. So if you're a carbon atom, your destiny is determined more by humans than it is by the other components of the Earth. I want you to think of the whole Earth as in movement, developing, changing. And the question is, what is really taking place? And you see that fundamentally, the human is involved.[69]

Swimme argues that there is a fundamental difference in looking at the human from an evolutionary perspective as opposed to more classical or even modern philosophical approaches which appear to posit a human mind as somehow *other than* the Earth. In fact, he points out, so much energy in Western civilization has been invested in showing the human mind as different, distinct, higher, and special. And yet we too are geological formations.

From an evolutionary perspective, our minds are largely the same as the other minds in the primate world. We arrived out of a billion-year shaping process with very particular kinds of minds, very particular kinds of consciousness. The nature of the primate mind, in terms of synergy, is two-fold: first, there is a deep focus on the level of the organizing mind, on the level of sentience, on sexual reproduction, creating the largest possible number of offspring; second, this focus will take place within emotionally bonded groups, either within the family or with closely related kin. The difference between other primates and the human is that the rate of development slowed down in the human. The word that biologists use for this is *neoteny*. It is a body-mind development that is slower than the previous generations of primates. The neotenic development of the human enabled the development of the imagination. ***It is the imagination*** *in particular that distinguishes the human from the other primates.* Although all primates have an imagination, in the human it became a huge capacity. The imagination, then, is the root of what it means to be human. For Swimme, imagination is the ability to seize possibilities that are otherwise invisible. And that made all the difference in what we have become:

> So then we invented flint and we invented grinding tools, and then the screwdriver and the compass, then we drew in the power of the wind and of the tides; then we had the steam engine. Then we had nuclear energy, then we had recombinant DNA. Each time the human, through the imagination, is drawing a new power of the Universe into the human project. The human then, through the imagination, draws in all the powers of the Universe, all the powers of the Earth community. And yet dealing with this we are using the same old primate mind. There has been no time for a change in anatomy; it has taken place that fast. The ratio between genetic invention and cultural invention is 100,000. That's the increase in creativity with the human imagination, compared to genetic mutation alone. That goes far beyond the capacity of the life process to stay with it or to catch up. So the human has become this planetary power, yet it does not have the understanding or the wisdom to organize this power within the total life complex.[70]

For Swimme, we are in a transition from a time when life was shaped by natural selection to a time when life itself begins to be shaped by something like a conscious selection. We are at a time when comprehensive compassion begins to take hold of the life process, through the human. Although it is not possible to predict what will take place, there are certain intuitions emerging. The phrase Swimme uses is "the emergence of a vibrant Earth community." Swimme is convinced that just as that which we hold in our imagination ultimately determines, personally, our life and our character; in the same way, for the species as a whole, that which fascinates the human imagination will become that which shapes life. He is convinced that we are in a space that enables the future to act in the present in a major new way. The question is, then, what goals, what purposes, what aims are we going to choose as humans? Whatever we choose will become a central shaping power of the life process. Swimme is convinced that we will choose that which deeply fascinates us. In this sense we will recognize in it our true destiny.

Swimme is also convinced that in order to develop what he calls "macrophase wisdom" we humans need the self-understanding that we are a mode of the Universe, of life itself, of evolutionary dynamics, as opposed to our prevalent understanding of ourselves as individuals. To begin to conceive of ourselves as a dimension or a mode of the whole would move us into another form of humanity. What would it mean to take on the mind of the Universe, the mind of life, the mind of the Earth community? Swimme's suggestion is that to move in imagination is to move into a new form of human existence. In this sense, we'd no longer be defining ourselves by the past. Rather, we'd begin to create ourselves by a vision that arrives out of the future, out of the not-yet. The more we become fascinated by that possibility, the more we would actually become that reality. The switch we would be making is from a fixation on the human project to a fascination with the Earth project. What's wonderful about this is that this becomes a new species project. And if that became our desire, our self-understanding, the first step toward accomplishing it would be to remove the impress of our industrial assault on the rest of the Earth community. Simply by drawing back our destructive imposition, it immediately sets into motion brilliant strategies that have been worked out over billions of years. As we identify with the larger Whole, then our withdrawal from destruction would bring a deep delight, as we see the Earth's ecosystems burst forth with life. On a deeper level, we would share in these ecosystems' own fulfillment, in their blossoming would be our own. This would be the first step toward bringing about the transformed human.

But Swimme suggests that there is a second step, which involves the invention and discovery of new forms of synergy: working with the Earth community so the wolves, the fish, the humans and the trees all feed on the Earth community in a way that is more abundant than now.

That is the meaning of synergy: mutually enhancing relationships. It is difficult for us even to imagine a form of interaction with the encompassing community that is truly mutually enhancing. But as his great friend Berry would say, "the dream drives the action."

Such seminal ideas presented by Berry and Swimme concerning how we view ourselves in relation to the wider earth community are profoundly influencing ecofeminist thought, as we shall see below.

Indigenous cosmology

The recent discoveries of the new science offer confirmation of what the original peoples of the earth have long known: that the earth is a living "mother" and all creatures, great and small, are her children. Therefore, we are all related. The variety and richness of indigenous cosmologies are once again being studied and embraced, now not as mere folklore, but as extraordinarily creative ways in which humanity has told its "story". Furthermore, their traditional love and care for the earth can now lead the rest of us to a deeper understanding of the land and its ecosystems. As Berry points out: "One of the significant historical roles of the primal peoples of the world is not simply to sustain their own traditions, but to call the entire civilized world back to a more authentic mode of being. Our only hope is in a renewal of those primordial experiences out of which the shaping of our more sublime human qualities could take place."[71]

Indigenous peoples everywhere are among the world's poorest; this is especially true in the case of indigenous women.[72] This situation will probably not improve until non-indigenous viewpoints of superiority and assimilation give way to respect and valuing of indigenous lifestyles. However, at this point the very structure of our technological civilization prevents us from communicating in depth with native peoples. Also, there is also a tendency of some spiritual seekers to trivialize and even exploit indigenous spiritualities. As Cherokee Andy Smith writes:

> The New Age movement has sparked a new interest in Native American traditional spirituality among white women who claim to be feminists. Indian spirituality, with its respect for nature and the interconnectedness of all things, is often presented as the panacea for all individual and global problems. Not surprisingly, many white "feminists" see the opportunity to make a great profit from this new craze. They sell sweat lodges or sacred pipe ceremonies, which promise to bring individual and global healing...our spirituality is not for sale.[73]

Non-indigenous are thus warned to differentiate between appropriating indigenous spirituality and learning from its insights. Berry, who as a cultural historian, has studied the North American Indians for many years. He points to their deep nature mysticism as necessary to reorient humanity toward a reverence for the earth. "Awareness of a numinous presence throughout the entire cosmic order establishes among these peoples one of the most integral forms of spirituality known to us," he says.[74] He also underscores indigenous peoples' interior communion with the archetypal world of the collective unconscious, revealed in their vision quests, the guidance they seek in dreams, and their connection to their own psychic powers in general—something most non-indigenous have lost in modern times.

> Indigenous wisdom is distinguished by its intimacy with and participation in the functioning of the natural world. The dawn and sunset are moments when the numinous source of all existence is experienced with special sensitivity. (...) This ever-renewing sequence of sunrise and sunset, of seasonal succession, constitutes a pattern of life, a great liturgy, a celebration of existence. In this context early humans discovered their food and sheltered themselves from the elements. Above all they developed an interpretation of life and pain and suffering and death, along with a feeling of security and joy in existence. A native wisdom was passed down through the generations, a wisdom carried in the lives of the people, in their thoughts and speech; in their customs, songs, and rituals; in their arts, their poetry; and in their stories not in any written form. In a special manner this wisdom is carried by the sacred personalities: the elders—both men and women, the chiefs, the shamans.[75]

In Latin America, there has been a resurgence of indigenous militancy since the anniversary of the European invasion of the Americas in 1992. The Zapatistas in Chiapas, Mexico, the Maya in Guatemala, the Quechua and Aymara of the Andean countries and the Mapuche of southern Chile have all mobilized in recent years to demand the return of their territorial lands usurped by colonial powers over the past 500 years. Their renewed sense of struggle is based upon a renewed sense of their own history as native peoples and in their own cosmovisions, which were often hidden or synchronized with the imposition of Christianity by the *conquistadores*. As Diego Irarrázaval, a Chilean priest working among the Aymara and Quechua peoples of Peru, writes:

> ….(these people) seek to survive within a cosmic harmony and wisdom. Such human groups are at the far edges of the modern world. They feel the sacred in their entire existence; they interact intensively with their ancestors and with benign and evil spirits; they see woman as a socializing and spiritual center; and they have devised warm rituals and mythical accounts having to do with life and death. (…) In doing so, they implicitly question a modernity that plunders nature and splits persons.[76]

Irarrázaval goes on to describe how very much alive this cosmic presence is, especially with regard to ritual and celebration. For instance, in prayer water, fire and vegetables are almost always used; there is ongoing interaction with those who have died; there is a sacred relationship with the surrounding living and inanimate beings; and there is a close relationship between bodiliness and spiritual energy. Here he mentions specifically the relationship between ritual and healing, noting that "much of the activity of believers has to do with handling illnesses and pain, with recovering emotional, bodily, communal and mystical equilibrium."[77] These beliefs flourish, despite the fact that colonial Christianity condemned them as demonic.

For some time now, I have been wrestling with the heritage of Latin America's indigenous heritage from a feminist perspective. Several years ago, I wrote an article entitled "After 500 years of mixings, who are we?

Walking in our dark grandmothers' feet,"[78] an attempt to summarize our work in Con-spirando surrounding what it means to be a "mix" between European and indigenous peoples. In light of the 1992 anniversary of 500 years since the supposed "discovery" of Latin America, we too were engaged in redefining Latin American identity. We asked the question, "Who are Latin American women after 500 years of resistance, adaptation and accommodation to wave after wave of foreign 'invasion'?"

A partial answer to that question is that we are a mix of European and indigenous peoples: and we are also a mix of mixes—Spanish, Portuguese, German, British and Irish men (who arrived alone, without women from their own culture) with Mapuche, Aymara, Quechua, Aztec women; Chinese and African male slaves with women from the first mixture. Not white or black or indigenous, Latin Americans are a new race, a new synthesis.

Given our *mestizaje*—our mix of mixtures—Con-spirando member Elena Aguila asked: "What is my responsibility to my ancestors, to my white as well as to my dark grandmother? I am a woman of both worlds; I refuse to deny one and adopt the other. I feel the urgent need to dialogue with the voices of all my grandmothers."[79] Aguila then asked why so many Latin American women ignore their indigenous roots in the mix and raise up those of their European ancestors. Her answer: Because 'white' is synonymous with 'power'—economic, political and cultural power. For example, power to formulate theological questions and suggest answers, power to define as holy your own image and likeness, power to institutionalize religious practices, power to establish myths and rituals for an entire culture. On the other hand, indigenous has meant oppression, poverty and a life of hardship. (It is undeniable that in Latin America, the greatest poverty is among the still-existing indigenous communities.) Aguila challenges Latin American women to rediscover the power in the "mixture"—without denying "the plurality written on our faces—to revindicate the wrinkles and scars of our dark grandmothers, because who knows what wisdom, power and secrets lie hidden there?".[80]

As *mestizo* women, we recognize that the cosmologies of our Mapuche, Aymara and Mayan ancestors profoundly color our emerging theology and spirituality. At the same time, as feminists, we firmly reject those indigenous movements that predict a kind of millennial catastrophe that will once again restore the lost worlds of indigenous empires. Our research and experience leads us to conclude that, although it is appears to be true that indigenous communities were more ecologically sensitive to their environments than our Western societies, these native communities cannot be construed as "paradise lost". Some of them, such as the Aztec and the Inca empires, had degenerated into a period of war, expansionism and rigid hierarchies by the time the Spanish colonizers arrived. Although women were esteemed and deities were both masculine and feminine, men governed.

We have no romantic illusions about returning to the past. However, this is a time of great change and we need a new synthesis, new energies, symbols and initiatives. Thus we return to our dark grandmothers. What might we learn from them? What do their voices whisper in our ears about our origins as well as our destiny? Perhaps an even more crucial question might be how their ancient beliefs—so long repressed as paganism by our European grandmothers—challenge and reshape our Christianity.

Our white grandmother has had the last word about who we are for too long. It is now time to listen to our dark grandmother—without rejecting our other ancestors. At Con-spirando we are attracted to holding our rituals under the trees, we feel moved to dance and sing to the sound of the drums while we try to listen to the rhythms of the Pachamama in our own bodies. We are attracted to the many modern-day "machis" (Mapuche holy women) and *curanderas* who walk our streets—wise old aunts and grannies who counsel us about what to do when our children suffer from asthma or some other ailment or when we have a migraine or a "women's problem". The sense of interconnection with the Mapuche and Aymara traditions, the need to reinstall the Aymara practice of reciprocity—to return to the earth what we take from her—feels right to us.

We sense that our current ecological crisis is based in our forgetting the reciprocity we owe the Pachamama.

We have only just begun this process of recovering our origins, our journey of walking in our dark grandmothers' feet. An ecofeminist perspective of our indigenous past must be accompanied with a good dash of caution against falling into fantasies of recovering a long lost world, of simplistic stereotypes that often surround re-engaging the wisdom of indigenous cultures. Also we are becoming more and more aware of the fact that so much of the context has been lost—how do we decipher and interpret the few images and artifacts that still exist? How can we extract a more truthful understanding of our indigenous myths and legends while making sure to not over-idealize our indigenous past—yet at the same time not dismiss it as "savage"? How can we begin a process of simply accepting these ancestors as part of ourselves? How can we let these ancient women who inhabit us speak to us today through our bodies, through our lives?" This search will engage us for some time to come.

Economic sustainability/Bioregionalism

Deep ecologists, armed with insights from the New Science and Cybernetics, inspired by "the new story" coming from cosmologists, and reclaiming earth-based wisdom traditions coming from indigenous peoples, put their vision into practice by trying to "come home to place".

The planet earth, of course, is not a uniform reality, but a highly complex web of differentiated bioregions that support local life communities. Again, quoting Berry: "A bioregion is an identifiable geographical area of interacting life systems that is relatively self-sustaining in the ever-renewing processes of nature. The full diversity of life functions is carried out as a community that includes the physical as well as the organic components of the region. Each of the component life systems must integrate its own functioning within this community to survive in any effective manner."[81] Bioregionalism, an alternative to viewing the planet as a collection of nation-states, can be described as a community that both in terms of species and in terms of members, maintains a certain numerical balance; can sustain itself in terms of food and well-being for all its members; can regenerate and adjust to seasonal changes; and that the inflow and outflow of energy are such that the community is sustainable over an indefinite period of time.

For ecofeminist Judith Plant, a leader in the bioregional movement in Canada, "bioregionalism means learning to become native to place, fitting ourselves to a particular place, not fitting a place to our predetermined tastes. It is living within the limits and the gifts provided by a place, creating a way of life that can be passed on to future generations."[82]

What becomes clear from a bioregional perspective, however, is that the current industrial economy is not sustainable. Industrial technologies are becoming more and more destructive of the earth's natural processes. All modern economic systems—whether socialist or capitalist—are anthropocentric, seeing the earth as a series of resources available for human use, instead of a finely tuned web of ecosystems where the human must discover its place as one species among many.

For David Korten, author of *When Corporations Rule the World*, we are currently experiencing accelerating social and environmental disintegration everywhere on the planet. "The continued quest for economic growth as the organizing principle of public policy is accelerating the breakdown of the ecosystem's regenerative capacities and the social fabric that sustains human community; at the same time, it is intensifying the competition of resources between the rich and the poor—a competition that the poor invariably lose."[83] For Korten, this growth is based on short-term financial gain for a handful of powerful corporations who claim that consumerism is the path to happiness—a myth propagated by the media and indeed by the very "air we breathe" to justify profligate greed.

> In the name of modernity we are creating dysfunctional societies that are breeding pathological behavior—violence, extreme competitiveness, suicide, drug abuse, greed, and environmental degradation. Such behavior is an inevitable consequence

> when a society fails to meet the needs of its members for social bonding, trust, affection and a shared sacred meaning. (...) Healthy societies depend on healthy, empowered local communities that build caring relationships among people and help us connect to a particular piece of the living earth with which our lives are intertwined.[84]

According to economist Herman Daly, environmentally sustainable societies must satisfy three conditions: First, the use of renewable resources must be based on a given ecosystem's ability to regenerate them; second, the consumption of non-renewable resources must not exceed rates as which renewable substitutes are developed and put to use; third, rates of pollution emission into the environment cannot exceed the ecosystem's ability to absorb them.[85]

As more and more of the earth's people become grounded once again in their local bioregional communities, it can be hoped that the creativity of imagining new possibilities for sustainability, predicted by Brian Swimme, will flourish and the "Ecozoic Age" envisioned by Thomas Berry will indeed dawn. This is also the promise of ecofeminism.

II. Radical/Cultural Feminism

Having developed the side of the chart on deep ecology, we now turn our attention to the radical/cultural feminism side.[86] Both radical and cultural feminism arose in what is referred to as the "second wave" of feminism in the 1960s and 1970s and took place principally—although not exclusively—within the United States (The "first wave" is associated with women's struggles to gain the right to vote; while women's suffrage movements took place at different rates throughout the world, this "wave" mainly happened in the first half of the 20th century.) In the second wave of feminism, women continued to struggle for a broadening of their civil, political and economic rights, and they also introduced feminist studies as a new academic discipline. At this stage, a variety of perspectives emerged within feminism, which can broadly be broken down into four major types:

- **Liberal feminism**: Emphasizes civil rights, including the right of women to freely make decisions about their own sexual and reproductive health. Seeks full equality of women with men in all facets of societal life, especially in economic political life.

- **Cultural or Spiritual Feminism**: Emphasizes the moral superiority of women over men and the values traditionally associated with women, such as compassion, nurturance, and peacemaking. Seeks the betterment of society by stressing the contributions made by women. Sometimes associated with women's "separatist" movements.

- **Radical Feminism**. Emphasizes the pervasiveness of male domination, which is seen as the cause of all societal problems, and the importance of "women-centered culture," characterized by nurture, closeness to nature and compassion. Seeks to eliminate patriarchy in order to liberate women from male control in every facet of life.

- **Socialist Feminism**: Emphasizes white male domination in the economic class struggles of capitalist societies. Believes that this dominance is the reason for the division of labor according to sex and race and the devaluing of women's work, especially the work of raising children. Seeks to end the economic dependence of women upon men and to achieve major social reforms that will end class divisions and enable all women and men to have the same opportunity to be gainfully employed and to be actively involved in parenting. [87]

The "third wave" of feminism, beginning in the 1980s and continuing to the present, seeks to attend to differences among women from different parts of the globe and at the same time build alliances that extend across these lines of differences. (Nowhere was this diversity more visible than at the U.N.'s Fourth Conference on the Status of Women held in Beijing in 1995, which I attended.) It is in this "third wave" that ecofeminism is situated, bringing together the domination of women and other subjugated groups with the exploitation of the earth.

Ecofeminism is seen as clearly flowing out of radical feminism because ecofeminists also identify **patriarchy** as the main source of global ecological destruction. However, ecofeminism's relationship with cultural and spiritual feminism is less clear. Some ecofeminists will tend to stress male domination *per se* as the cause of ecologically destructive and socially oppressive behavior and hold up women's ways of knowing as more ecologically sound. These cultural and spiritual ecofeminists tend to stress an elemental connection between women and nature. This has led to charges of essentialism. Those ecofeminists coming from a socialist feminist background would argue that the division of power between men and women results in unsustainable patterns of development. (Most socialist feminists have not embraced ecofeminist thought, charging that ecofeminists basically divert energies to struggling against what they would see as the major oppression: that of economic exploitation under capitalism.) It is liberal feminism that would be most criticized by ecofeminists who maintain that there is simply no purpose in fighting for equal opportunities within the present political and economic system. Or as ecofeminist Ynestra King has written: "The piece of the pie that women have only begun to sample as a result of the feminist movement is rotten and carcinogenic...What is the point of partaking equally in a system that is killing us all?"[88]

Ecofeminist Charlene Spretnak, in a now classical essay, *Ecofeminism: Our Roots and Flowering,*[89] maps out three different paths women have taken toward ecofeminism: The **first path** was the study of Marxist political theory in the 1960s and dominance theories in the 1970s by radical and cultural feminists. These scholars rejected the Marxist assertion that domination is based solely on economic oppression and class exploitation, pointing out that if ever there was a universally dominated class, it was women. They also explored the roots of patriarchy in their studies of dominance theory, identifying the dynamics of fear and resentment behind the dominance of the male over the female. The **second path** was exposure to nature-based religion. In the mid-1970s, many radical/cultural feminists, examining historical and archaeological studies, discovered pre-patriarchal myths and goddess cults that honored the female and portrayed the divine as immanent. Spretnak notes that this discovery "was utterly earthshaking for us Judeo-Christian women of a thoroughly modern culture (…) and inspired rituals of our own creation that express our deepest feelings of a spirituality infused with ecological wisdom and wholeness."[90] The **third path** is through environmentalism and/or green politics, where women encounter theories of ecofeminism or deep ecology, which give their activism a more coherent philosophy.

For Spretnak, there are many variations on these three paths, but she find that ecofeminism's promise lies not only in addressing "the interlinked dynamics in patriarchal culture of the terror of nature and the terror of the elemental power of the female, but also the ways out of the mesmerizing conditioning that keeps women and men so cut off from our grounding in the natural world, so alienated from our larger sense of self in the unfolding story of the universe."[91]

And King concludes:
> In ecofeminism, nature is the central category of analysis. An analysis of the interrelated dominations of nature—psyche and sexuality, human oppression, and nonhuman nature—and the historic position of women in relation to those forms of domination is the starting point of ecofeminist theory. We share with cultural feminism the necessity of a politics with heart and a beloved community, recognizing our connection with each other—and with nonhuman nature. Socialist feminism has given us a powerful critical perspective with which to understand, and transform, history. Separately, they perpetuate the dualism of "mind" and "nature." Together they make possible a new ecological relationship between nature and culture, in which mind and nature, heart and reason, join forces to transform the systems of domination, internal and external, that threaten the existence of life on Earth.[92]

All ecofeminists agree that patriarchy is the root cause of our present unsustainable situation. Patriarchy can be defined as "the social construction of reality and of thinking that is based on domination of women and of all groups considered inferior because of race, gender, class, sexual orientation, disability, etc. These structures of domination and subordination are woven into a *double web of oppression* created by structures of political, economic, cultural and intellectual power distribution in society, and of a dualistic system of thought that justifies this unjust distribution of power."[93]
Patriarchal culture has several characteristics:

- Appropriation and control over goods, persons (especially women), and nature.

- A culture of domination, centered on authority, obedience, and the use of force: males develop a kind of "psychological armor" that manifests "strong" emotions like anger and aggression and expresses contempt for "soft" emotions such as love, compassion, and tenderness. Self-control is strongly emphasized, and sensuality and pleasure are seen as sinful or as expressions of weakness. Pain and fear are used as central motivators.

- Justification of appropriation and control through the appropriation of the truth. Insistence that there is only one "correct" way in religion, politics and the social order. Alternative ways of thinking and acting are regarded as threats and are duly punished. "I am a jealous God." (Yahweh) "Error hath no rights." (St. Augustine)

- Hierarchical relationships in all areas: church, politics (monarchy), economic institutions, educational institutions and the family. Everything is ranked and compared; competition is a way of life. There are hierarchies of wealth and power, of strength and intelligence, of beauty, and even of merit and sanctity. Each person's dignity and worth tends to be related to their position in the "pecking order" rather than in their intrinsic human qualities.

- Linear rather than process thinking and action. Even God is seen as having a fixed, linear "plan" for creation.

- Patriarchal religion: a monarchical God, clothed in patriarchal robes. A warrior God (Lord God of hosts), a judge who metes out severe punishments, a distant and immutable deity. In keeping with its need for control and self-control, this religion often emphasizes asceticism and even self-mutilation.

- Violence needs to be controlled and suppressed. Peace is to be found only in domination: "Pax Romana" or "Pax Americana." There is peace only when everything is under control.[94]

Based on my own reading and research,[95] I have developed a timeline of the development of patriarchy as in four stages summarized below:

Stages in the development of patriarchy

I. The Paleolithic or Hunter-Gatherer Stage (2 million-10,000 BCE—99% of human history)

Some 30,000 years ago *homo sapiens* had spread to all parts of the planet. We lived in tribes of 25-30. We were nomadic and had few possessions. There were occasional fights among tribes, but wars of conquest were unheard of. Men hunted larger animals, while women stayed closer to the campsite in charge of the children. There was much time devoted to religious ceremony.

In terms of our psychic development, we conceived everything as a complex of interconnecting spiritual forces. We were animists: everything—the mountain, the river, every living being—had its spirit or "totem". Ours was a world of profound participation, magic, intuition. And all was a manifestation of the Great Mother from which we came and to which we would return. The Medicine Wheel (still seen in many indigenous cultures) expressed our primary experience of living in a world of amazing fecundity with its sequence of seasons which entailed a cyclical autumn dying and spring rising. To this generosity of the earth we responded with gratitude. There was no distinction between nature and spirit, between religious and "ordinary" life. The first "images" of our religious sensibilities were expressed in the multitude of "Venus figures" found throughout the planet—the image of the pregnant or fertile woman, symbol of the origin of life. To the Paleolithic mind, the Great Mother was manifest in the body of a woman. Sexuality, birth, death and resurrection were all of one piece, both natural and spiritual.

II. The Neolithic Revolution: The Age of Agriculture (10,000 – 3,500 BCE)

Gradually, we began to "domesticate" plants and animals. With the development of agriculture, we move from a "wild" planet to a "domesticated" one—there was a change in relationship on the entire planet. We were able to cultivate much more food in a small space and to "control" flocks of animals. We lived in villages of about 150 people. There was a growing division of labor: women domesticated plants and small animals and were in the forefront of subsistence agriculture. Men were more associated with plow agriculture and with pasturing and herding animals. With the development of agriculture, accumulation became possible; surpluses in food developed, which allowed some to dedicate themselves to tasks other than agriculture and herding. There was growing specialization in ceramics, art, architecture, weaving and ritual.

In terms of psychic development, our major spiritual energies continued to be expressed in a complex feelings of both gratitude and fear of the Great Mother—her power to both give life and to give death. She was venerated as that feminine power connected with the earth and its fertility and was responsible for both the creation and the destruction of life. Sexual union between man and woman was seen as a sacred ritual reflecting those mysterious powers that sustain life. The *Hieros gamos*, or "Sacred Marriage", a public enactment of sexual union, was considered the most important yearly rite of the Neolithic period. In imitation of the earth, the ritual honored the source of life by enjoying sexual pleasure, joy and gratitude. Sexual pleasure was considered sacred and pleasing to the Great Mother, in all her forms.

There is a growing body of evidence that between 4,300 and 2,800 BCE at least three waves of invasions dramatically altered earlier Neolithic societies around the Fertile Crescent. Pastoral, warlike tribes from what is now Northern Europe and the Russian steppes began to invade these agricultural settlements in search of food and fertile women. They came on horseback and began to sack the villages, killing the men and capturing the women. The invaders apparently had an altogether different psychic experience from that of inhabitants of the more matristic villages and had a different relationship with the Earth than did the agriculturalists. They had learned to domesticate animals and turn them into herds. This also meant protecting them from other animals, such as the wolf, which came to be seen as an "enemy".

Procreation, rather than sexual union for pleasure, came to be an overriding value: more than their agrarian counterparts, herders valued women's and animals' ability to procreate and sought to control that procreation. The gradual appropriation over women's ability to reproduce offspring changed what had been a more egalitarian relationship between the sexes. Fertile women came to be seen as a highly prized resource and were often exchanged or captured. Men, as a group, began to have a power over women, who, as a group, did not have power over men.

Exposed to the vastness of the plains, the immensity of the heavens, and the harshness of the climate, herding peoples felt awe and fear in the presence of powerful, invisible forces in the cosmos: total submission to these forces was seen as the only possible response.

In the end, the patrifocal invaders subdued the more matristic world and their gods overthrew the Great Mother. This is recorded in the many myths of the ancient world.

III. The Classical Civilizations (3500 BCE—1500 AD)

This era was marked by major leaps in production and technology, especially in fertile valleys where large surpluses allowed greater specialization. This was the age of bronze and iron, the rise of the ancient classical cities. It was the age of the wheel, development in transportation by land and sea for exchange of goods, migrations, the age of the great temples. A stage marked by division among social classes based on property ownership. Kings ruled empires and recruited armies both for defense and to conquer other empires. War became chronic. The patriarchal family became the norm, with the patriarch owning his wife, his children, his slaves, his property. The subordination of women was now seen as "natural" and was institutionalized in all religious and legal codes. The earth was now a resource to be exploited by humans and accumulation gave us our sense of security. In this period, hierarchical, militaristic societies governed by religious and/or political elites became the norm throughout the entire planet.

In terms of our psychic development, the earlier sense of coming from and returning to the Great Mother was replaced by belief in deities representing the patriarchal "power-over" mindset.

IV. The Modern Period (1500 to the present)

The modern period has been characterized by the rise of empirical science and technology, and by the appearance of movements that have challenged the four patriarchal dominations described above: the appropriation of most economic resources by a small elite; the political-military rule of kings and emperors; male domination over women and children; and the domination and exploitation of the Earth.

While emancipation movements have not yet been successful in eliminating these dominations (some actually intensified under the colonial system, with the application of fossil fuel-based technology to the exploitation of the earth, and with the increasing power of transnational corporations), they point to a new awareness of the problems and have unleashed an enormous energy and growing expectations that change will come about. Patriarchal structures and values are being questioned all over the world, and growing masses of people have become aware that they need not last forever.

Feminist anthropology: Goddess images

Ecofeminism is above all a movement that offers a spirituality that is earth-based—and it is from immersion in this spirituality of the connectedness of all things that ecofeminists find the energy to chart new directions that are clearly utopian. Much of this energy comes from the realization that before the male, monolithic God of Judeo-Christian tradition, there were countless representations of the divinity in female form.

Nowhere has this discovery been more clearly documented than in the work of feminist archaeologist Marija Gimbutas. Gimbutas devoted her life to an exhaustive study of images and symbols to discover their inner coherence. It was not until after she had directed several excavations where 90 percent of the images dug up were female that she had a flash of insight that something was lacking in traditional theories about religion and culture in the Neolithic period. She found it necessary to widen the scope of descriptive archaeology, an expanded approach she called "archaeomythology," which included the study of linguistics, mythology, comparative religion and the study of historical records. Using this "meta-language," Gimbutas discovered a sacred relationship between human society and the natural world. The female form, expressed in thousands of images, reflects the centrality of women in religious and cultural life.[96] As ecofeminist scholar Carol Christ writes: "the work of Marija Gimbutas has the potential to bring about a paradigm shift in the way we study religion: it pushes the time of cultural and religious origins far back before the Sumerians, the Hebrews, or the Greeks and challenges us to rethink the roles of women and of female symbolism in religion."[97]

Gimbutas was the first scholar to describe an overview of Neolithic cultures on a pan-European scale and the first to articulate the differences between the matristic Old European and the patriarchal Indo-European systems. In her view, these contrasting systems underwent a hybridization that determined the development of all subsequent European cultures. In her major work, *The Civilization of the Goddess*[98] —a summary of her life's work that names Old Europe as a civilization without war or male domination—Gimbutas provides an essential key for deciphering the sources of contrasting cultural elements that become tangled and fused over time. She writes: "Celebration of life is the leading motif in Old European ideology and art. There is no stagnation; life energy is constantly moving as a serpent, a spiral, or whirl... One form dissolves into another... There was no simple death, only death and regeneration. And this was the key to the hymn of life reflected in their art."[99]

Gimbutas' theory can be described in three stages:
1. There flourished in Neolithic Europe (6,500-3,000 BCE) a pre-Indo-European Goddess civilization that was matristic, socially egalitarian, communal, peaceful, and highly artistic and primarily Goddess-worshiping.

2. This indigenous European civilization was overrun and dominated by patriarchal, horse-riding, Indo-European, sky-god-worshiping invaders (called "Kurgans" for their burial mounds) from the Russian Steppes in three successive waves, beginning around 4,400 BCE, 3,500 BCE and 3,000 BCE.

3. The subsequent culture of Europe was a hybridization of the Indo-European and Old European cultures, the dominant patriarchal warrior culture and the peaceful matristic culture. The latter was partly destroyed, partly subordinated, partly assimilated.[100]

Gimbutas maintained that while the symbolic structures of the Indo-Europeans prevailed, those of Old Europe survived as an undercurrent. She further maintained that without this insight into different symbolic structures, the ideologies of European peoples and the genesis and meaning of their symbols, beliefs, and myths couldn't be comprehended.

Gimbutas believed that women played central roles in the religion and society of Old Europe. Evidence from graves shows no great disparities among individuals or between women and men. This stands in sharp contrast to the royal graves of later periods and suggests that all members of the societies of Old Europe were equal. The clearest marks of patriarchal societies—implements of war and the celebration of warriors, the warrior king and the warrior God—are lacking. Gimbutas interpreted the civilization of Old Europe as "matrifocal", worshiping the Goddess and honoring women, and probably "matrilineal", with family ties traced through the female line. However, Gimbutas did NOT call Old European civilization "matriarchal," because this would imply that women dominated men. She insisted that men played important and valued roles within the culture, especially with regard to trade.

Gimbutas writes: "The Old European culture took keen delight in the natural wonders of *this* world. Its people did not produce lethal weapons or build forts in inaccessible places, as their successors did, even when they were acquainted with metallurgy. Instead, they built magnificent tomb-shrines and temples, comfortable houses in moderately sized villages, and created superb pottery and sculptures. This was a long-lasting period of remarkable creativity and stability, an age free of strife. Their culture was a culture of art."[101] Gimbutas taught that it is very difficult for people from modern European-based cultures to understand the religion and culture of Old Europe because our worldview is shaped by the ideas of those who overthrew Old Europe. She believed that we are still living under the sway of an aggressive male invasion beginning around 4,400 BCE and are only now discovering our long alienation from our authentic European heritage, which was "gylanic, nonviolent and earth-centered."[102] Recently, Gimbutas' theory of Kurgan invasions from the Russian steppes into eastern Europe has been corroborated by the work of Italian geneticist Luigi Cavalli-Sforza, who has discovered genetic evidence for a population expansion into what is now Europe stemming from an area that matched almost perfectly with Gimbutas' projection for the center of Kurgan culture.[103]

Gimbutas' research has come under fire from more orthodox anthropologists because she did not find what she should have found in Old Europe, that is, an inferior, primitive, barbarian prelude to civilization. Instead, Gimbutas argued that embedded in the symbolic language of Old Europe is a culture and a worldview that is not only comprehensible but also "civilized." Old Europe was nonhierarchical, in tune with nature, peaceful, highly artistic, and in many ways superior to the cultures and worldviews that followed it in Europe. She rejected the assumption that civilization refers only to androcentric warrior societies and felt that it was a gross misunderstanding to contend that warfare is endemic to the human condition.

Carol Christ suggests that we should look at the deeper reasons why some scholars are uncomfortable with Gimbutas' claim that the culture of Old Europe was violently destroyed. Christ points out that we know from the conquest of the Americas that better-armed, well-trained armies can easily defeat less well-armed, less militaristic populations over several generations and may also succeed in largely eradicating traditional values. Nonetheless, proponents of the myth of progress insist that cultures proceed onward and upward by a kind of internal logic, with new and superior ideas replacing old and inferior ones. She notes: "Most of us continue to think that Christianity became the dominant religion of Europe owing to the inherent superiority of its ideas about human life and because paganism was in decline and decadent, rather than because it took control by the sword and by violent suppression of the practitioners of all other forms of religion."[104]

Gimbutas caused further discomfort among scholars when she placed the female at the center of her work. She believed that at the root of Old Europe's artistic creations and at the heart of its ability to live in harmony for thousands of years was a spiritual world view anchored in the understanding of the Goddess as Giver, Taker, and Renewer of Life.

The Goddess as Giver of Life was symbolized as bird and chevron, as the letter V, as water, stream, zigzags, and the letter M, as meanders and water bird, as breasts and eyes, as mouth and beak, as spinner, metalworker, and music maker, as ram, as net, as the power of three, as vulva and birth giver, as deer and bear, as snake.

The Goddess as Taker and Regenerator of Life was symbolized as vulture, owl, cuckoo, hawk, dove, boar, as the Stiff White Lady (bone), the stiff nude, the egg, the column of life, the regenerative vulva, the triangle, the hourglass, the bird claw, the ship of renewal, the frog, hedgehog, fish, bull, bee, and butterfly.

As Renewing and Eternal Earth, she was Earth Mother, pregnant Goddess, lozenge and triangle with dots, sow, sacred bread, hill and stone as omphalos (belly), tomb as womb, holed stones, the power of two and doubling. As Energy and Unfolding, she was spiral, lunar cycle, snake coil, hook and ax, opposed spiral, caterpillar, snake head, whirls, comb and brush, standing stone and circle.[105]

Gimbutas has inspired a whole new generation of feminist researchers to look with new eyes at so-called "pre-history" and to document that before God the Father, "God was a woman". Gimbutas was the first to connect archaeology with mythology; scientific research and spirituality. Furthermore, her findings are consonant with the "new science" being developed by physicists, biologists, mathematicians, systems theorists, eco-psychologists, ecofeminists, and others as they come to terms with the mysterious interface of mind and matter, body and spirit, reason and intuition. Gimbutas herself addressed the relevance of her discoveries to contemporary life: "This material, when acknowledged, may affect our vision of the past as well as our sense of potential for the present and future. We must refocus our collective memory. The necessity for this has never been greater as we discover that the path of 'progress' is extinguishing the very conditions for life on earth."[106]

Another view of why the goddess has been displaced has been put forward recently by Dr. Leonard Shlain, a brain surgeon. Shlain posits the thesis that with the invention of writing the Great Goddess began to lose power. He says:

> In their attempts to solve the mystery of the Goddess's dethronement, various authors have implicated foreign invaders, the invention of private property, the formation of archaic states, the creation of surplus wealth and the educational disadvantaging of women. While any or all of these influences may have contributed, I propose another: the decline of the Goddess began when some clever Sumerian first pressed a sharp stick into wet clay and invented writing. The relentless spread of the alphabet two thousand years later spelled Her demise. The introduction of the written word, and then the alphabet, into the social intercourse of humans initiated a fundamental change in the way newly literate cultures understood their reality. It was this dramatic change in mind-set, I propose, that was primarily responsible for fostering patriarchy.[107]

Shlain holds that the goddess's demise is directly related to the development of monotheistic religions that offered an imageless Father deity whose authority rests on his Word ("in the beginning was the Word..."). Conceiving a deity who has no concrete image prepares the way for that abstract thinking that we find in law codes, dualistic philosophy and mechanistic science, Shlain contends. He finds that wherever a culture elevates the written word at the expense of the image, patriarchy dominates; when images are more important than the written word, feminine and egalitarian values flourish.[108]

Shllain's work contributes to the work feminist scholars are pursuing to "re-write history" from a feminist viewpoint. Today, there is overwhelming archaeological and historical evidence that during a long period of our history, we worshiped goddess figures as manifestations of the

Great Mother. In Sumer, she was Inanna, in Egypt, Isis, in Canaan, Asherah, in Syria, Astarte, in Greece, Demeter, in the Andean cultures, Pachamama. Everywhere she was recognized as the Creatrix of life, nurturer of the young, source of vitality for both animals and humans. She presided over the great mysteries of living, dying and rebirth. Everywhere we look, during the pre-patriarchal period we find a deity who personified the Great Goddess or Great Mother.

There is a tremendous allurement and joy in discovering the lost mystical world where women were honored as the life-givers. As Charlene Spretnak so poetically writes: "What was cosmologically wholesome and healing was the discovery of the Divine as immanent and around us. What was intriguing was the sacred link between the goddess in her many guises and totemic animals and plants, sacred groves, and womblike caves, in the moon-rhythm blood of the menses, the ecstatic dance—the experience of knowing Gaia, her voluptuous contours and fertile plains, her flowing waters that give life, her animal teachers."[109]

Ecofeminists from the Christian tradition, like myself, do not take the discovery of the pre-patriarchal goddess tradition as a call to a literal return to worship her. Rather, this discovery invites us toward liberating ourselves from the ultimacy of the biblical image of the patriarchal god. A growing number of women who have gone through a process of realizing that there was an evolution in our root image of the Holy—that is, that before God there was a more primal image of Goddess—look for new images more appropriate to how we might now image Ultimate Mystery. When emphasis is placed on the goddess as a symbol, there is a revaluation of both our bodies, as women, and of the earth. Carol Christ reminds us that we have a deep human need for symbols and rituals that enable us to cope with those limit situations—death, evil, suffering—and to pass through life's key transition moments—birth, sexuality, death. When women's key image of the divine is the goddess, they are tremendously empowered, finding "the fierce new love of the divine in themselves."[110] Christ continues:

> For me the divine/Goddess/God/Earth/Life/It symbolizes the whole of which we are a part. This whole is the Earth and sky, the ground on which we stand, and all the animals, plants, and other beings to which we are related. We come from our mothers and fathers and are rooted in community. We come from the Earth and to the Earth we shall return. Life feeds on life. We live because others die, and we will die so that others may live. The divinity that shapes our ends is life, death, and change, understood both literally and as metaphor for our daily lives."[111]

Jungian psychology

To understand the importance of the goddess as a symbol, many ecofeminists have been influenced by the work of Swiss psychiatrist Carl Jung and his work on archetypes.

For the past two years I have been part of a study group on Jung, and have found that my horizons about reality and about who we are as humans have widened dramatically. I have discovered that I am acting on a much larger stage than that of which I am aware. I have become more attuned to the archaic psychic components (archetypes) that have entered my psyche without any direct line or tradition. From Jung, I have learned that the *imago dei* in the human psyche is a symbol of our quest for psychic wholeness. And I have also learned that we (our bodies as well as our psyches) emerge from the unconscious and return to it, linking us with those who have gone before us as well as to those who will come after us. We are indeed both memory and possibility.

In contrast to Freud, who held that each person is a unique, independent phenomenon, Jung believed that people are unique not in their own right, but in terms of the larger entities to which they belong. All of us are, of course, products of our relationships, but Jung held that our interconnectedness is not simply interpersonal, but also cosmic. Based on this insight, he offered his idea of the collective unconscious, which he saw as a vital force permeating all creation, an energy containing all the thoughts, feelings and dreams of the past and all the hopes and aspirations of the future, even the evolutionary "aspirations" of the universe itself.

For Jung, our psyche is set up in accord with the structure of the universe, and what happens in the macrocosm likewise happens in the infinitesimal and more subjective reaches of the psyche. He writes in his autobiography:

> Natural history tells us of a haphazard and casual transformation of species over hundreds of millions of years of devouring and being devoured. The biological and political history of man is an elaborate repetition of the same thing. But the history of the mind offers a different picture. Here the miracle of reflecting consciousness intervenes...The importance of consciousness is so great that one cannot help suspecting the element of meaning to be concealed somewhere within all the monstrous, apparently senseless biological turmoil, and that the road to its manifestation was ultimately found on the level of warm-blooded vertebrates possessed of a differentiated brain—found as if by chance, unintended and unforeseen, and yet somehow sensed, felt and groped for out of some dark urge... We do not know how far the process of coming to consciousness can extend, or where it will lead. It is a new element in the story of creation, and there are no parallels we can look to.[112]

Jung distinguishes between the personal unconscious—things we simply do not remember or that we repress— and the collective unconscious, qualities that are not individually acquired but which are inherited, such as instincts, impulses and archetypes. The collective unconscious forms an "omnipresent, unchanging and everywhere identical quality or substrate of the psyche *per se*. (...) The deeper 'layers' of the psyche lose their individual uniqueness as they retreat farther and farther into darkness. 'Lower down'—that is, as they approach the autonomous functional systems, they become increasingly collective until they are universalized and extinguished in the body's materiality; that is, in chemical substances. The body's carbon is simple carbon. Hence 'at bottom' the psyche is simply 'world.'[113]

Jung's notion of the collective unconscious is part of the paradigm shift affecting science. Jung worked closely with physicist Wolfgang Pauli, who pointed out that c .. idea of the evolution of life requires a revision that would take into account the interrelation between the unconscious psyche and biological processes. Marie Louise von Franz, one of Jung's closest collaborators, believed that the most promising field for future study in a Jungian perspective is in the area of microphysics:

> At first sight, it seems most unlikely that we should find a relationship between psychology and microphysics.... The most obvious aspect of such a connection lies in the fact that most of the basic concepts of physics (such as space, time, matter, energy, continuum or field, particle, etc.) were originally intuitive, semi-mythological, archetypal ideas of the old Greek philosophers, ideas that then slowly evolved and became more accurate and that today are mainly expressed in abstract mathematical terms.[114]

What Jung calls archetypes (those patterns of emotional and mental behavior coming forth from our collective unconscious) could be referred to as "probabilities" or "tendencies" in quantum physics. These archetypes tend to become manifest in a "synchronistic arrangement" (Jung's term) or as a "complementarity" (a term from quantum physics) that includes both matter and psyche. A final example von Franz uses to show parallel developments in microphysics and psychology is the Jungian concept of meaning or purpose. Just as quantum physicists are looking for the connections in nature rather than for hard and fast laws, so Jung, rather than asking what causes something, asked: what did it happen for?[115]

Like Bateson's "pattern that connects" and Bohm's "folding and unfolding universe," Jung's "deeper stratum" or collective unconsciousness from which all has come and to which all returns offers a clue toward a closer understanding of ultimate mystery. For Jung, meaning and purposefulness are not the prerogatives of the mind. Rather, they operate in the whole of living nature. There is really no difference between organic and psychic growth; each will respond to its instinctual/archetypal coding. A plant will produce a flower; the psyche will create a symbol.

It is the concept and experience of the archetype that engages ecofeminism. According to Jung:

> The concept of the archetype is derived from the repeated observation that, for instance, the myths and fairytales of world literature contain definite motifs that crop up everywhere. We meet these same motifs in the fantasies, dreams, deliria, and delusions of individuals living today. These typical images and associations are what I call archetypal ideas. They impress, influence and fascinate us. They have their origin in the archetype, which in itself is an irrepresentable, unconscious, pre-existent form that seems to be part of the inherited structure of the psyche and can therefore manifest itself spontaneously anywhere, at any time.[116]

For Jung, psychology could not be founded on the study of a seemingly infinite variety of individual differences: it was necessary to establish the ways in which humans are all psychologically similar. In other words, what are the archetypal features of human nature? Jung believed that the human psyche, like the human body, has a definable structure that shares a phylogenetic continuity with the rest of the animal kingdom. In the unconscious, Jung believed, there resided the collective wisdom of our species, the basic program enabling us to meet all the demands of life. He believed that the collective unconscious contains the whole spiritual heritage of human evolution, born anew in the brain structure of every individual. Archetypes have the capacity to initiate, control and mediate the common behavioral characteristics and typical experiences of our kind, even though we are, for the most part, unaware of them. The archetypes transcend culture, race and time. Thus, in Jung's view, the mental events experienced by every individual are determined not merely by one's personal history, but by the collective history of the species as a whole, which is biologically encoded in the collective unconscious, reaching back into the primordial mists of evolutionary time.

Archetypes, then, are biological entities. Like all biological entities they have a natural history and are subject to the laws of evolution. Archetypes are the neuro-psychic centers responsible for coordinating the behavioral and psychic repertoires of our species in response to whatever environmental circumstances we may encounter. The archetype is an inherited mode of functioning, an innate predisposition toward something which is then responsible for patterns of behavior.[117]

The archetypal endowment with which each of us is born presupposes the natural life-cycle of our species—being mothered, exploring the environment, playing in the peer group, adolescence, being initiated, establishing a place in the social hierarchy, courting, marrying, child-rearing, hunting, gathering, fighting, participating in religious rituals, assuming the social responsibilities of advanced maturity, and preparation for death. *Ultimately every individual life is the same as the eternal life of the species.* The human is therefore a psychophysical system with a built-in biological clock: our lifecycle is predetermined by the evolutionary history of our genes.

Jung believed that throughout the whole cycle of one's life, the archetypal function stands behind the scenes as a kind of author-director. According to British Jungian analyst, Anthony Stevens, Jung's model proposes a *phylogenetic* (that is, related to the species) structure, the interstices of which are filled out in the course of *ontogenetic* (that is, individual) development. The phylogenetic structure is made up of archetypal units which posses the dynamic property of seeking their own actualization in the behavior and the developing personality of the individual as she or he lives out their lifecycle within the context of their environmental circumstances.[118] To this overall process of archetypal actualization and personality development Jung gave the name *individuation*. For Jung, individuation is an expression of that biological process by which every living thing becomes what it was destined to become from the beginning. Nevertheless, for Jung, archetypes have meaning only when you take into account their relation to the living individual. Ultimately, he said, you cannot define an archetype, any more than you can define meaning. You can only experience it. Finally, Jung held that archetypal structures were fundamental to the existence of all living organisms, and that they were continuous with structures controlling the behavior of inorganic matter. The archetype is, then, the bridge to matter in general. What is passed from generation to generation is a structure, a characteristic patterning of matter: it is this pattern, then, which forms the replicable archetype of the species.[119]

Jung's concept of archetype is a useful tool for us to employ in the service of meaning while still respecting the unfathomable mystery of the cosmos. Jung speaks of the archetype as a formative process, more properly understood as a verb than a noun. The psyche has an apparent desire to render a raw flux of atoms intelligible and meaningful by sorting them into patterns: archetypes create primal forms, which are then filled with the contents unique to a particular culture, a particular artist, a particular dreamer.

According to U.S. Jungian James Hollis, our capacity to form *images which carry energy* constructs the requisite bridges to those infinite worlds which otherwise lie beyond our rational and emotional capacities. Without the archetypal imagination, we would have neither culture nor spirituality. The archetypal function is the means by which the individual participates in those energies of the cosmos of which we are always a part.[120]

According to Hollis, perhaps life is meaningless, but we are meaning-seeking creatures who are driven to understand it. We attempt to form some meaningful relationship to life. We learn from archetypal psychology, from the core of primal religious experiences, from quantum physics and from the artist's eye that all is energy. Matter is a dynamic, temporary arrangement of energy. Apparently, a religious symbol or prayer, a work of art, or an expressive practice can so act on our psyche as to move that energy when it has been blocked, deadened, or split-off. The archetypal imagination seeks, through affectively charged images, to connect us to this flow of energy at the heart of the universe. With such images, we have provisional access to Mystery. Apparently what is real and omnipresent is energy: what allows us to stand in relationship to that mystery is image; and what generates the bridge is an autonomous part of our own nature, the archetypal imagination. Jungians would argue that we are never more profoundly human than when we express our yearnings, nor closer to the divine than when we imagine.[121]

Jung noted that psychology was the last so-called social science to be invented because the insights that it seeks were previously the domain of tribal mythologies and institutional religions. Affective linkage to the cosmos, nature and the community were once available via tribal creation stories, heroic legends and transformative rituals. With the loss of these connective rites and mythic images, the problem of identity and the task of cosmic location or spiritual grounding, becomes an individual dilemma.

As we know, myth is not created; it is the dramatization of our encounter with depth. The divine life is expressed through the psyche's archetypal process, which lifts images up and out of the flux of nature to serve as mediatory bridges to the cosmos. Just as there are instincts for biological survival and social interaction, there are instincts (archetypes) for spiritual connection as well.

According to Hollis, we live in a spiritually impoverished time, in the Great In-Between, when our current gods no longer give us meaning. We live in the waning days of some larger historical period, but cannot yet glimpse the rebirth that will spring forth later. But although we have lost our spiritual connection, we have not lost our spiritual desire. Hollis maintains that the problem is simply that the images generally available to us have lost their power to point beyond themselves and thus fail to connect us to Mystery, although we may cling to certain "image husks" with fundamental fervor. Hidden in the etymological recesses of the gods and goddesses are fundamental insights into the nature of reality. In fact, Jungians would define these divine beings archetypically as the affect-laden, highly charged, numinous images that arise out of a depth experience. The development of modernism represents the diminishment of the numinosity of these root metaphors and their incremental replacement with artifacts of the intellect that no longer stir the heart.[122]

Jung held that a condition of our mortality is the fact that there are webs of programmed tissues and autonomous energies which move us to rhythms not consciously ours. Who or what invents our dreams, our religions, our patterned choices? What powers urge us to reproduce, build civilization, to long for meaning? These are the archetypal powers, more ancient than we can imagine. Hollis believes that this little incarnation we call our life is but the vehicle for a larger journey which divinity makes through us. We are asked to become the individual in order that our small portion of the unfolding of the divine may be achieved.[123] He concludes:

> To summarize, a primal experience begets an image, which is the carrier of Mystery. For a time—a moment or a millennium—that image remains suffused with energy. As time is the enemy of symbol, and the deities have their own agenda, the energy leaves the image, which remains an artifact of the mind, a husk that once the gods and goddesses inhabited. The oldest of religious blasphemies is the literalization of the husk and its worship, when the energy has already gone elsewhere. This is idolatry and its servant is that reification which protects itself against the gods and goddesses by worshiping their graves. When such vital linkage leaves the individual, he or she suffers neurosis: when it leaves the tribe, it occasions a cultural crisis, with all those sociopathies that beset us today. The suffering occasioned by the loss of the light is what made analytic psychology necessary. It is a means of helping the individual find his or her own way back to the precincts of numinosity.[124]

Although Jung's insights into the nature and function of archetypes have been essential to the development of ecofeminist philosophy, some ecofeminists are critical of the patriarchal lens with which Jung applied his theories. Feminist Jungian analysts struggle with the concept of archetypes, attempting to adjust Jungian insights to feminist theory. No one has wrestled more with Jungian archetypes and their applicability for contemporary women than feminist psychologist and social philosopher, Madonna Kolbenschlag. A close collaborator of Con-spirando's, she was our visiting lecturer on "Myths and Archetypes" during our Summer School of Ecofeminist Spirituality and Ethics in 2000.

For Kolbenschlag, "the history of the goddess archetypes and images reflects an evolving psychological sense of self: from a holistic primordial image, to fragmentation and demonizing by the patriarchal gaze, to the validation and reintegration of women, contemplating her self and her many gifts of power. Women can find the highest aspirations of their whole being mirrored in the goddess images: their tenderness and caring, their passion, their delight in their bodies, their intelligence, their playfulness, their political, spiritual, artistic power."[125]

In explaining Jung's concept of archetypes, Kolbenschlag described them as experiences, along with their accompanying emotions and affects, which then form a residual substratum in the subconscious. In a kind of feedback system, new experiences tend to be organized according to the pre-existing pattern. The process is somewhat like ski paths in the snow or in the woods: the first tracks of the day are reinforced by subsequent skiers, and it is finally very difficult to deviate and start a new set of tracks. Like ski paths, archetypes are traces of crystallized experience that constellate new experience and engage us in the search for correspondence in the environment. She found in her research that some of Jung's theories have acquired more credibility in the light of the studies of the persistence of memory in human DNA and in human cells, as well as from the evidence of morphogenic fields and holographic theory.[126]

Kolbenschlag found that the so-called feminine archetypes have been described primarily from the point of view of a patriarchal imagination; but today women are deconstructing these archetypes and re-constructing them to reflect women's reality: "Archetypes of the feminine became categories to contain women—and most destructively because of their reputed origin in a transcendent and religious realm, the archetypes had acquired an irrefutable numinosity. An archetype can never be thought of as an image whose content is frozen but must be thought of as a dynamic process that forms and reforms images in relation to repeated experiences," she insisted.[127]

Rather than Jung, Kolbenschlag found the work of Toni Wolff to be more applicable to women. Wolff was a protégé and lover of Jung's. In 1956 she proposed a typology of the feminine psyche with four archetypes: Mother, Hetaria (Lover), Amazon (Warrior) and Medium. Working with Wolff's schema, Kolbenschlag has shown how the many goddess figures of the past reflect these four archetypal yearnings.[128] She concluded:

> If we see through the patriarchal gaze to the dynamic energy fields that represent the experience of being woman, being feminine, then the archetypes and the images of them we have

> inherited—in our soul, as well as in the representations of human art—can be a mirror for discovering lost or repressed aspects of our own power. We can invoke them as oracles. We can question them. They can speak to us. The archetypes look backward (through evolutionary, anthropological and cultural history). They can look forward (through dreams, creative imaginations, artistic transformations and the real experience of women). The archetypes do not remain static. They have a dynamic aspect that only women can fully discern. In our own search for wholeness, the fragmented images of the Goddess become one again.[129]

Like eco/feminist anthropologists, Jungian eco/feminists find the discovery of the goddess in her many forms to be deeply liberating. As Kolbenschlag writes:

> We are like orphans, descended from a Great Mother, whose teaching and values we have forgotten. We are ignorant of our true ancestry. So we must think back through Eve, rethink the "fall," the eclipse, the fragmentation, the displacement. She demands recognition and we must rediscover her. The paradigm of the future begins there... The image of Eve, symbol of our lost birthright of power and our lost connection with the Mother of All, will fade as the goddesses reappear. (...) In the theophany of feminine archetypes in our time we are discovering our "original face" and a map for the future of the human community...Remember, you are a goddess, and all the goddesses dwell within you.[130]

Body as Source of Wisdom

Closely linked to the discovery of the existence of the goddess both in history and in psychology and to the shift in perceiving the earth and indeed the entire universe as a one inter-related, ongoing cosmogenesis, is ecofeminism's revaluation of the wisdom residing in our bodies. Ecofeminists explicitly value the connection between women and nature to counterbalance the long patriarchal era where the human species' material dependence on both was denied. In the words of Charlene Spretnak, "Earth body and the personal body are sacred."[131]

Recovering the sacredness of the body is largely a reaction against Christianity's deeply-engrained misogyny where the flesh, particularly that of women, is seen as an occasion of sin and where Eve, as that great temptress of Adam in the Genesis myth, is still somehow regarded as bringing evil into the world. Celebrating female embodiment also attempts to cut through the dualistic split that equates women with nature and men with culture. This separation, inherent in patriarchal mentality, sets the male apart from nature and from women in a way that allows for the development of cruel and oppressive behavior toward both. Ecofeminists would remind us that we all share a universal kinship with nature and that human embeddedness in the earth is directly related to our own human embodiment. As ecofeminist Mary Mellor writes: "Ecological impacts and consequences are experienced through human bodies, in ill health, early death, congenital damage and impeded childhood development. Women disproportionately bear the consequences of those impacts within their own bodies (dioxin residues in breast milk, failed pregnancies) and in their work as nurturers and caretakers."[132] For ecofeminists, then, concern for the planet's well being is directly related to women's embodied experiences. Revaluing that experience is key to establishing a post-patriarchal world.

Ecofeminism is in conflict with a postmodern social deconstructionist position that accords all agency to human society and culture. The physical materiality of human life is real: we as a species form part of the earth and the universe, which as we have seen, has its own dynamics that are beyond human "construction". Embodiment is a universal human condition. An ecofeminist analysis points out how gender inequality has been used to create a false division between "nature" and "culture". Clearly, female humans are no closer to the earth than male humans. Nevertheless, according to anthropological studies, it appears that the division associating women with nature, the body, sexuality, mortality and the propensity to "sin" on the one hand, and men with culture, the spirit, the mind and the power to dominate women and nature on the other, is very ancient. According to ecofeminist theologian Rosemary

Radford Ruether, a key element in identifying women with nature is her reproductive role: it is the woman who gives birth and then nurtures her offspring by producing and preparing food, clothing, shelter, etc. The man, in contrast, took on the harder work of hunting, which because it was dangerous also came to be considered prestigious. But these tasks were done more occasionally than the tasks done by women, which gave men more leisure time. For Ruether, this leisure time was historically monopolized by men to "make culture" as some sort of privilege of a superior order. With time, women's work of maintaining the material basis of the home and the well being of the family came to be seen as inferior work, both by men and by women themselves. The domestic work of caring for home and children became exclusively the realm of women. The earth, as the birthplace of animals and plants, was associated with women's bodies, the birthplace of the human cub.[133]

The nature/culture argument is also reflected in the patriarchal distinction between transcendence and immanence. Culture is created through transcendence of the immanence of humanity's embeddedness in nature and in our biology. Rejection of immanence means that human society can always be constructed over against the natural world. Ecofeminism calls for embracing our immanence.

Ecofeminist emphasis on embodiment and on celebrating our link with nature has rankled socialist and liberal feminists who view women's liberation as freedom from our biological constraints. As feminist Cecile Jackson writes: "Ecofeminist prescriptions are for women to reject transcendence, embrace the body, bond to our mothers, remain embedded in our local ecosystems, abandon the goals of freedom and autonomy, rely on and care for our kin and community and remain in subsistence production. Such conservatism can hardly claim empowerment for women."[134] Jackson's underscoring of the feminist struggle for women's freedom and autonomy calls attention to the contradictory aspects of ecofeminism as it tries to bridge feminist and ecological perspectives. Ecofeminists must convince their socialist and liberal feminist sisters to let go of their Enlightenment-based commitment to individual freedom and autonomy in favor of belonging to a larger web of life. At the same time, we must convince our mostly male deep ecologist friends that male dominance and patriarchy are root causes of the present state of affairs.

However, radical feminists such as Adrienne Rich argue that when feminists have recoiled from their bodies, they are reflecting the patriarchal rejection of female biology. Rich calls upon women to reclaim and gain control over their bodies, to explore and understand "our biological grounding, the miracle and paradox of the female body and its spiritual and political meanings... to think through the body so that every woman is the presiding genius of her own body. (...) In order to live a fully human life....we must touch the unity and resonance of our physicality, our bond with the natural order, the corporeal ground of our intelligence. In so far as (some) men have transcended their physicality, they have lost contact with the natural order."[135]

Failure to confront our human frailty—our immanence—is leading humanity into deep pathology created by the patriarchal mindset. As ecofeminists point out, we are the only species that is aware that it will die, a realization that creates a tremendous existential anxiety unless we realize that we are finite—from the earth we have come, and to the earth we will return—which is the destiny of all who form the web of earthly life. Embracing embodiment is a way out of such pathos.

Another criticism leveled at ecofeminists is that ecofeminism holds that women have "epistemic privilege" in relation to the natural world. Because women are mothers and nurturers, because our bodies are more in tune with nature's cycles, and/or because we have been oppressed, our "lived experience" makes us more in sinc with the earth. As Spretnak writes: "What can't be said, though, is that women are drawn to ecology simply because we are female."[136] Indian ecofeminist Vandana Shiva makes the same point when she talks about "women as knowers"—they know how to survive because they have learned from nature, which is "the very basis and matrix of economic life".[137] Shiva finds that present day development programs treat poor women as "non-knowers" despite their lived experience. Whether or not women have more knowledge of the earth than men remains an open question. Ecofeminism invites us to remember that we are embedded and embodied human beings, male and female, who "know" the natural world because we are part of that world.

Ecofeminism then, sees all humanity as embodied, yet those bodies are gendered—and therein lies the contradiction. Women are materially associated with—and largely responsible for—human embodiment, whether as paid or unpaid work. The needs of human embodiment are shared by all humanity but are disproportionately borne in the bodies and lives of women.[138] As Mellor says:

> Women do have particular bodies that do particular things, but what matters is how society takes account of sexual differences and the whole question of the materiality of human existence. Women are not closer to nature because of some elemental physiological or spiritual affinity, but because of the social circumstances in which they find themselves—that is their material conditions. Women's disproportionate responsibility for human embodiment is partly expressed in the work that women do, but also in their availability for biological needs... Whatever social lives people construct they are always delimited by bodily existence. Equally, social lives are delimited by the ecosystem.[139]

Even more to the point, Ecofeminist Ynestra King writes:

> It is as if women were entrusted with and have kept the dirty little secret that humanity emerges from non-human nature into society in the life of the species and the person. The process of nurturing an unsocialized, undifferentiated human infant into an adult person—the socialization of the organic—is the bridge between nature and culture. The western male bourgeois then extracts himself from the realm of the organic to become a public citizen, as if born from the head of Zeus. He puts away childish things. He disempowers and sentimentalizes his mother, sacrificing her to nature. But the key to the historic agency of women with respect to the nature/culture dualism lies in the fact that the traditional activities of women—mothering, cooking, healing, farming, foraging—are as social as they are natural.[140]

Concretely, celebrating embodiment has triggered an irruption of rituals, meditations, and other practices that are watering ecofeminist spirituality. These celebrations—generally linked to the earth's cycles—are marked by embeddedness, by a remembering of our belonging to the earth and to the universe. Inspired by a cosmovisión that now offers a broader sense of self, practical ecofeminists find themselves planting gardens where they spend a good deal of time contemplating the growth cycle of their medicinal herbs, their organic vegetables and spices. Many practice Tai Chi or other forms of body movement to begin or end their day, greeting the sunrise or sunset, or as a form to commune with the moon, the planets and the stars. They engage in sacred dances both ancient and new. They celebrate their own life cycles—the arrival of a young girl's first menstruation, the croning of a post-menopausal woman. Many practice the ancient custom of walking the labyrinth.

Reconnecting with the wisdom of the body has also raised criticisms of the current "mechanistic" health system and the way contemporary society views health and disease. Ecofeminists know that "we cannot have healthy people if the planet is sick" and are committed to holistic health practices. Convinced that the mind-body split must be healed, many ecofeminists—inspired by the insights coming from the new science—connect health and well being to the larger energy flow of the universe itself. In this view healing ourselves and healing the earth are seen as inseparable. Many are learning and using Eastern healing practices such as acupuncture, Reiki, Chakra work, etc. (I have been deeply involved in holistic health and spirituality since 1993. I am a member of Capacitar-Chile, a team of women committed to teaching these practices to grassroots women.)

Attempts at forming post-patriarchal communities

Just as deep ecologists hold up bioregionalism and local, community-based economies that are geared toward sustainability rather than growth, so too do radical and cultural feminists long for local communities where relationships are based on justice, equality and respect for women, men and children and where a post-patriarchal gestalt is the norm.

An ecofeminist society, as described by Mellor, "would be egalitarian and ecologically sustainable. There would be no sexual/gender division of labor, and any necessary work would be integrated with all aspects of communal life. Relationships between humans and between humans and nature would be harmonious and co-operative. (...) Most ecofeminists are at pains to include men in these utopian dreams and hold up diversity of gender, race, age and sexual orientation as essential for a viable community."[141]

Ecofeminist theologian Ruether also maps out a vision for a post-patriarchal time in her book, *Gaia and God*. She calls us to build "communities of celebration and resistance"—which she defines as local face-to-face groups with which one lives, works, and prays. There are three interrelated aspects of these communities:

> One is shaping the personal therapies, spiritualities, and corporate liturgies by which we nurture and symbolize a new biophilic consciousness. Second, there is the utilization of local institutions over which we have some control, our homes, schools, churches, farms and locally controlled businesses, as pilot projects of ecological living. Third, there is the building of organizational networks that reach out, regionally, nationally and internationally, in a struggle to change the power structures that keep the present death system in place.[142]

For Ruether, healing therapies and spiritualities need to concentrate on inner growth, on learning how to just "be," learning how to rejoice in the goodness and beauty of life. She calls upon these communities to recover our body-psyche-spirit nexus, "to learn to breath again, to feel our life energy…to get back in touch with the living earth. We can start to release the stifled intuitive and creative powers of our organism, to draw and to write poetry, and to know that we stand on holy ground."[143]
These communities should create their own liturgies both to mourn together and to celebrate healing and new birth. Ruether believes these communities, if they organize in an ecologically healthy way, can become pilot projects for consciousness-raising on a larger scale, gradually

affecting energy use, waste disposal, transportation, and agriculture—indeed the whole way in which society is organized. While utopian, these communities of celebration and resistance offer—to my way of thinking—our best hope to live "justly and rightly" into the future. As she concludes: "Being rooted in love for our real communities of life and for our common mother, Gaia, can teach us patient passion, a passion that is not burnt out in a season, but can be renewed season after season."[144]

Attempts to forge sustainable, post-patriarchal communities are sprouting up around the globe as more and more people realize that humanity must find alternative, sustainable ways of surviving other than the current system of runaway capitalism. While the range of these communities is as varied as the people involved in them, I would like to underline the amazing growth of "ecological learning centers"—or sometimes called "eco-spirituality centers" or even "eco-monasteries" –being set up by more and more groups of Catholic religious sisters. While this phenomenon is taking place chiefly in the United States, I see these centers popping up in the Third World as well as a result of the influence of US missionary sisters on their native counterparts.

Women's religious congregations seem to be the group most susceptible to embracing the new cosmology. Especially influenced by the thought of Thomas Berry and his invitation to "re-inhabit the earth" by learning from the Earth itself, nuns are fast becoming organic farmers and gardeners, vegetarian cooks, Reiki masters and holistic health practitioners, grassroots botanists, astronomy buffs, and teachers/learners of ecology and cosmology—all within the new centers they are founding. Everywhere I go, I see ramifications of these ecological learning centers: there are three (that I know of) in my home state of Ohio—one founded by my old community, the Sisters of the Humility of Mary, another founded by the Akron Dominicans, and a third founded by Sister of Charity of Cincinnati, Paula Gonzalez. I have visited such centers in Brazil, Nicaragua and Costa Rica and am part of two such centers here in Chile.[145]

Much of the inspiration for these centers comes from "Genesis Farm," an ecological learning center located in the State of New Jersey and founded in 1980 by Dominican Sister Miriam Therese MacGillis. A passionate disciple of Thomas Berry, MacGillis not only has a viable organic farm, but has sparked projects such as community gardens, a local elementary school where the "new cosmology" is taught, a university-degreed Masters program in ecological sustainability, and a movement to both learn about and then protect the region's ecosystem. She also holds rituals to mark the changes of the seasons. (I participated in the Summer Solstice ritual in 1997, where MacGillis linked John the Baptist to that archetypal personality that comes from the margins to invite the community to a new sense of itself. As part of the ritual, each of us made our own crowns from summer flowers and danced the spiral dance, led by Miriam Therese.)

MacGillis is inspiring a whole generation of religious to return to rootedness. Quoting Berry, who maintains that to garden is to activate the deepest mysteries of the universe, she sees gardening "as an invitation into the journey of the cosmos as it unfolds and reveals itself in a cauliflower. To enter into the interior spaces of the natural world is to be confronted with our own arrogance. We must disarm ourselves of so many of our attitudes of inner dominance or of indifference if we are to discover the divine."[146]

MacGillis is calling for a new way of living religious life—a call to what Irish eco-theologian Diarmuid O'Murchu calls "liminality." For O'Murchu:

> The task of a liminal community is to both clarify the structure of society and to be instrumental in changing it. In a sense, every society creates its own liminal groups. Usually unconsciously, a society sets aside certain individuals and groups and endows them with intensive value systems. It projects upon these liminal groups its deepest hopes, dreams and aspirations and requests the liminal person or group to embody and articulate for society at large the deepest values the society finds sacred. Put more simply, we seem to need models that will embody for us the ideals we deeply believe in. Yet society can be very ambivalent about such persons or groups. Sometimes it dismisses them as totally irrelevant, often persecuting—even executing—them, while at the same time admiring

them, however begrudgingly. We use these liminal groups to articulate our archetypal values. Society has always done this and there is good reason to believe that it always will. It is often in hindsight that a specific person, group or movement is deemed to be liminal. Liminality is not something one sets out to create. Rather, it is the product of the creative imagination, seeking to respond to the pressing needs of the contemporary world, fueled by a new vision of the future. It is a call to provide a mirror image in which people can see reflected their own searching, struggles, and hopes for a more meaningful existence.[147]

For MacGillis, the call to liminality can be lived out in endeavors such as Genesis Farm. However, these eco-spirituality centers being founded by mostly women religious are also inspired by a renewed sense of the meaning of the vows of poverty, chastity and obedience. Poverty becomes the call to be satisfied with the community of life and the human's place within it:

We will be content and joyful when we recognize our own place in that community. Thus, we will be able to restrain our addiction to consumption, which is eating the planet alive. From this perspective, we will be able to tap the energy necessary to create the new forms of sustainability so needed at this time. We will have the energy to bring human needs into harmony with the community of life.[148]

Chastity is seen as the human need for bonding. MacGillis notes that today there is a tremendous brokenness in the construction of the self. The shadow side of this is that we often manipulate others for our own self-esteem. The call here is for humans to be "pure of heart," to be "chaste" –which is a way of seeing. It is about *how* we bond with others —and has nothing whatsoever to do with celibacy. For MacGillis, a lack of chastity results in sexism, racism, and militarism: "We are called to witness against the fact that the whole planet has been brought into a pornographic objectification. But now the whole planet will have to become "chaste" to survive—will have to see all as subjects, not as objects."[149]

Finally, obedience is seen as a call to respond to the creativity at the heart of the universe. We must be obedient to that process.

MacGillis sees this understanding of poverty, chastity and obedience as a call to all humans. The vows now must be seen as a covenant with the land to protect, defend and foster the earth's journey into the future. She advises religious communities to convert their motherhouses into bioregions and invites religious congregations to re-found themselves into the larger community of life. She says:

> We are invited to be a presence in the region. To develop the capacity to hear the voices of this sacred community. To listen to the scriptures of the natural world. To form new communities in our bioregions. We must remember that the earth is primary; the human is derivative. We must come home to our bioregions and make food a sacrament again; to sense the spirit in food lovingly nurtured. I suggest that we are coming once again to "the fullness of time". Perhaps we are not at the end of religious life. I suspect we are just beginning![150]

As exciting as this new vision is, however, it is still a very small mustard seed and is not as yet influencing institutional religious life in the slightest. And again, it is more of a phenomenon within the United States than within Latin America.

What does seem to be happening among Latin American religious women is their attraction to learning about natural medicines and treatments to heal those they work with—be it with victims of violence, people suffering from AIDS, malnourished children or the indigent and elderly. There are a growing number of religious sisters working in the region's slums or in impoverished rural areas or with indigenous people who have been quietly training themselves as "medicine women" to treat specific diseases. They are also becoming experts in herbal medicine and treatments. Although they may not necessarily agree with being called as such, they are assuming an ancient and revered role among Latin America's indigenous people: that of the *curandera,* or *machi,* or *bruja.* Just as their counterparts of old, they too know that healing involves the body as well as the spirit and use not only their skills of midwifery and herbal remedies, but also their training in psychology and counseling to offer wholeness to the people they serve.[151]

These two bodies of thought, then—deep ecology and radical/cultural feminism—with all their ramifications, form the basis of ecofeminist theology, the subject of the next chapter.

---

[20] Kolbenschlag, p. 126.
[21] Mary Judith Ress, "Las Fuentes del ecofeminismo: una genealogía", *Ecofeminismo: hallazgos, preguntas, provocaciones. Revista Con-spirando, No. 23,* Santiago, Chile, marzo, 1998. What follows is based on this article.
[22] Kuhn as quoted in Ress, Ibid., p. 5.
[23] Mary Mellor, *Feminism & Ecology.* New York: New York University Press, 1997, p. 15.
[24] Ibid., p. 44.
[25] Vandana Shiva, *Staying Alive.* London: Zed Press, 1989., p. xvi.
[26] Mellor, p. 21.
[27] Ibid., 21.
[28] Fritjof Capra, *The Web of Life.* New York: Doubleday, 1996, p. 7.
[29] Mellor, 132.
[30] Michael E. Zimmerman, "Deep Ecology and Ecofeminism", *Reweaving the World: The Emergence of Ecofeminism.* Irene Diamond and Gloria Orenstein, eds. San Francisco: Sierra Club Books, 1990, p. 141.
[31] Capra, p. 7.
[32] Michael Dowd, *The Big Picture.* On-line article posted by author. No date.
[33] Joanna Macy, *World as Lover, World as Self.* Berkley: Parallax Press, 1991. pp. 15-27.
[34] Ibid., pp. 5-11.
[35] Ibid. p. 14.
[36] Ibid. p. 192. Bold-faced type is mine for emphasis.
[37] Mellor, p. 140
[38] Ibid., 139.
[39] Ibid., 141
[40] Marti Kheel, "Ecofeminsim and Deep Ecology: Reflections on identity and difference", *Reweaving the World,* p. 129.
[41] Brian Swimme and Thomas Berry, *The Universe Story.* HarperSanFrancisco: 1992. Thomas Berry. *The Dream of the Earth.* San Francisco: Sierra Club Books, 1988. Brian Swimme. "Canticle to the Cosmos" (12-part video series) Holy Name College, 1988.
[42] Diarmuid O'Murchu, *Quantum Theology.* New York: Crossoad, 1998.
[43] Capra, p. 27.
[44] Ibid., p. 30.
[45] Werner Heisenburg, as quoted in Capra, p. 30.

[46] O'Murchu, pp. 66-69.
[47] Ibid., p. 28.
[48] David Bohm, quoted in Moni McIntyre, "Toward a Theological Perspective on the Implicate Order of David Bohm," *Readings in Ecology and Feminist Theology*. Mary Heather MacKinnon and Moni McIntyre, eds. Kansas City: Sheed & Ward, 1995, pp. 382-383.
[49] O´Murchu,, p. 58.
[50] Elisabet Sahtouris, *Gaia: The Human Journey From Chaos to Cosmos*. New York: Pocket Books, 1989, p. 9. This is an excellent text describing the evolution of the planet with the passion of an involved biologist who is also a feminist.
[51] I have found Bateson.s works very difficult to read and have relied largely on the detailed summary of his thought found in Morris Berman. *The Reenchantment of the World*. Ithaca: Cornell University Press, 1981), esp. Chapters 7-9. Berman relies on Gregory Bateson. *Steps to an Ecology of Mind*. New York: Ballantine, 1972.
[52] Ibid., p. 238.
[53] Ibid., p. 244-245.
[54] Ibid., p.259.
[55] Ibid., p. 257.
[56] Humberto Maturana and Fransciso Varela. *The Tree of Knowledge*. Boston: Shambala, 1987. I have been to workshops with Maturana and try to follow the development of his thought.
[57] Capra., pp. 100-110.
[58] Ibid., p. 50.
[59] O´Murchu, p. 197.
[60] Berry, *The Dream of the Earth*, pp. 13-14.
[61] Ibid., p. 21.
[62] Ibid., p. 132-133.
[63] Thomas Berry, *The Great Work: Our way into the future*. New York: Bell Tower, 1999.
[64] Ibid., p. 165.
[65] Berry, *The Dream of the Earth*, p. 81.
[66] Berry, *The Great Work.*, p. 201.
[67] Swimme, *The Canticle to the Cosmos* (12-part video series). Each video program is dedicated to developing one of these 12 principles.
[68] Brian Swimme, *The Earth's Imagination* (8-part video series). Mill Valley, CA: Center for the Story of the Universe, 1998.
[69] Ibid., first video.
[70] Ibid.
[71] Berry, *The Dream of the Earth*, p. 4.
[72] "Platform for Action", Fourth UN Conference on the Status of Women. Beijing, China: 1995.
[73] Andy Smith, "For all those who were Indian in a former life," *Ecofeminism and the Sacred*. Carol J. Adams, ed. New York: Continuum, 1993, p.168,171.
[74] Berry, *The Dream of the Earth*, p. 184.
[75] Berry, *The Great Work*, p. 177.
[76] Diego Irarrázaval, *Inculturation: New Dawn of the Church in Latin America*. Maryknoll: Orbis, 2000, p.20.
[77] Ibid., p. 90.
[78] Mary Judith Ress, "After Five Centuries of Mixings, Who Are We?: Walking with our Dark Grandmothers' Feet," Women Healing Earth, Rosemary Radford Ruether, ed. Maryknoll:

[79] Orbis, 1996. What follows is a summary of that article.
Elena Aguila, "Mestiza, champurria, revoltijeada," *Revista Con-spirando*, No. 2, October, 1992, pp. 2-5
[80] Ibid. p. 5.
[81] Berry, *The Dream of the Earth*, p. 166.
[82] Judith Plant, "Searching for Common Ground: Ecofeminism and Bioregionalism", *Reweaving the World*, p. 156.
[83] David Korten, *When Corporations Rule the World*. West Hartford: Kumarian Press and San Francisco: Berrett-Koehleer Publishers, 1995, p. 11.
[84] Ibid., pp. 261-262.
[85] Herman Daly, quoted in Korten, p. 272.
[86] Once again, I must stress that Cultural/Radical Feminism is deeply marked by US feminist history, which is also my own experience. This history is not the same for Latin America.
[87] This chart was mapped by feminist theologian Maria Riley, as cited by Clifford, Anne M. *Introducing Feminist Theology*. Maryknoll: Orbis, 2001,23.
[88] Ynestra King, "Healing the Wounds: Feminism, Ecology, and the Nature/Cultural Dualism"
Reweaving the World, p. 106.
[89] Charlene Spretnak, "Ecofeminism: Our Roots and our Flowering," *Reweaving the World*, pp. 3-14.
[90] Ibid., p. 6.
[91] Ibid., p. 6
[92] King, pp. 117-118.
[93] Letty M. Russell, "Patriarchy". Handout. Yale Divinity-School, 1996.
[94] David Molineaux, Unpublished notes on patriarchy.
[95] I have been influenced in the development of this outline by the works of Berry and Swimme, cited above, as well as by feminist anthropologist Marija Gimbutas, as described in Riane Eisler. *Sacred Pleasure*. HarperSanFrancisco: 1995. An earlier summary of my work on the development of patriarchy appeared in *Revista Con-spirando*, # 11 (marzo, 1995), "La historia del *homo economicus*: una version ecofominista en cuatro actos".
[96] Mary Judith Ress, "Redescubriendo quienes somos: En memoria de Marija Gimbutas (1921-1994). *Revista Con-spirando*, No. 19 (marzo, 1997). Pp. 10-15. This article was based on a special issue of the *Journal of Feminist Studies in Religión*, Vol. 12, No. 2 (Fall, 1996) dedicated to the work of Gimbutas.
[97] Carol Christ, "Introduction: The Legacy of Marija Gimbutas." *Journal of Feminist Studies in Religion*, p. 33.
[98] Marija Gimbutas, *The Civilization of the Goddess: The World of Old Europe*, Joan Marler, ed. HarperSanFrancisco, 1991.
[99] Ibid., p. 324.
[100] Ibid., p. viii
[101] Ibid., p. 321.
[102] Ibid. p. xxi.
[103] Mara Lynn Keller, "The Theory of Early European Origins and the Contemporary Transformation of Western Culture." *Journal of Feminist Studies in Religion*, p. 83.
[104] Carol Christ, "A Different World." *Journal of Feminist Studies in Religion*, pp. 57-58.
[105] Ibid., pp. 53-54.

[106] Gimbutas, *Civilization of the Goddess*, p. vii.
[107] Leonard Shlain, *The Alphabet Versus the Goddess*. New York: Penguin Books, 1998, p. 7.
[108] Ibid., p. 7.
[109] Charlene Spretnak, *Reweaving the World*, p. 5.
[110] Christ, quoted in Mellor, p. 53.
[111] Carol Christ, "Rethinking Theology and Nature", *Reweaving the World*, p. 65.
[112] Carl Jung, *Memories, Dreams, Reflections*. Aniela Jaffe, ed. New York: Vantage Books, 1965, p. 339.
[113] Ibid, p. 402.
[114] M.L. von Franz, "Science and the unconscious." *Man and his Symbols*. New York: Doubleday, 1964, pp. 306-307.
[115] Ibid., p. 309.
[116] Jung, p. 392.
[117] Dr. Anthony Stevens, *Archetypes. A Natural History of the Self*. New York: Quill, 1983. pp. 29-47.
[118] Ibid., , p. 14.
[119] Ibid., pp. 21-62.
[120] James Hollis, *The Archetypal Imagination*. Texas A&M University Press, 2000. pp.10-11.
[121] Ibid., pp. 4-12.
[122] Ibid., pp. 18-25,
[123] Ibid., p. 24.
[124] Ibid., p. 26.
[125] Colectivo Con-spirando. *Diosas y Arquetipos: En Memoria de Madonna Kolbenschlag*. Santiago: Colectivo Con-spirando, 2000, p. 16.
[126] Madonna Kolbenschlag, Unpublished notes. Much of Kolbenschlag's work on the Jungian archetypes can be found in *Eastward Toward Eve*.
[127] Kolbenschlag, unpublished notes.
[128] Colectivo Con-spirando. *Dioas y Arquetipos*. Santiago, 2000. This publication contains Kolbenschlag's last lecture summarizing her work on Toni Wolff's typology.
[129] Ibid., pp. 14-15.
[130] Kolbenschlag. *Eastward Toward Eve*, pp. 134-135.
[131] Charlene Spretnak, "Earthbody and Personal Body as Sacred," *Ecofeminism and the Sacred*. Carol Adams, ed. New York: Continuum, 1993. .
[132] Mellor, p. 2.
[133] Rosemary Radford Ruether, quoted in "Una critica al ecofeminismo: el esencialismo". Mary Judith Ress. *Revista Con-spirando*. No. 23 (marzo, 1998). Pp. 40-41).
[134] Cecile Jackson, quoted in Mellor, p. 73.
[135] Adrienne Rich, quoted in Mellor, pp. 87-88.
[136] Spretnak. *Reweaving the World*, p. 4.
[137] Vandana Shiva, as quoted in Mellor, p. 104.
[138] Mellor, p. 188-183.
[139] Ibid., p. 184.
[140] Ynestra King, "Healing the Wounds: Feminism, Ecology and Nature/Culture Dualism," *Reweaving the World*, p. 116.
[141] Mellor, pp. 69-70.
[142] Ruether, Rosemary Radford. *Gaia & God: An Ecofeminist Theology of Earth Healing*.

London: SCM Press, 1993., p. 269.
[143] Ibid., p. 270.
[144] Ibid., p. 273.
[145] My own Maryknoll community has begun an eco-spirituality center in cooperation with the St. Joseph Sisters of Corondelete in Vilches in southern Chile and I am part of the founding of an holistic health and eco-spirituality center in the Cajon de Maipo, outside Santiago with my team, Capacitar.
[146] Miriam Therese MacGillis, "Genesis Farm links wholistic living with envisioning a new world order" *IDOC Internazionale*. Rome: July-August, 1990, p. 39.
[147] Diarmuid O'Murchu. *Poverty, Celibacy and Obedience: A Radical Option for Life*. New York: Crossroads, 1999, pp. (check)
[148] Miriam Therese MacGillis, Taped reflections on the religious life.
[149] Ibid.
[150] Ibid.
[151] It was Ivone Gebara who, after reading this section of my thesis, pointed this phenomenon out to me.

«Tu eres una diosa y todas las diosas habitan en ti.»
—Madonna Kolbenschag[1]

Chapter III

Ecofeminist theology

From its beginnings, ecofeminism has had a strong link to spirituality and many of its writers have described ecofeminist intuitions in impassioned poetic—often-mystical—language. Indeed, this orientation toward spirituality gives ecofeminism much of its vitality.

In general, ecofeminists can be classified—although not rigidly—on a scale running between Christian and post-Christian postures. Here, however, we walk a thin line because there is a tendency among Christian theologians to classify as "post-Christian" ecofeminists who challenge key concepts of Christianity as being unredeemably patriarchal. Personally, I resent this: unless one actually proclaims that she is "post-Christian," it seems to me an injustice to label her as one. The task of re-imaging the body of Judeo-Christian theology within the new cosmology and as post-patriarchal is truly daunting. Looking "back" on this heritage from the lens of the new paradigm and rediscovering what can still be considered core teachings is an enormous theological task for ecofeminist theologians who do not "throw in the towel" in exasperation with a tradition riddled with the patriarchal mindset.

This caveat aside, I find that most of the better-known spiritual ecofeminists are "post-Christian." Included here would be Starhawk, Charlene Spretnak, Carol Christ and Susan Griffin—all of whom are drawn to an earth-based spirituality where the figure of the goddess, as either a literal divinity or as a symbol, is essential. Starhawk is a practitioner of Wicca, which she describes as the "old religion of Paganism"[2] Spretnak, although she lifts up the Judeo-Christian heritage of social justice for the oppressed in her book *States of Grace*, is convinced that the God of Christian revelation supports dominance of both women and the Earth. She argues that the Christian God is thoroughly transcendent with a hierarchical understanding of the human as autonomous to and higher than the non-human.[3] Carol Christ, who calls herself a *thealogian,* finds Christianity to be male-centered and anti-body, in that it rejects the flesh, especially when it comes in the form of a woman. She argues that the goddess legitimatizes female power as beneficent and independent; when women identify with the goddess as symbol they find "a fierce new love of the divine in themselves."[4] Poet Susan Griffin was one of the first to hold up women's deep identification with nature: "This earth is my sister: I love her daily grace, her silent daring, and how loved I am…and I do not forget: what she is to me, what I am to her."[5]

Griffin, like other contemporary ecofeminists, has been deeply influenced by the writings of radical feminist philosopher and former Catholic theologian Mary Daly. Daly's commitment to reclaiming women's spiritual history from patriarchal theology also led her to search for an alternative mythology present in pre-patriarchal times. Her famous statement, "if God is male, then the male is God" has resonated with a whole generation of feminist theologians. In her 1973 classic, *Beyond God the Father,* Daly declared that it would be impossible to redeem Christianity from patriarchy and literally "left" the church. She called upon feminists to opt out of patriarchal cultures while at the same time documenting the evils of "the Most Holy Trinity: rape, genocide and war". Daly continues to create her own symbolic language system in anticipation of a post-patriarchal consciousness and the creation of communities of women connected to the "elemental world" of our familiars—cats, cows, trees, the dark side of the moon—where we can touch the world of mystery that we communed with before the arrival of patriarchy.[6]

An organic vision of nature leading to a spirituality that affirms the sacredness of the entire earth community is shared by both Christian and post-Christian ecofeminists. But whereas post-Christian ecofeminists such as Starhawk, Spretnak and Chirst would see the divine as totally immanent, Christian ecofeminists search the tradition for a theology of God compatible with an organic vision of the Earth. I will examine the contributions of Christian ecofeminists Sallie McFague (briefly) and Rosemary Radford Ruether (more at length) before turning to the contributions coming from Latin America—namely those of Ivone Gebara and of the Con-spirando collective. (I choose these two women because of their influence on Gebara and on Con-spirando.)

Ecological theologian Sallie McFague uses the terms mother, lover and friend in her search for a new naming of the experience of God in this era of anguish over the planet's devastation.[7] She is interested in the language about God contained in the Bible, arguing that it is metaphorical and expressive of relationship. As such, it is fluid and can evolve. McFague is also committed to a recovery of immanence in our metaphors to describe the divine. She believes that "without a sense of the nearness of God, the overwhelming sense of the way God pervades and permeates our very being, people will not find the God of Christian revelation relevant to their lives and concerns."[8] For this she offers the metaphor of the world as the Body of God, which reflects a theological model where all entities in the cosmos are united symbiotically in levels of interdependence but are also separated as centers of action and response.[9] Critical of post-Christian ecofeminist insistence on the immanence of the divine, McFague argues that God cannot be reduced to the world any more than humans can be reduced to our bodies. She (like Ivone Gebara, as we will see below) proposes a pan*en*theistic understanding of God—that is a god-world relationship where the world exists **in** God. She is careful not to equate God with the cosmos, insisting in the classical scholastic argument that God is more than the sum of the parts. But while God transcends the world, nothing exists without God. At the same time, God is being "bodied forth" in the evolutionary process of ever more complexity. She understands creation as the continuing, dynamic, growing embodiment of God, an embodiment that counterbalances centuries of overemphasis on God's transcendence. Indeed she describes a cosmos wherein "immanental transcendence or transcendent immanence is the model of the universe."[10] This unity between immanence and transcendence is realized in the incarnation of Jesus Christ. The Son of God is embodied in our world and becomes the sign of God's involvement with the created universe.

While McFague argues convincingly that "bodies matter" in Christian theology, her theology is, in the end, a variation of classical incarnational theology—and is still dualistic, in my opinion. She remains caught up in the bind of imaging God as an external agent directing the evolutionary unfolding of creation, thus separating Creator and creation. McFague has great difficulty describing a non-dualistic God. She "resists the ultimate, immanent identification of God with the world. She feels that pantheism would take her too far beyond Christianity. As a Christian reformist, she wants God to identify and suffer with creation, yet retain a transcendence unlimited by it."[11] As post-Christian ecofeminists point out, there is a real problem besetting religions of transcendence in that they lead us to look for the grounding of this world **somewhere outside it**. Emphasis remains on a God who creates "out of nothing" (*ex nihil*), or as "prime mover" and therefore as external to the created order. Even with McFague's incarnational emphasis, where God/Sophia becomes human flesh, emphasis is still on a transcendent, Ultimate Source.

Rosemary Radford Ruether, one of the "mothers" of contemporary feminist theology, in the last decade has moved toward ecofeminism. *Gaia & God* is, to date, her major attempt to situate ecofeminism within classical as well as feminist theological discourse. This work has been translated into Spanish where my Collective Con-spirando spent an entire semester studying it in 1995.

Nowhere have I found a better development of the links between the subjugation of women and the rape of the earth than in Ruether's work. She says: "Domination of women has provided a key link, both socially and symbolically, to the domination of earth, hence the tendency in patriarchal cultures to link women with earth, matter, and nature, while identifying males with sky, intellect, and transcendent spirit."[12] Ruether says that a healed relation to each other and to the earth calls for a new consciousness, a new symbolic culture and spirituality. It also calls for a new vision of a source of life that is "yet more" than what presently exists, continually bringing forth both new life and new visions of how life should be more just and more caring. Ruether finds that we have constructed an idea of ourselves as over against all that is not human, thus creating a sense of the natural world that is both nonhuman and nondivine.

In *Gaia and God*, Ruether reviews the interlocking relations of domination of women and domination of nature throughout history. The central question she explores is how the human community might be healed from both its sexism and its alienation from the rest of nature, which is the "sustaining matrix "of all life. Because she seeks to be faithful to the Christian tradition, she raises up two patterns of biblical thought she believes can be important resources for an emerging ecofeminist theology: covenantal ethics and sacramental cosmology.

Covenantal ethics offers a vision of a rooted community of humans—the farmer and his family, other farm workers—with the land, all living in a covenantal relation with a caretaking God. Ruether points out that while the patriarchal/slave-holding overlay of this local covenantal unit must be rejected, what is insightful is the sense that humans, even the farmer, does not own this land and cannot do with it what he wills.

Humans are only caretakers of a land that ultimately belongs to God; and they are accountable to God for the well-being of all that dwell there—humans, animals, the soil itself. This caretaking demands periodic rest and restoration—every seven days, every seven years, and even after seven times seven years. In that Jubilee Year there must be the great restoration, which includes the revolutionary dismantling of the systems of unjust accumulation of land and exploitation of labor that have occurred over the past two generations. Debts must be cancelled, slaves must be freed, and land alienated from peasants through debt and enslavement must be restored. There must be a land reform that recreates a society where each household has the land for its own maintenance. Unjust social and economic relations are cancelled, as well as animals and land given rest so all can be restored to a just and sustainable balance between humans with each other and humans with animals and soil.

For Ruether, covenantal ethics is complemented by a sacramental cosmology, which she finds in both the Jewish Wisdom tradition and in a cosmic Christology found in the New Testament. Here she discovers a deep respect for the body as the sacramental bodying forth of the creative Spirit, not simply as human body, but as the whole body of the cosmos that surrounds us and sustains our life: For Ruether, the God in whom we live and move and have our being is not some detached spiritual being in heaven, but the one who is in and through and under the whole life process. The whole cosmos is God's body. For Christians it is the Body of Christ as the overcoming of our alienation and separation from God's sacramental presence in creation. We are called to commune with God, not by turning away from body, but in and through the mystery of bodies, which are sacramental presences of the divine.[13]

> In these two traditions, covenantal and sacramental, we hear two voices of divinity from nature. One speaks from the mountaintops in the thunderous masculine tones of "thou shalt" and "thou shalt not." It is the voice of power and law, but speaking, at its most authentic on behalf of the weak, as a mandate to protect the powerless and to restrain the power of the mighty. There is another voice, one that speaks from the intimate heart of matter. It has long been silenced by the masculine voice, but today is finding again her own voice. This is the voice of Gaia. Her voice does not translate into laws or intellectual knowledge but beacons us into communion.
>
> Both of these voices, of God and of Gaia, are our own voices. We need to claim them as our own, not in the sense that there is "nothing" out there, but in the sense that what is "out there"

> can only be experienced by us through the lenses of human existence. We are not the source of life, but are latecomers to the planet. Our minds didn't fall from the skies, but are the flowering of organic body and its capacities to know itself. We can touch our fellow beings, and intuit the source of all life and thought that lies behind the whole. This contact, though humanly imaged, can be true. Its truth lies in the test of relationships; do our metaphors bear the fruits of compassion or of enmity?[14]

Ruether does not believe a feminist ecological culture can be recovered from past pre-patriarchal cultures. She questions the assumption of an earlier matristic, peace-loving "paradise" suggested, for instance, by Gimbutas. She finds efforts to recover such pre-patriarchal ecofeminist cultures as imaginative efforts of people in advanced industrial societies driven by new crises of our times to find a more meaningful myth. "Some see the Jewish and Christian male monotheistic God as a hostile concept that rationalizes alienation from and neglect of the earth…I agree with much of this critique, yet I believe that merely replacing a male transcendent deity with an immanent female one is an insufficient answer to the 'god-problem'".[15] She calls for a more imaginative solution to these traditional oppositions than simply their reversal.

For Ruether, the weakness of such matristic societies lie in their difficulties in finding satisfactory roles for adult males that neither support male dominance over women, or produce demoralized males deeply resentful of women:

> While the female role is built into the process of life-reproduction and food gathering, the male role has to be constructed socially. Societies that fail to develop an adequately affirmative role for men, one that gives men prestige parallel to that of women but prevents their assuming aggressive dominance over women, risk developing the resentful male, who defines his masculinity in hostile negation of women.[16]

Deeply influenced by the new cosmology coming from Berry and Swimme, Ruether is firmly convinced of humanity's need to recognize our utter dependency on the life-producing matrix of the planet in order to learn to reintegrate our human system of production, consumption and waste into the ecological feedback patterns by which nature sustains and renews life. A transcendent God who is outside the world does not infuse human consciousness into human bodies. Rather, human consciousness is an intensification of that awareness that exists to some degree on every level of reality, from subatomic physics, to organic molecules, to photo-synthesizing plants to increasingly self-aware and communicating animals. "We might think of our particular gift of symbol-making consciousness as where all nature becomes conscious of itself in a new self-reflective way, not in the sense of separating us from other species, but in the sense of celebrating the whole cosmic creative process, as well as learning to harmonize our needs with those of the rest of the earth-community."[17]

This vision reshapes the concept of God. God in patriarchal thought has been modeled after alienated male-identified mind or soul that has been thought of as prior to body, existing in an unoriginated, unembodied mental realm outside of and ruling over the physical cosmos. By contrast, Ruether´s ecofeminist theology embodies God *in and though and under the whole cosmic process*. God in this sense can be imagined neither as exclusively male nor as anthropomorphic, but rather as the font from which the variety of plants and animals well up in each generation, the matrix that sustains and renews their life-giving interdependency. Answering the charge that such a description of God will be seen as smacking of immanentism, of a concept of God that lacks transcendence, Ruether invites us to rethink the whole concept of transcendence.

She argues that transcendence-immanence has been understood for too long in dualistic terms of either-or, mind-body, male-female splits. Ecofeminist theology sees transcendence not as a concept that implies a God who is a male disembodied mind outside the universe, but as a renewing divine Spirit radically free from our systems of domination and distortion. The patriarchal God, who rules from outside the universe, is not transcendent in this ecofeminist sense, but is the ultimate captive justification of patriarchal domination and delusion. The true spirit of renewing life is free of all such rationalizations of injustice, but also closer to us than we are to ourselves. An ecofeminist understanding of divine Wisdom both sustains daily life processes and also grounds the creative transformations by which we free ourselves from such distortions to rediscover the real nexus of just relations.[18]

Like McFague, Ruether also uses the image of the universe as "God's body," but I find that Ruether escapes McFague's dualism. For Ruether:

> We humans are the evolutionary growing edge of this imperfectly realized impulse to consciousness and kindness. But this does not separate us from the common fate we share of organisms that grow and then die. An ecological ethic must be based on acceptance of both sides of this dilemma of humanness, both the way we represent the growing edge of what is "not yet" of greater awareness and benignity, and our organic mortality, which we share with the plants and animals. We pass on our ideals to the future not by escaping personal death, but by partly reshaping "nature" to reflect these human ideals. But this reshaping is finally governed by the finite limits of the interdependence of all life in the living system that is Gaia.[19]

Nowhere is Ruether more visionary in her short section called "Toward an ecofeminist theocosmology". She underlines the urgent task of our times to convert human consciousness to the earth in order to live within the web of life as sustainers, not destroyers. Alongside of mentors such as Teilhard de Chardin, Berry and Swimme, she reminds us that human self-awareness is where we recognize our kinship with all other beings. At the same time while our sense of self is enlarged, we become aware of the fragility of our own individual self. She sees the need to let go of the ego on the one hand, by affirming the integrity of our personal center of being, but always in mutuality with the personal centers of all other beings across species.

> Like humans, the animals and the plants are living centers of organic life that exist for a season. Then each of our roots

shrivels, the organic structures that sustain our life fail, and we die. The cutting of the life center also means that our bodies disintegrate into organic matter, to enter the cycle of decomposition and re-composition as other entities. The material substances of our bodies live on in plants and animals, just as our own bodies are composed from minute to minute of substances that once were parts of other animals and plants... Our kinship with all earth creatures is global, linking us to the whole living Gaia today. It also spans the ages, linking our material substance with all the beings that have gone before us on earth and even to the dust of exploding stars.[20]

Ruether calls on us to relinquish the illusion of permanence and to accept the dissolution of our physical substance into primal energy, to become matter for new organisms. She reminds us that this relinquishment will fill us with a deep compassion for all living things, breaking down our illusions of otherness. And here she speaks once again of her sense of Gaia/God: "At this moment we can encounter the matrix of energy of the universe that sustains the dissolution and re-composition of matter as also a heart that knows us even as we are known (...) Surely, if we are kin to all things and offspring of the universe, then what has flowered in us as consciousness must also be reflected in that universe as well, in the ongoing creative Matrix of the whole.(...) But we also know this as the great Thou, the personal center of the universal process, with which all the small centers of personal being dialogue in the conversation that continually creates and recreates the world. The small selves and the Great Self are finally one."[21]

Latin American ecofeminist theology

Ivone Gebara

What ecofeminist theology proposes is, without a doubt, a very radical—some would even say "post-Christian"—restructuring of ultimate meaning. However, its tenets not only appear to make sense to a growing number of poor women in Latin America, but ignite great passion and joy!

As we have seen in Chapter I, ecofeminist theology in Latin America emerges in the "third stage" of feminist theology, which begins in the 1990s. Without exception, those of us working in this field in Latin America have been deeply influenced by the thought of Ivone Gebara, the region's foremost ecofeminist theologian. Indeed, she is the architect of what she terms "holistic ecofeminism" which characterizes this third stage. An overview of her life and work, then, is in order.

Gebara, always admitting that ecofeminism "is not a native flower of Latin America" but takes on the region's specific tonalities and contexts,[22] has been influenced by the shift in cosmology based on the new science as expressed by thinkers such as Teilhard de Chardin, Fritjof Capra, Thomas Berry and Brian Swimme and from feminist theologians such as Mary Daly, Rosemary Radford Ruether, Sallie McFague and German theologian Dorothee Soelle. (She is especially influenced by Ruether´s feminist and ecofeminist thought and was recently the keynote speaker at Ruether´s retirement celebration from Garrett Evangelical Seminary in Chicago.) A quick summary of Gebara´s "credentials:" She is a religious sister, a member of the Canonesses of St Augustine, a French congregation. She holds doctorates in both Philosophy and Religious Sciences and is the author of many books, including her opus on ecofeminism, *Longing for Running Water: Ecofeminism and Liberation* (1999) and her recently released *Out of the Depths: Evil and Salvation in a Feminist Perspective* (2002). While she hails from Sao Paulo, Gebara has lived in Brazil's Northeast for the past 20 years. She taught epistemology and philosophy in the Catholic Theological Institute in Olindo/Recife for 14 years, under the direction of Dom Helder Cámara, one of Latin America's most famous "liberation" bishops. When Cámara retired, he was replaced by Dom José Cardoso, a conservative bishop who—acting on orders from the Vatican—ended the Institute, as Cámara had conceived it, and fired all the professors. Gebara has since become a "nomad," as she describes her current ministry of traveling throughout the region—and beyond—giving courses and workshops on feminist and ecofeminist theology to grassroots communities, women's groups, religious communities and solidarity organizations of all kinds. But she continues to live in a slum outside Recife in Northeastern Brazil. It is the daily life of her neighbors, most of whom are poor women, from which she constructs her theology. Those who attend her courses or read her books and articles feel they know her well because, true to feminist methodology, she always speaks from her own experience and shares her life and her feelings with her audiences—so much so that everyone considers her a personal friend. In 1994, Gebara was "silenced" by the Vatican for her unorthodox opinions, especially with regard to abortion. She was ordered "back to school" for doctoral studies in theology at a Pontifical Catholic University in Europe. The result of this "punishment" is her recent book, *Out of the Depths*. Since returning from "exile" she continues to be a "nomad."

In characterizing the "third phase" of Latin American feminist theology, Gebara says that it began with a suspicion about the very definition of God:

> We began to criticize the concept of God, Father Almighty, all-powerful, omnipotent, and Being-unto-himself who out of his goodness created heaven and Earth, men and women. We didn't notice that the story we were presented was a power struggle between God and humanity—and that every time humanity deviated from God's will, a 'catastrophe' occurred because we had broken with God, we had gone against God's will. Our image of ourselves was of *fallen beings*. And the only way we could be saved was for God to send His son, who was also God, to rescue us from our original sin. But who decided what was God's will, which has throughout history favored the rich, the white race, and the male? Our religious leaders, who said they were more capable of discovering what was God's will for us. Even more insidiously, we were told and came to believe that we were God's chosen people, and in God's name Christianity took on a messianic, missionary triumphalism: we were superior to all other peoples and all other religious expressions that had developed through the ages.[23]

According to Gebara, liberation theology begins with the question: "How to speak of God in the face of hunger, injustice, misery, dictatorship and the destruction of entire peoples?" Its major contribution is a more collective understanding of God as well as a sense of the social nature of sin. God becomes the God of life and of justice who has a preferential love for the poor. However, liberation theology has not challenged the **patriarchal anthropology and cosmology** upon which Christianity is based. Nor has it challenged the underlying patriarchal structure of Christianity itself. Gebara wonders whether Christianity will be flexible enough to change the foundations of its anthropology and cosmology to respond to what she calls "holistic ecofeminism." She says it must if it is to survive.

In *Longing for Running Water*, Gebara describes her "holistic ecofeminism:"

> With ecofeminism I have begun to see more clearly how much our body—my body and the bodies of my neighbors—are affected not just by unemployment and economic hardship but also by the harmful effects the system of industrial exploitation imposes on them. I have begun to see more clearly how the exclusion of the poor is linked to the destruction of their lands, to the forces that leave them no choice but to move from place to place in a ceaseless exile, to racism, and to the growing militarization of their countries. To defend the unjust monopoly of a minority, the poor countries have become more intensely militarized: they arm themselves to kill their own poor. I have come to see how much all this fits in with the inherent logic of the patriarchal system, especially in its current form...I sense that ecofeminism is born of daily life, of day-to-day sharing among people, garbage in the streets, bad smells, the absence of sewers and safe drinking water, poor nutrition, and inadequate health care. The ecofeminist issue is born of the lack of municipal garbage collection, of the multiplication of rats, cockroaches and mosquitoes, and of the sores on children's skin...This is no new ideology. Rather, it is a different perception of reality that starts right from the unjust system in which we find ourselves and seeks to overcome it in order to bring happiness to everyone and everything[24]

I would like to examine four areas where I believe Gebara is standing traditional theology on its head from an ecofeminist point of view.

These are: her definition of "person"; her reflections on ethics; her definitions of God, Trinity and Jesus; and finally, the relationship between ecofeminism and the option for the poor.

Gebara insists that we must first change our **understanding of men and women** within the cosmos before we turn to a reconstruction of God. She argues that because any image of God is a reflection of the understanding or experience we have of ourselves, an ecofeminist view would re-situate the human within—not above—the universe. She shows how this is diametrically opposed to a Christian anthropology that insists that humanity is "lord of creation" ordered by the Creator to "dominate the Earth." In our current anthropology, the human's right to dominate, control and possess has been legitimatised by the Creator and thus has become part of our definition of ourselves. Gebara, however, argues for a new understanding of "relationality" which she sees as the primary reality: Relationality "is constitutive of all beings. It is more elementary than awareness of differences or than autonomy, individuality, or freedom. It is the foundational reality of all that is or can exist. It is the underlying fabric that is continually brought forth within the vital process in which we are immersed. Its interwoven fibers do not exist separately, but only in perfect reciprocity with one another—in space, in time; in origin and into the future."[25]

We are, then, fundamentally "relatedness." Gebara then goes on to develop relatedness as a human condition, as an earthly condition, as an ethical reality, as a religious experience and as a cosmic condition. She wrestles with the notion of consciousness and implies that liberation theology limited consciousness to the realm of a social, political and religious project. Anything that fell outside of the consciousness-raising project was rejected because it did not square with the project's model of rationality.[26]

In addressing relatedness as an ethical reality, she argues that no transcendent principle or higher divinity should act as some sort of moral grounding for our actions. Since relatedness is a constitutive experience of the very universe in which we live, we appeal to ethics because we see it as the vital foundation of our personal and collective lives as we evolve. Ethics, then, is the fruit of our own humanization process, of our collective growth in our attempts to construct a world in which shared life can become more and more a reality.

Gebara argues that an **ecofeminist ethics** seeks to open spaces for women and for the earth's ecosystems to assume their rightful place in the building of new relationships based on respect and reciprocity. Both have become ethical non-subjects under patriarchy. She is especially critical of the ethical posture of the Catholic church with regard to the treatment of women, noting that "we are talked to; guidelines for living are imposed on us as if these guidelines were laws, of more importance than our own history."[27] This is especially true in the area of women's sexuality where the belief in the superiority of men and an all-male leadership allows legislating the behavior of women and their bodies. She notes: "In Catholic morality, evil and sin are defined and legislated in advance. (…) It produces 'guilty' persons and 'victims,' rather than citizens who seek to assume risks and responsibilities in history. In this scheme, women often are guilty parties and victims at the same time."[28] Gebara calls for an ethics of life that takes account of the diversity of both humanity and the planet's ecosystems as well as the dynamic, changeable character of human relations and human earth relations. That is why ethics can never be a static system of laws, but must always be attentive to the complexity of situations as they occur. Ethical decisions must be made in context, beyond pre-established universals. She insists that an ethics of life aims at creating a society in which every person and species has the right to life within a collectivity because each one has a vital need for the other. This is a major departure from traditional Christian theology, which has projected that everything good has already been present from the beginning in the "eternal truths" of that Tradition. Today, she says, "we are presented with an invitation from the history of Life—the Life of different peoples, the Life of ecosystems, the Life of the planet. Christian tradition must join a larger movement, beyond the old frontiers, cosmologies and anthropologies. In re-encountering the Wisdom of nature, that of native peoples and marginalized groups, the Christian tradition will learn, as others have, to find a new place for itself in the Universe."[29]

Gebara's chapter on **God** in *Longing for Running Water* contains some of her most radical and most brilliant insights. She says that questions about God are really questions about ourselves:

> To seek God is to seek our own humanity, in an attempt to speak of ourselves beyond our own limitations and contingencies and to heal a kind of wound that we feel within us always. To seek God is to seek meaning.... We set up pure and perfect beings to contrast them with our own experiences of impurity and imperfection. We set up powerful beings to contrast them with our own fragility and weakness.[30]

Gebara argues against a personal God because if God were a person, God would be an autonomous being, which supports the patriarchal concept of God who is "above" and "over" life itself. Although God is not a person, we humans are persons, so this is how we tend to relate to Divine Mystery. Therefore, analogously, I speak to God as a person. She uses the analogy of "praying to my double". We attribute the qualities of a person to our double, but it is really one's "I" talking to one's "I".[31] It is here where Gebara levels her harshest criticism of patriarchy. She maintains that a metaphysical, anthropomorphic and anthropocentric God became a necessity within the psychological structure that evolved throughout the history of patriarchal culture. God was regarded as another "I"— an ego of infinite excellence whose designs were inaccessible to human beings. And there was always the hope that this ego would listen to me and respond, offering a sense of paternal or maternal security. She says that: "The need to affirm a higher power—a power presented as being in ***discontinuity*** with all the powers of the cosmos, the earth, human beings, animals, plants, and even life itself—appears to be of fundamental importance in maintaining the hierarchical organization of the society in which we live."[32]

Gebara's ecofeminist perspective does not spend time reflecting on God as a Supreme Being because we can no longer envision such a being as an autonomous, separate person. Ecofeminists are convinced that we are a single Sacred Body; we dwell in Mystery larger than ourselves. We are part of this Mystery, which, like us, is evolving. In this Body, the individual is not annihilated, but is instead related to a wider whole without which life would be impossible. Holistic ecofeminism, then, holds that God is in all—and therefore all is sacred. A view Gebara, like McFague, calls "pan-en-theism".[33]

With regard to the **Trinity**, Gebara reminds us that since it is we ourselves who construct meaning, so too have we, through our ancestors, construed the Trinity as "three different persons in one God." For Gebara, the Trinity is a metaphor we use to explain the unexplainable: "The experience of the Trinity brings multiplicity and the desire for unity into a single and unique movement…Trinity is the name we give ourselves, a name that is the synthesis of our perception of our own expanded existence."[34] She reaffirms the Trinity as the expression of the Mystery that envelops us, which is both one and multiple. However, she also insists that, as an expression of our single/multiple reality, it will also have to contain evil within it:

> An ecofeminist, Trinitarian vision of the universe and of humanity does not identify evil, destruction, and suffering as realities that are outside ourselves and need to be eliminated by the use of violence, nor does it say they should be accepted as "God's will." Rather than pointing to "the other" as the source of evil, it recognizes that what we call evil is in ourselves; in a certain sense, evil is also our body. Evil is a relationship we ourselves construct. It leads to the unraveling of the entire fabric of human life.[35]

With regard to **Jesus**, Gebara shares her own journey, telling us that she was often bothered by the excessive centrality of Jesus in liberation theology which gave so little space to other initiatives—especially those coming from women. At the same time she finds the figure of Jesus profoundly alluring. He is the symbol of what we seek, of how we long to be. She develops the idea of symbol:

> To say that Jesus is a symbol means that, although he is Jesus of Nazareth, he is really more than Jesus of Nazareth. He becomes the possession of the community of his followers, a collective construct representing a way of life, a path to the meaning of our existence. Jesus as a symbol is in a certain sense greater than Jesus of Nazareth as an individual, because in him millions and millions of persons are encompassed.[36]

Within an ecofeminist perspective, Jesus does not come in the name of some "superior will" that sent him; rather he comes from here—he is an earthling just like us. He came from the same evolutionary process as we did. He is not the powerful Son of God who dies on the cross and becomes the "king" who reigns over his kingdom here on earth. Rather, he is a symbol of the vulnerability of love who ends up being murdered, but who rises again in those who love him.

This said, Gebara also examines the manipulation of the Jesus symbol within our present globalized world. Discourse about the power of Jesus, which is over every other power, appears paradoxically as a way out for those without power. Jesus is that power who can find a solution to all problems, but in exchange he demands conversion and submission. This Jesus becomes, then, the Great God-Man who helps all who call upon him, and with his powerful help one can stop drinking, stop smoking, stop prostituting and become a "third-rank citizen, a little client of the system."[37]

Gebara admits that there is little dialogue with feminist Christology in Latin America, where the figure of Jesus continues to be central—whether as liberator (Liberation theology) or as Lord (the Pentecostal and Charismatic movements). She takes up the challenge to reject what she sees as a type of idolatry in relation to the figure of Jesus and calls upon us to look for the salvific dimensions of other figures in biblical and Christian history. Jesus, she says, is no longer the only "way," or the "resurrection and the life" or the only one who has "the words of life" for those who hunger and thirst for justice. Today, there are a wide variety of choices.[38] She reminds us that each of us can be the "resurrection and the life" for others—resurrections experienced daily, which are provisional and a continual process. She invites us to a Christology of gratitude: a capacity to gratefully contemplate the mysterious beauty that surrounds us, to feel our common belonging to the same universe. Such a Christology is understood as a pluralistic salvific effort—tenderness of humanity for humanity, tenderness of humanity for the earth, tenderness of the earth for humanity and the entire community of life. This Christology is present when two or three are gathered living out this gratitude; indeed, it is in those moments that the presence of Great Mystery is manifest.[39]

However, Ivone Gebara's overriding concern, as she travels around Latin America offering workshops on ecofeminism, is for **the oppressed**—those "voiceless of history"—who by the very fact of where they are born are excluded from the chance to live a full life. She is keenly aware that it is the poor who are the greatest consumers of patriarchal religion because of the consolation it provides and she is determined to stay close to these voiceless ones, and do her theology from this posture.

It is from the perspective of these excluded that Gebara also responds to the critiques of "essentialism" within ecofeminist thought. Like Ruether, she says that we must stop thinking that humans are not a part of nature or that culture exists somehow in opposition to nature. She reminds us that we are not supernatural creatures who somehow are destined to escape our own human nature. Gebara concentrates on colonization of both women and nature in this debate, arguing for an historical approach. Locating herself in the Latin American context, she calls attention to the huge numbers of Africans who were submitted to slavery during the 16th and 17th centuries to fulfill the labor needs of the new Portuguese and Spanish colonies in the Americas. She notes that women and men were "colonized" differently, with women's bodies being subject to both a sexual and work-related colonization. This is not a matter of "essence;" it is a historical, cultural, economic, political and religious matter:

> Colonization is the occupation of others, through the dimensions of time and space, and the reduction of the identity of the colonized to that of the colonizer... The worst part of colonization is the loss of awareness of being colonized and no longer knowing one's roots, or who he or she was or is. The worst part of colonization is losing self-confidence and one's cultural values, placing oneself in the hands of the other in a submissive and uncritical way.[40]

For Gebara, it is patriarchal society with its male division of social labor that is essentialist, in that—from a perspective of the "colonized"—women's bodies are producers, both biologically and culturally, to the extent that women give birth and nurture the young of the species. They require no tools to produce. Domestic work is not recognized as work basic to the maintenance of human life—indeed the rearing and feeding of children is comparable in the patriarchal mindset to other mammals' activities. Under capitalism this situation has become exaggerated: women's role of procreation and nurturing is not valued or remunerated.

At the symbolic-cultural level, Gebara notes that masculine symbolism is dominant even when representing the female body. In the last 20 years, however, women have realized that their absence from the production of cultural symbols is the result of an imbalance in the distribution of work and a relegation of women to the domestic sphere. "This is why I hold that women are colonies," she argues. "Women have been colonized to stay home and allow men the grand flights of fancy required for the production of culture, politics and religion. We assist in the reproduction of a culture that makes men feel they are the center of history, and its organizers."[41] She insists that Christian theology must take major responsibility for imposing a powerful ideological colonization of women's bodies in that the behaviors of the virtuous woman have been predetermined as the "will of God". If we change what is considered "natural" for women, we challenge the very construction of Christianity itself—which, Gebara suspects, is beginning to happen. She calls for a new symbolism to reflect the vital web of interdependence in which we exist.

In her most recent book, *Out of the Depths: Evil and Salvation in a Feminist Perspective*, Gebara grapples with the understanding of evil, especially as it is understood in theology, in relationship to women's experience and their lack of power. While not explicitly an ecofeminist work, her ecofeminist perspective is clearly present. It seems to me that by tackling evil from a radical feminist perspective, Gebara is trying to offer poor women some clues for understanding their age-old oppression. She again raises the nature/culture dilemma, but in terms of masculine evil, which seems somehow less evil than feminine evil. "For men, evil is an act one can undo. But for women, evil is in their very being. Being female is from the start something bad, or, at least, something limiting—so there is at bottom an anthropological question that reveals a conflict in the very way we understand what it means to be human."[42] She asks: why do women need a twofold mediation to be saved—that of God and that of men—while men need only one? Something fishy here! And so, as always, she brings the working tool of suspicion to her analysis of evil.

Gebara spends a good deal of time in analyzing sacrifice, especially the Christian concept of Jesus' sacrifice on the cross. Here her thought can be closely identified with womanist theologian Dolores Williams and Asian feminist theologian Rita Nakashima Brock. Just as with poor women everywhere, the sacrifice of Jesus on the cross validates their own suffering and gives meaning to their lives. She notes that: "The ideology of sacrifice, imposed by patriarchal culture, has developed in women a training in renunciation. They must give up their pleasure, thoughts, dreams, desires, to put themselves at the service of others or to live as others think they should (...) This attitude leads most women to endure and accept suffering as if it were part of God's design... It is still common to hear women in great trouble say: 'Jesus suffered more than this'".[43] Such attitudes hide real injustices and fail to allow women to distinguish between suffering caused by wrongdoing and that angst present in the ordinary lives of all humans.

Gebara calls attention to the fact that in Latin American popular culture, there is a deeply rooted sense among women that it is a curse to be born female. Most women will admit that they often wished they had born male, and long for male children so they will not suffer the "cross" that comes with being born a woman. However, they also believe that, as Christians they are to bear and even welcome their crosses rather than look for ways to get rid of them.

Searching for ways to deliver women from this theological quagmire of bearing crosses willingly, Gebara reminds us that while suffering is an ever-present reality, so too are creative forms of redemption. She calls these "provisional escapes in our tentative lives".[44] They are experienced in sharing a meal together, in acts of tenderness, in the straightened posture of a stooped woman, in the birth of a child, in a good harvest. To broaden the meaning of salvation and resurrection is, for Gebara, an ethical necessity: "Concretely, it means listening to the wisdom of our bodies, even with all its contradictions, because it is our bodies that point out the places of resurrection, the sites of pleasure and the paths that lead to happiness."[45] She also exhorts women to relativize the agony Jesus suffered on the cross. This suffering, though indeed great and unjust, is no greater than that of a mother whose child is wrenched from her, of women who see their children die of hunger because of the greed of those who hold economic power. The centrality of Jesus' death on the cross has been used to exclude or minimize other sufferings.

Gebara cautions us to remember that there is not universal salvation, but that the powerful of this world need universal salvation or an all-powerful God as a way to consolidate their own power. No, there is no salvation once and for all; there is no resurrection once and for all. Both come in small doses that remind us of who we really are. They are lived in our concrete bodies, our flesh of today. This doesn't mean the death of political projects for change. The private and the public, the micro and the macro, the individual and the collective are dependent on one another.

Gebara admits that there is a tendency to identify ecofeminism with "new age" groups and that, for the most part, Latin American progressives think that ecofeminism fails to offer solid religious grounding for popular emancipation struggles, which are regarded as struggles for liberation on the journey toward establishing the reign of God here on earth. She challenges these critics to see that what they call "grounding" is more often than not based on a specific sociological reading of Christianity. What they call a solid foundation is "the anthropocentrism and Theo centrism that have long marked our thinking. What they call groundedness is the continuation of a theology based on a hierarchical religious system."[46] She insists that ecofeminism's invitation to love and mercy does not come from a reality that is external to us. Rather, it is an urge present in our very humanness. There is an incredible attraction toward other beings written within our very flesh. She also insists she is creating an ecofeminism that:

> ...is based on the experience of those who have diminishing access to green things and clean water; of those who breathe an ever-greater amount of the air pollution that has spread everywhere. My ecofeminism is pregnant with health: not health as we understood it in the past, but the health of a future that promises deeper communion between human beings and all other living things. My ecofeminism is shot through with the staunch conviction that beauty is important in healing people. It might be the beauty of sounds, of colors, of words, of faces, of food and drink, or of embraces. Like my friend Rubem Alves, I too can vouch for "salvation through beauty."[47]

In the end, Ivone Gebara is a poet, a shamanic figure of our times who spins new visions that captivate the imagination. Her writings and her teaching is shot through with allurements that imagine a post-patriarchal world where salvation does indeed come through beauty. A final quote, addressing the ultimate patriarchal fear: our mortality:

> There is something that resembles a non-acceptance of our mortal reality, a reality shared with all living beings. There is a lack of any sense of belonging to a Unique Body, a Living Body in transformation, a Body, which is mortal and open to endless possibilities. (...) I prefer to stay enmeshed in the dust of the earth rather than to mount to a sky white and perfect. I prefer, for my last sigh and my last repose, the arms of the Earth—which, according to Genesis, is the place where God walks. Beyond what is imagined by reason, there is something imagined by desire, poetry, beauty (...) It is so little, but it is so beautiful! It is beautiful in its fragility, and everything beautiful has something fragile in it and something ephemeral. This

eschatology commingled with earth, the cycle of life, the year's seasons, the bodies of animals, plants and flowers, this human and larger-than-human eschatology, warms the heart a great deal.[48]

Yes, it does, it does.

Con-spirando's contribution to ecofeminism

Ivone Gebara is one of Con-spirando's midwives and has greatly influenced our thinking. She writes in her Introduction to *Longing for Running Water:*: "At the moment, in my view, the liveliest ecofeminist group in Latin America is the Con-spirando Collective in Santiago, Chile."[49] She was also the keynote speaker at our 10th anniversary celebration in April 2002. In her talk on Con-spirando's contribution to Latin America's ecofeminism she held up the fact that we are not a purely academic organization, nor are we associated with any church organization, which frees us from the control of both. She also extolled Con-spirando's way of organizing itself as a collective: we are a non-hierarchical, multicultural team that has both Latin American members as well as members from other countries where relations of justice and tenderness are the goal. She noted that Con-spirando has become that space where the questions of many women of Latin America were echoed—our frustrations with both the patriarchal society and church in which we live. Priority has always been given to women's voices, she stressed. Gebara listed five major contributions of the Cons-spirando Collective:

- First, the belief in the wisdom of our bodies and the priority of knowing through our corporality in relationship. Here feeling becomes a way of knowing.
- Second, efforts to search out non-hierarchical ways of being that model "power with" rather than "power over".
- Third, the sharing of new ways to celebrate, new rituals that nurture our emerging spiritualities and our commitments.

- Fourth, the re-examination of those foundational myths upon which Western, Christian culture is based in order to relativize them and search for new myths that can water our emerging spiritualities, theologies and ethics.
- And fifth, all of us are one. All are my kin, from the folks in the barrio to the animals, the mountains, the rivers.

Gebara says that Con-spirando epitomizes a new cosmology, a new anthropology, a new epistemology and a new ecology needed for our times.

Con-spirando is a women's collective working in the areas of ecofeminism, theology and spirituality which began in 1991. I am a founding member of this collective. We publish a quarterly journal, *Con-spirando: Revista latinoamericana de ecofeminismo, espiritualidad y teologia,* hold workshops, seminars and an annual summer school on ecofeminist theology, spirituality and ethics, and offer a yearly cycle of rituals. In our magazine's first issue, we set out our purpose, which more than 10 years later, still very much defines what we are about:

> In the patriarchal culture in which we live, women's contributions are not taken seriously. This is particularly true in the area of theology. Women are absent as subjects doing theology and also as a major subject matter of this theological reflection. Our lives, our everyday religious practice and our spirituality is simply not present In current theological reflection. Absent too, are our experiences of suffering, joy and solidarity — our experiences of the Sacred. Besides expressing our criticism of patriarchal culture, we also seek to contribute to the creation of a culture that allows theological reflection to flower from our bodies, our spirits—in short, our experiences as women.
> We seek theologies that take account of the differences of class, race and gender that so mark Latin America. We hope to open new spaces where women can dig deeply into our own life experiences without fear. These experiences are often negative, even traumatic, in terms of the religious formation we have received. We seek spaces where women can experience new ways of being in community; where we can celebrate our faith more authentically and creatively; where we can rediscover and value our roots, our history and our traditions—in short, to engage in an interreligious dialogue that helps us to recover the

essential task of theology, which is to search out and raise the questions of ultimate meaning.

We are convinced that, to bring about relationships marked by justice and equality, we must celebrate our differences and work toward a greater pluralism worldwide. To this end, we need theologies that unmask the hierarchies in which we live, theologies that, rather than seeking to mediate Mystery, celebrate and explore the Holy without reductionisms or universalisms. We call for theologies that question anthropocentrism and that promote the transformation of relationships based on dominance of one race, nationality, gender or age group over another and of the human over other forms of life. Such theologies will have profound political consequences.

Such a feminist perspective based on our diversity of class, race, age and culture must also take up our love as well as our anguish for all life on the planet that we feel is so threatened today. We call this posture ecofeminism. It is within this perspective that we seek a spirituality that will both heal and liberate, that will nourish our Christian tradition as well as take up the long-repressed roots of the native peoples of this continent. We want to explore the liberating dimensions of our experience and imagination of the Holy. To do this, we *"con-spirar juntas"*.[50]

Without a doubt, Con-spirando would be located in the "third stage" of the development of Latin American feminist and ecofeminist theology. What has been our specific contribution to theology? First, several of us are uncomfortable with the very word "theology" to define us because it is such a patriarchal term and links us in the popular mind to "religion," "church," "morality," "doctrine" and, of course, to "the science of God". Sometimes we think we should just drop the term "theology" from our name altogether! However, at other moments, we renew our commitment to push the definitions of theology past their patriarchal confines by broadening the term to grapple with "constructs of meaning" as concretely experienced by women. We are dedicated to bringing to bear the insights coming from anthropology, psychology, literature and gender analysis to our understanding of theology.

Although not exhaustive, I believe Con-spirando has made a significant theological contribution in the following four areas: in unmasking some aspects of theological violence toward women; in renaming and connecting with the Sacred; in offering an embodied theology; and in bringing an ecofeminist perspective to theology. All four are inter-connected and relate to our work in developing ecofeminism from a Latin American perspective.

- **Unmasking theological violence toward women**

Influenced by feminist/womanist theologians such as Dolores Williams, Rita Nakashima Brock, Joanne Carlson Brown and Rebecca Parker,[51] we have been working toward a non-sacrificial reading of redemption in order to liberate Christianity from patriarchy. With these theologians, we too have been challenging Christianity's core doctrine that Jesus' death on the cross was essential to redeem humanity from sin. Indeed, helped by their analysis, we are seeing that the theme of atonement and redemption in Christ may be directly related to "allowing" violence and child abuse. According to Dolores Williams, "if we as Christians understand that our redemption happened through a violent act and that God in some sense intended this to happen, is that not giving a sacred status to violence?"[52] And according to Rita Nakashima Brock, "the father allows, or even inflicts, the death of his only perfect son. The emphasis is on the goodness and power of the father and the unworthiness and powerlessness of his children, so that the father's punishment is just, and the children are to blame"[53] We have translated the essay "For God So Loved the World" by Joanne Carlson Brown and Rebecca Parker into Spanish and have used in our workshops. This essay argues that the central image of Christ on the cross as the savior of the world communicates the message that suffering is redemptive—a message that is further complicated by a theology that holds that Christ suffered in obedience to his Father's will. The authors criticize Christianity's central belief of Christ's suffering and dying for us as accepting and even encouraging suffering and ask if it is really so strange that there is so much abuse in society when the predominant theological image of our culture is that of divine child abuse!

In 1994, Con-spirando dedicated an entire issue to the underpinnings of violence, paying particular attention to theological violence.[54] In our June 1996 issue, two of our members grappled with the theme of child abuse and of images of God related to the concept of power. Their reflections grew out of a workshop on images of the Sacred in our understanding of power. Participants discovered that the patriarchal image of an all-powerful God who rules over humans had impeded them from understanding that "all of us form part of each other and we co-create each other in the depths of our being."[55]

Violence and "beyond violence" was also the theme of our *Shared Garden* theological education program held in 1997-98. This program was a cooperative educational effort among WATER, Women's Alliance for Theology, Ethics and Religion, based in Washington DC and co-founded by feminist theologian Mary Hunt and feminist liturgist Diann Neu, Ivone Gebara and her team in Recife, Brazil and the Con-spirando Collective. During each of the three "Gardens," participants worked with Ivone Gebara on unmasking the myth of Adam and Eve's "fall" from Paradise; they also were exposed to Elisabeth Schüssler Fiorenza´s concept of kyriarchy to describe the system of hierarchical power relationships that impinge upon us at every level. At each stage, women were encouraged to untie the knots of violence embedded in the memory of their individual bodies, as well as in the "bodies" of church, society and theology. At the same time, they were encouraged to move "beyond violence" to nurture new theologies based on women's experience to offset those theologies that support kyriarchy and allow for "contexts of violence".[56]

- **Renaming and celebrating the Sacred**

To speak one's own theological word, to name and reflect upon one's own experience of the Holy is essential in the process of elaborating our own theology. Offering new images of the Sacred—out of which evolve both new ethical demands as well as new spiritual practices—has been part of Con-spirando's work since our beginnings. In our magazine, workshops and rituals, we try to empower women to rename the Sacred according to their own lights. New images which have surfaced include: a pregnant woman giving birth; a great uterus as the body of God; a nest;

a tree; a mountain; a flowing river; the ocean; a gentle breeze and a wild wind; a web; a hungry child, an elderly invalid; a circle of laughing children; the sunset —to name a smattering. In workshops we invite women to draw, mold and dance their sense of the Sacred. We often use the following chart, which each woman fills in for subsequent group sharing:

My personal evolution of images/symbols of the Sacred

	Image/symbol	Ethical demands	Spiritual practices
Childhood			
Adolescence			
Adulthood (now)			

In March 1997 we dedicated an entire issue of *Con-spirando* to the creation and evolution of symbols.[57] In the lead article, one of our members describes how symbols of the Sacred reflect the belief system of an entire people, an entire historical period, and as such contain tremendous power over that people and historical context. However, the author, Con-spirando member Josefina Hurtado, stresses that symbols of the Sacred are created by we humans in response to our experiences—and therefore can and should evolve.[58]

Yeta Ramirez of Nicaragua expresses that evolution quite clearly in the following testimony:

> Ever since I was eight years old, I was surrounded by images of the saints and of the Virgin in the homes of my aunts. I remember one aunt in particular who lived in the country and every afternoon she would sit in front of her altar with all of her statues and pray the rosary and other prayers. We kids used to laugh at her because she was always interrupting her prayers to give orders about domestic matters, etc. At that same time, every Saturday I had to go to catechism classes to receive instructions for making my First Communion. What symbols of the Sacred did I receive then? The image of Christ on the Cross-, Christ in his casket that was paraded through the streets ev-

ery Holy Week. The Sorrowful Virgin was also very present; she was dressed in black and was crying at the foot of the cross. Later on, as an adolescent, I began to work with the Catholic Action movement. At that time, I was very impressed by colors—the white of the Virgin and of the Resurrection. In the 1960 liturgical reform, I began to discover the Risen Jesus who was with us, and the historical Mary, the campesina woman who baked bread. Work became a sacred symbol as well as the tools we used for work. We also began to integrate the struggle for liberation into our symbol system. The color green was important—giving a green light for Latin America to take over the land, for agrarian reform. Green was present in our liturgies as a symbol of commitment, hope, and the struggle for land.

Then, in the 1980s, I began to go deeper into nature and incorporate this in liturgy. In my time with Catholic Action, a symbolism of God in nature was present as well as a certain contemplative dimension. More recently, I have taken up an ecological perspective as if I was finally remembering something that I had somehow forgotten. Also, in this past decade, there has been a renewed interest in rediscovering our own cultural roots that have been repressed. Now we no longer speak of father god, but also of mother-god and of the goddesses.

All this symbolism comes out when I work in the area of ritual and liturgical celebration. In the women's group that I belong to (which is a group committed to stopping violence in all its forms), we have celebrated rituals of healing where we use oils and plants, water, flowers, candles, food, etc. We are now at a stage where we are reclaiming our bodies as sacred in order to combat all the physical and psychological violence we have been subjected to. We have come to see that the concept of "god" is very closed and that really the divinity is much, much broader. We have come to understand that the churches do not have the power to name sacred symbols—power is in the people and so it is we ourselves who must discover those symbols that speak of the divinity for us. This allows us to build spirituality from our own conception of what is divine. The religious symbols of my childhood were all given to me from outside; now, however, I mold them and give them meaning based on my own experience.[59]

- **Embodied theology**

Con-spirando's third theological contribution is in the area of methodology. We espouse an embodied theology holding up women's bodies as "sacred text". Our method has developed out of years of working with the *concientizacion* methodology developed by Brazilian educator Paulo Freiri where oppressed groups, through concentrating on their own experience, engage in social analysis for change *(praxis)*.[60] What we have learned through our work with women, however, is that our bodies are social and cultural constructs, that our history of violence and pain as well as joy and pleasure is stored in our body's memory. The body, then, becomes our theological starting point: to counteract the patriarchal mindset that women's body is the source of evil; to heal the dualistic split between body/spirit; and to learn to love our bodies, discovering that we are indeed embodied "temples" of the Holy.

Much of our pastoral work has to do with healing. In workshops where we introduce simple practices such as Tai Chi, deep breathing exercises and hand, foot, back, head and shoulders massage techniques, real transformation takes place. Healing touch more often than not awakens new life. Participants tell of feeling loved and cared for, as well as safe and protected. We promote learning about and returning to some of the age-old healing practices of our indigenous ancestors who did not separate physical and psychological illness because their concept of health was based on a power to heal that comes from within.

We have also discovered the intrinsic connection between our bodies and our spirituality. Since our beginnings we have celebrated the link between wholeness and holiness and have developed rituals where we pray through body movement, dance and chant. We have learned to believe in this embodied methodology as a more holistic, intuitive way of learning where we become aware of the interconnectedness of all in all. Again, we have dedicated an entire issue of *Con-spirando* to the theme of embodiment as a method for both personal and cultural transformation.[61]

- **Ecofeminist perspective**

Finally, the fourth contribution we make to theology is our growing commitment to an ecofeminist perspective. We try to offer an ecofeminist perspective to every theme we cover in the *Revista Con-spirando*, as well as dedicate entire issues specifically to ecofeminism.[62] We give workshops on ecofeminism and ecofeminist theology and spirituality, which have been and continue to be our strength. Our annual summer school on ecofeminist spirituality and ethics also has a strong ecofeminist component to its content and methodology. Our rituals, in a myriad of creative forms, convey that we are one Sacred Body, with all its welcome diversity!

To put flesh on Con-spirando's work, I would like to describe the summer school process in more detail, because it is a microcosm of what we are trying to accomplish. Starting in 2000, Con-spirando has organized an annual summer School of Ecofeminist Spirituality and Ethics, which brings together approximately 40 activist women leaders from Latin America. This initiative grew out of an earlier project called the Shared Garden, mentioned above. It was during the Shared Garden process that the theme of "myths and their power over us" first surfaced. Participants enacted and then analyzed the creation story of Adam and Eve as found in Genesis 2, the foundational myth that undergirds our current patriarchal Christian culture. It was during this process that we began to realize how much we have internalized this myth—which sustains both our cultures and our cosmologies—and continues to operate within us at a very deep, although frequently unconscious level.

Our need to delve more deeply into how myths originate as well as how they can operate to uphold patriarchy as "normal" or "God-given" led to Con-spirando's commitment to hold an annual summer school. This "school" would offer, for 10 brief days, a contained space and time where women could ask their theological questions without fear. It would be a "safe space" allowing participants to search together for more life-giving theologies, cosmologies and ways of celebrating our emerging spiritualities. It would be a space to search together and formulate our own body of thought, study and reflection as Latin American women engaged in the religious debates of our region.

As a collective, we were convinced that, as a first step, it would be absolutely key for women in Latin America to deepen both our analysis and our theoretical deconstruction of both the Genesis myth and myths in general to be able to see how they act in our sub-consciousness, determining how they affect the way we relate to one another. At the same time, we were convinced that we needed to begin to build new practices and power relations as we look for ways to sustain ourselves in terms of constructs of meaning both at the personal and at the communal level. This entails searching for new stories of meaning, new myths and rituals.

During our first School, then, we chose as our central theme, *Myths and their power over us* and began the all-important process of deconstruction. During that school in January 2000, we developed our own understanding of myth based on our own experiences—looking especially hard at those myths dealing with women's bodies. We also looked at myths as they evolved in the human psyche, as well as how they develop in an individual woman's life cycle. We analyzed both our cultural and psychological need for myth and how we might transform myths and use their power over us to empower ourselves. We honed in on the four basic archetypes that shape us as women—Mother/Life-giver; Lover/Companion; Amazon/Warrior; Wise Woman/Medium—and saw these archetypes reflected in the many goddesses who have appeared throughout the ages.

Because both participants and the team found these themes to be so gripping for their lives, *Myths and their power over us II* was unanimously chosen as the central theme for our second School held in January 2001 and built upon the previous year's process. From a gender perspective, we concentrated specifically on the four feminine archetypes, as developed by Toni Wolff, close collaborator of Carl Jung. When we looked at the Mother/Life-giver archetype, we traced our own lineage of women in our lives and honored those who gave us life, whether physically, intellectually or spiritually. It was here where we discovered how strong the overriding image of the Virgin Mary, Mother of God, is throughout Latin America. We began to look behind her image to older, more indigenous images of the Mother. This, we recognized, is a major area for further research. In the Companion/Lover archetype, we looked at the evolution of sexual pleasure. When, we asked, did pleasure/eroticism and spirituality become separated—indeed, set in opposition? Another area for further research! In examining the Amazon/Warrior archetype, we came face to face with the whole issue of power. Here we looked at how women's power has been symbolized in different periods of history and in different cultures and how, from a gender analysis, "man" and "woman" are social constructs and yet how difficult it is for us to use power in new ways. So often women "warriors" have been those who have sacrificed their lives for their people. We concluded that there is an urgent need to search for new ways of being Amazons in today's world that move beyond the stereotyped role we are expected to play. Finally, to delve deeply into the Wise Woman/Medium/Witch archetype, we were invited to meet our shadow-side—that part of us we often repress or ignore. Here it became evident that what has been kept in the shadows, repressed –which is so often related to the powerful but devalued feminine—is a deep source of wisdom for us waiting to be tapped.

Again, based on the evaluations of participants and facilitators, the Con-spirando team chose to stay with this theme for our third School, held in January 2002, but this time concentrate on the shadow side of each of the four archetypes as well as looking at the process of stereotyping the original energy of each. We also decided to examine how the many ethical norms related to women and our bodies developed over time, as the patriarchal gaze became to be the norm. Thus, the theme for the third School was: ***Myths and Power III: Women's Bodies-Ethical Implications***

With regard to the shadow side, the mother/container archetype presentation asked participants to look at their own history of being contained—by mother, church, political party, movement, etc. and see how they were both nurtured as well as "devoured". Specific attention was given to the Virgin Mary in Latin America and how she may be a domesticated form of earlier, more sexual, "dark" goddesses. The shadow side of the companion/lover archetype surfaced in terms of the patriarchal need to control eroticism, placing it safely within the confines of marriage or subjugating it to the "bad woman," or prostitute. To touch into our erotic powers and feelings, we invited two women from the feminist collective Newen Kuche in Concepción, Chile to lead us in a workshop on Belly Dancing. Their explication of how this dance—always a dance among women to the goddess and often a dance to help women at the time of childbirth—was really liberating! To connect with the shadow side of the warrior archetype, we chose to be a certain animal and enacted a battle for territory. Most of us didn't like to attack, but were aroused to defend our territory. It is worth mentioning here, that most participants recognized that they were indeed "warriors", that is, leaders of their different communities and that they were "tired" of always having to "lead the charge" and fight for their rights. As the School progressed, many discovered that they had overdeveloped their warrior energies at the expense of their erotic and wise woman energy fields. In working with the Wise Woman or Medium archetype, we concluded that this energy is seen as totally "shadow" by the patriarchal gaze. Elderly women are simply invisible and irrelevant in modern society. And yet, it is precisely in times of crisis that the vision of the Wise Woman is needed. We concluded with a Paleolithic shamanic ritual.

Ritual is a key ingredient of the Schools. One of the most powerful is the re-enactment of the part of the Sumerian myth of Inanna, the queen who descends to the underworld to meet her "dark sister" Ereshkigal. On the descent to the underworld, each participant was invited to leave a sign of her power at each of seven gates marking the decent. (The gates represented the powers related to the seven charkas, which we had been working on throughout our days together). Once below, each saw herself—her essence, now stripped of all of her powers—reflected back as she gazed into a mirror; and behind her she also saw her dark sister, a masked figure clothed in black. The task: to integrate this dark sister into our psyche. After time to process the descent, we then began our ascent, donning again our seven powers, now transformed by contact with Ereshkigal. This ritual was very powerful for the participants and team alike.

Another powerful ritual is walking the labyrinth, an ancient, pre-Christian symbol and practice that has been rediscovered in our times. The invitation is to slowly walk in silence to the center, which symbolizes journeying to one's own center. It is an exercise in integration and a chance for participants to pull together all they had learned. We formally conclude the School around the labyrinth, in a circle where we thank the spirits for accompanying us and ask them to move on to accompany other groups in similar quests for wisdom.

What follows is a list of "learnings" gleaned from participants from the three schools:

New perspectives:

- An ability to relativize the Christian myth and situate it within the broader sweep of our evolution as a species. A much larger sense of the history of the universe, of the antiquity of our roots.
- When the feminine is absent from the image of the divinity, women are devalued, affecting the entire social fabric. When the feminine is not present, honored in ritual or in a culture's sacred image of the divine, violence against women is common.
- We do no want to return to some ancient past—we are concerned with synthesizing and moving toward a post-patriarchal future. In this process, there are often moments of chaos, uncertainty—a necessary space to be able to bring about a new ordering of one's thought and beliefs.
- Listening to what our bodies are saying has become our methodological starting point.
- We are committed to staying profoundly connected to our dreams, intuitions, emotions, sensations, the wisdom we find in

women's rituals, in recovering lost myths as sources of wisdom and guidance.
- A renewed appreciation for the wisdom of our ancestors; a need to critically examine our own mestiza roots.

Ethical implications:

- Courage to critically look at the Christian myth and reinterpret/relativize it. (At the same time we need to know how to protect ourselves in this task to avoid new witch hunts. We need "safe spaces" to do this work of deconstruction and recycling.)
- We are committed to diversity, accepting our differences, being flexible; refusing rigid postures.
- We assume responsibility to continue educating ourselves in these areas.
- Our ethical positions grow out of our experiences of the tears, desolation and vulnerability of so many women, including ourselves. This leads to solidarity, sisterhood and compassion among women as we journey toward wholeness, empowering each other in the process.
- Our ethical decisions are grounded on our own bodily experiences, our experiences of ordinary daily life, always in communion with other women.
- "More and more the good/evil dichotomy is inadequate! There is only today—the here and now." Nevertheless, we agree that the Human Rights Charter is a key framework for a universal ethic, which includes a gender perspective.
- Ethical postures are always evolving.
- We are capable of making our own ethical decisions and being responsible for the consequences. Let us empower ourselves to do this in our daily lives! Our current patriarchal society makes laws but does not assume the consequences of these laws.

Call to action:

- Work from the micro toward the macro. Priority should be given to small groups as well as to networking. The image here is the spider web, which is strong but flexible, many-centered. We feel called to work for deeper cultural change at the local level.
- This work requires that we nurture ourselves with ancestral wisdom—through ritual dance and music, small-scale organic gardening, bartering, local experiments of economic sustainability. We are committed to developing spiritual practices of using natural medicines, herbs, eating lower on the food chain.
- We are committed to work for small changes without taking on patriarchy in a confrontational way. We will build and strengthen links with others. We will continue to search for "spaces" where we can be renewed and discover new methodological tools for cultural transformation. Spaces and groups that help us recognize and affirm the power we have to be "creative resisters". [63]

Although we are very proud of our accomplishments, we know that ecofeminist thought is only beginning to have an impact on theology and feminist theory in the region. Mainline patriarchal theologians, as well as liberation theologians, are threatened by ecofeminism because of its challenge to orthodox definitions of God, and of the human in relation to the divine. Feminists criticize ecofeminism as being too "eco" and not "feminist" enough. They also warn against identifying women with nature, which would be falling into an essentialist trap that, in the end, would unwittingly support patriarchal dualistic constructs.

For us, a major transformational tool is our commitment to embodied learning. Body prayer, ritual, intuition, and healing practices all offer new ways of learning— for not only women, but for all humanity. And with our yearly cycle of rituals, we give flesh to our commitment to empower women to celebrate the Sacred as we see fit.

There are, of course, voices that caution us to water our Latin American ecofeminism with the streams coming from the lives of the region's poor majorities. We also must beware of essentialism, that is, depicting women as closer to nature because of our cycles, our relationship with the moon and the tides, etc. We must avoid the label of being "New Age" with an individualist, "make me feel good" spirituality. And we must respond with visible actions to the accusation that an ecofeminist posture avoids justice and human rights issues. We are also fragile in terms of financial resources and even after 10 years, still depend heavily on outside funding. We are also a very small collective—we are now only six, and one of us is in the US studying for her doctorate and another is semi-retired. There is real concern that we will not bring in new members, but whither on the vine. However, a guiding metaphor of ecofeminism is the seed. Instead of the predominant "power over," the seed suggests "power within." The seed lies dormant; it breaks open, sprouts forth, blossoms, bears fruit, matures, withers, and falls to the ground again. It will be what it is meant to be. We too are seeds, called to be what we are meant to be. And so is Con-spirando. May it be what it is meant to be—nothing more, nothing less.

This, then, is an overview of the current thought underlying ecofeminism and ecofeminist theology, from my point of view and from my location within the feminist theological world of Latin America.

[1] «You are a goddess and all the goddesses dwell within you.» This was the phrase Madonna used to close her workshop on the goddesses as archetypes at Con-spirando's first Summer School of Ecofeminist Spirituality and Ethics in 2000. Con-spirando continues to use this phrase in our rituals.
[2] Starhawk. "Power, Authority and Mystery: Ecofeminism and Earth-based Spirituality." *Reweaving the World.*
[3] Charlene Spretnak, *States of Grace: The Recovery of Meaning in the Postmodern Age.* San Francisco: HarperCollins, 1991, pp. 114-154.
[4] Carol Christ, "Repensando la teología y la naturaleza", *Revista Con-spirando #4*, (Junio, 1993), pp. 28-29.
[5] Susan Griffin, *Woman and Nature: The Roaring Inside Her*, quoted in Mellor, p. 49.
[6] Mary Daly, *Outercourse: The Be-dazzling Voyage.* HarperSanFracisco, 1992. This is Daly's autobiography where she herself tells the story of her evolution and her contributions to radical feminist thought.
[7] Sallie McFague, *Models of God: Theology for an Ecological Age.* Philadelphia: Fortress 1987 and *The Body of God: An Ecological Theology.* Minneapolis: Fortress Press, 1993.
[8] McFague, quoted in Anne M. Clifford. *Introducing Feminist Theology.* Maryknoll: Orbis, 2001, pp. 236-237.
[9] McFague, *Models of God*, p. 11.
[10] Carr, p. 238.
[11] *God's Living Body: A Pantheist Reading of Sallie McFague*, a thesis by Jennifer M. Molineaux. Graduate Theological Union, Berekely, California, February, 1997, p. 12.
[12] Ruether, *Gaia and God*, p. 3.
[13] Rosemary Radford Ruether, *Ecofeminism and Healing Ourselves, Healing the Earth.* A lecture in the series **Keeping the Spirit Alive**, presented by St. Stephen's College and given in Edmonton and Calgary, Alberta on June 2 and 3, 1998.
[14] Ruether, *Gaia and God*, p. 254.
[15] Ibid., p. 4.
[16] Ibid., p. 167.
[17] Ruether, Lecture, *Ecofeminism and Healing Ourselves.*
[18] Ibid.
[19] Ruether, *Gaia and God*, p. 31.
[20] Ibid., p. 252.
[21] Ibid., p. 252-253.
[22] Ress, Interview with Ivone Gebara, p. 208.
[23] Ibid., p. 209
[24] Ivone Gebara, *Longing for Running Water: Ecofeminism and Liberation.* Minneapolis: Fortress Press, 1999, p. 2.
[25] Ibid., p. 83.
[26] Ibid., pp. 85-87.
[27] Ivone Gebara, "Eco-feminism: An Ethics of Life," *Sacred Earth, Sacred Community: Jubilee, Ecology and Aboriginal Peoples.* Canadian Ecumenical Jubilee Initiative. Toronto: 2000, p. 33.
[28] Ibid., p. 33.
[29] Ibid., p. 45.
[30] Gebara, *Longing for Running Water.* Pp. 101,111-112.
[31] Ress, Interview with Gebara, p. 212.

[32] Gebara, *Longing for Living Water*, p. 114.
[33] For Gebara, "to speak of pan-en-theism is to consider the potentialities of the universe, the potentialities of life, and the potentialities of human life as always open-ended. Thus we escape from the close circle of immanence and transcendence, of "being in itself," to become part of the reality we cll the process of life,in which transcendence and immanence are mere expressions that point to the dynamics that draw us forth." Ibid., p. 124.
[34] Ibid., p. 148.
[35] Ibid., p. 164.
[36] Ibid., p. 187.
[37] Ivone Gebara, "¿Quién es el Jesús liberador que buscamos?" *Palabras claves sobre Jesús de Nazaret*. J. J. Tamayo Acosta, Ed. Estella (Navarra): Editorial Verbo Divino, 1999 pp. 158-160.
[38] Ibid., p. 178.
[39] Ibid., p. 184.
[40] Gebara. "Ecofeminism: An Ethics of Life," p. 37.
[41] Ibid., p. 39.
[42] Ivone Gebara, *Out of the Depths: Evil and Salvation in a Feminist Perspective*. Minneapolis: Fortress Press, 2002. (I am working from the manuscript version), p. 3.
[43] Ibid., p. 92.
[44] Ibid., p. 141.
[45] Ibid., p. 141.
[46] Gebara, *Longing for Running Water*, p 129.
[47] Ibid., Preface, p. vii.
[48] Gebara, *Out of the Depths*, pp. 150-151.
[49] Gebara, *Longing for Running Water*, p. 14.
[50] *Con-spirando: Revista latinoamericana de ecofeminismo, espiritualidad y teología*. Santiago de Chile. No. 1. March, 1992. pp. 2-5.
[51] Dolores Williams, *Sisters in the Wilderness: The Challenge of Womanist God-Talk*, New York: Orbis Books, 1993; Rita Nakashima Brock, *Journeys by Heart: A Christology of Erotic Power*, New York: Crossroad, 1991; Joanne Carlson Brown and Rebecca Parker, "For God So Loved the World?" in J. Carlson Brown and C. Bohn, eds., *Christianity, Patriarchy and Abuse*, Cleveland: The Pilgrim Press, 1989.
[52] R. Solari, "Just another conference?" (sidebar in: "In her own image,", pp. 18-27, *Common Boundary*, July/August, 1995.
[53] Nakashima Brock, p. 56.
[54] "Desarmar la violencia," *Revista Con-spirando*, No. 8, Junio, 1994. Specifically see "Tanto amó Dios al mundo: violencia y abuso en la tradición crisitana," por Ute Seibert-Cuandra, pp. 2-8.
[55] "Afectos y poderes", *Revista Con-spirando*, No. 16, Junio, 1996. cf. Bridget Cooke, "Nuestra relación con las/os niñas/os: más allá del palo y la zanahoria", pp. 18-25; Ute Seibert-Cuadra, "Dios: Poder en relación?", pp. 40-43.
[56] *Sistematización: Más allá de la violencia: solidaridad y ecofeminismo*. Summary of Shared Garden held in Santiago, Chile, Jan 27-Feb. 8, 1998. (Manuscript prepared by Con-spirando)
[57] "Por sus símbolos los conoceréis", *Revista Con-spirando*, No. 19, marzo, 1997.
[58] Ibid, Josefina Hurtado, "Por sus símbolos los conoceréis", pp.2-9.
[59] Ibid, Yeta Ramírez, "El poder de los símbolos", pp. 35-35.
[60] Paolo Freire, *Pedagogy of the Oppressed*, New York: Herder & Herder, 1970.

[61] "(trans) formación y cambio cultural", *Revista Con-spirando*, No. 26, diciembre, 1998.
[62] "El ecofeminismo: reciclando nuestras energías de cambio", No. 4 (junio, 1993); "Etica y ecofeminismo", No. 17 (setiembre, 1997); and "Ecofeminismo: hallazgos, preguntas, provocaciones", No. 23 (marzo, 1998).
[63] Final Report: Third School of Ecofeminist Spirituality and Ethics. Con-spirando Collective, p. 6.

People do not change because of intellectual convictions or ethical inclinations, but rather through transformed imaginations.
—Madonna Kolbenschlag[1]

Chapter IV

Charting the change: 12 women's reflections

While Ivone Gebara and the Con-spirando Collective have been working in ecofeminist theology, spirituality and ethics for the past decade, ecofeminist thought is still very new to Latin America. However, while the term may not be very familiar to most Latin Americans, I have a growing "suspicion" or hunch that the vision and perspectives described in Chapter II are being embraced by an increasing number of Latin American women. To recall my hypothesis for this research:

> In Latin America during the 1990s, a growing number of activist, faith-based women who had historically aligned themselves with liberation theology and its practice are now describing themselves as "ecofeminist". This is evident in the way they perceive themselves in relation to the rest of the Earth community and to the Universe as a whole; in the way they are re-imaging/re-naming Ultimate Mystery; in their beliefs about death and rebirth; and in their spiritual and ethical practice. On the whole, the region's liberation theologians are not acknowledging this shift. *I propose to document the process that is bringing about this change by interviewing—in depth—a representative sample of*

women throughout Latin America who now call themselves ecofeminist.

To document this hypothesis I interviewed 12 Latin American women who have been engaged in the field of feminist theology for a number of years. The majority of these women have been activists in liberation theology and in liberation movements in their respective countries. I believe I chose a representative sample of interviewees whose commitment to the poor and oppressed, based on their Christian faith, is obvious from the stories they share of their life journeys. The majority identify with ecofeminist thought, but not in its entirety or with their own reservations, questions, and descriptions. Those interviewed represent a variety of countries (several were born in one country, but have been living in another for much of their adult lives—a reality of the region's internal migration patterns), ages and religious denominations. At the same time, while there is a wide range of diversity among these women in terms of their experience, temperaments and points of view, all of them work with poor and disadvantaged women in the field of theology, and all of them recognize the influence of Ivone Gebara on their own theology and spirituality. I must also confess that these women are not strangers to me—I know all of them personally; indeed they are friends and colleagues that I have met in my own comings and goings in the small but lively circles of feminist theology in Latin America. During 2000 and 2001 I journeyed throughout Latin America interviewing these women—which for me became deeply sacred moments of sharing.

By profession I am a journalist, and I immensely enjoy interviewing people to try to elicit from them those "dearest, deep down" intuitions of the soul. My goal during these interviews was to ask the women to describe their evolving convictions/intuitions in five areas:

- their sense of themselves as humans; "who am I?" at this juncture of my history;
- their images/names to describe Ultimate Mystery (the Divine, God/Goddess);

- their beliefs about death and afterlife;
- their ethical practices (especially in the area of sexuality/reproductive rights);
- their spiritual practices or disciplines that nourish their beliefs.

I felt that these questions, which grapple with the theological quests of all time, namely the definition of the human (anthropology), of the divine (cosmology), of "how" we know (epistemology), ethics and spirituality, would be an adequate barometer to chart the theological evolution of these women. Because all feminist theology starts from lived experience, I always began the interviews by asking each woman to describe her own journey within the larger political, social and theological context of her country. My intention was to elicit from each a somewhat systematic description of her process through the three stages of feminist theology in Latin America. I had hoped to show, on the one hand, why liberation theology and its practice is no longer as appealing to faith-based women activists as it once was during the 1970s and 1980s and, on the other hand, demonstrate why these same women are now attracted to ecofeminist theology and spirituality. While this shift is present in the interviews, in actual process both the interviewee and the interviewer became so absorbed in the story that I admit that I often abandoned a rigorous question/answer methodology in favor of pursuing reflections that were not part of the original project. The result, however, is a rich "coat of many colors" –a collection of "sacred texts" that reveals the inspiring journeys of 12 remarkable women as they search to be faithful to themselves and to their deepest intuitions. I have published these interviews in a book called *Lluvia para florecer: Entrevistas sobre el ecofeminismo en América Latina*. I will summarize the results of my research below. However, I lament the fact that in summarizing and translating from the Spanish, much of the lived experience as recounted by each woman has been lost.

After interviewing the women and sending them the collection of interviews to read and mull over, I gathered them together for a workshop on the texts, with Ivone Gebara, so that we might together reflect on our collective journeys and see what they might mean theologically. In the second part of this chapter I will summarize those reflections.

Summary of the interviews

Description of the women interviewed:

- **Agamedilza Sales de Oliveira** (b. 1950) is from Manaus, a frontier town deep within Brazil's Amazon jungle. She is from the Catholic tradition. A teacher by profession, she also has extensive training as a biblicist and calls herself a grassroots feminist biblicist. She is the founder of *Maria Sem Vergonha*, a grassroots women's organization dedicated to the empowerment of women. Her passions: writing poetry and composing feminist rituals.
- **Marcia Moya** (b. 1965) is from Quito, Ecuador. She is from the Catholic tradition. A dentist by profession, she has done graduate work in theology and teaches feminist theology and biblical studies at the university level. She also works with grassroots women as well as religious congregations. She is the author of the book *Propuesta pedagógica de Jesús* (Ediciones Abya Yala, 1999). Her passions: reading, writing, taking time to play with her small son, Victor Alberto who "keeps me grounded."
- **Coca Trillini** (b. 1951) is from Buenos Aires, Argentina. She is from the Catholic tradition. A teacher by profession, and a feminist theologian and biblicist by choice, she is currently part of the coordination team for Catholics for the Right to Choose in Latin America. She is the author of *¿Qué son las Comunidades Eclesiales de Base en la Argentina?* (Ediciones Paulinas, 1993) and *De la pirámide al arco iris: Cuaderno de Trabajo sobre Mujer y Biblia* (Ediciones Paulinas, 1995). Her passions: Writing, reading, dreaming, walking along the seashore, playing with her grandson, cooking, cultivating friendship.

- **Sandra Duarte** (b. 1966) is from Sao Paulo, Brazil. She is from the Methodist tradition. She has recently completed her doctoral studies in ecofeminist theology, spirituality and ethics, which focused on an analysis of this discourse from a biosocial as well as from a social constructivist perspective. She is currently a member of the religious studies faculty at the Methodist University in Sao Paulo. Her passions: spending time in indigenous communities in order to understand them better, photography and reading.
- **Fanny Geymonat-Pantelís** (b. 1940) is originally from Uruguay where she was raised in the Waldensian tradition, but has been living and working in La Paz, Bolivia for many years. She is now from the Methodist tradition. A religious educator, she has advanced degrees in religious education and ecumenism and is currently working on her doctorate in feminist theology. The title of her thesis is: *Naming God in the Andes*. She is currently the national coordinator of UDIFOM, a women's ecumenical movement in Bolivia. She has had a long history of representing the Latin American Council of Churches in the Southern Cone as well as working in the area of Christian publications and educational materials. Her passions: poetry, photography, gardening. She has published two books: *De Cipotes y Guerra* (poetry) and *Entre el Obelisco y la Cruz* (short testimonies by Central American exiles living in Washington, DC).
- **Sandra Raquew** (b. 1973) is from Brazil's Northeast. She was born in the interior, but now lives in Joao Pessoa where she earned a degree in journalism. She is now studying in a Masters program in Popular Education, Communication and Culture. She is from the evangelical tradition. She is a member of the feminist theology collective Chimalman, initially mentored by Ivone Gebara. Her passions: painting, writing, photography.
- **Graciela Pujol** (b. 1950) is from Montevideo, Uruguay. She is from the Catholic tradition. An architect by profession, she has also studied social psychology and feminist theology. She is the

past editor of *Conciencia*, the Spanish publication of Catholics for the Right to Choose and now runs her own publishing house. She is the founder of the ecofeminist organization Caleiscopio. Her passions: Spending quality time with her children (now grown), going out with friends, dancing, reading, studying the Eneagram.
- **Alcira Agreda** (b. 1955) is from Santa Cruz, Bolivia. She is from the Catholic tradition. A nurse by profession, she now has her licentiate in biblical studies and works as a feminist theologian and biblicist. She teaches theology and biblical studies at the university level in Bolivia and also gives classes to grassroots groups. Currently she is the academic dean and a professor at the Instituto *Superior de Teología Andina* in Santa Cruz. Her passions: dancing, ecological cooking, talking to the trees—and reading.
- **Clara Luz Ajo** (b. 1949) is from Matanzas, Cuba. She is from the Anglican tradition. A religious educator, she has her doctorate in feminist theology from the Methodist University in Sao Paolo, Brazil. Her thesis topic was on "The Body in the feast of the Sacred: An analysis of how the body is seen in the divinities, symbols, myths and rituals of Santeria in Cuba." She is currently a member of the faculty at the Evangelical Theological Seminary in Matanzas. She and her partner Pedro have composed the well-known *Misa cubana*. Her passions: music, dancing.
- **Doris Muñoz** (b. 1958) is from Santiago, Chile. She is from the Catholic tradition. A popular educator, she has a licentiate in Catholic theology. A teacher of holistic health and spirituality through understanding the body, Doris is co-founder and co-coordinator of Capacitar-Chile, a grassroots health and education project. She teaches theology and biblical studies from a feminist perspective to grassroots communities as a member of the Diego de Medellin Ecumenical Center in Santiago. Her passions: Body work, such as Tai Chi, Reiki, Polarity Massage.
- **Gladys Parentelli** (b. 1935) is originally from Uruguay but has been living in Caracas, Venezuela for the past 30 years. She is

from the Catholic tradition. A grassroots organizer, journalist and documentalist, she has a long history of working with both ecumenical and UN-related organizations in the Third World. A longtime Catholic feminist, she has fostered the foundation of a number of local and regional feminist organizations and feminist periodicals. She is now retired. She tells her remarkable theological journey as an activist Latin American Catholic in the 1950s through the 1980s in her autobiography *Mujer, Iglesia, Liberación* (Caracas, 1990). Her passions: reading (always and at every moment), photography, climbing Mt. Alba daily.

- **Silvia Regina de Lima Silva** (b. 1962) is originally from Rio de Janeiro, Brazil but is now living in San José, Costa Rica. She is from the Catholic tradition. A teacher and social activist in Latin America's Afro movement, she has a Masters degree in biblical studies. She defines herself as a black feminist theologian and is now the dean of studies and a member of the faculty at the Universidad Bíblica Latinoamericana in San Jose. She is the author of *En Territorio de Frontera: Una lectura de Marcos 7:24-30* (Dei: 2001). Her passions: writing poetry, creating ritual, the Afro-Latin American movement.

These short sketches, written by the women themselves, do not begin to convey the depth of each, which is captured in the interviews. For instance, the elder of the interviewees, Gladys Parentelli, comes from campesina stock. A local priest in her small town in Uruguay spotted her leadership talents when she was a teenager. Gladys rose in the Young Catholic Agrarian Movement to become a national leader, then a regional leader, and finally she was elected as one of the international coordinators of the movement and sent to headquarters in Belgium. There she was invited as one of three Catholic lay women to be an observer at the sessions of the Second Vatican Council. The story of her dawning feminist consciousness within the Catholic church in the sixties and seventies is one of both anger and courage. Her countrywoman, Fanny Geymonat-

Pantelís (they grew up in the same small town in Uruguay and Fanny's first boyfriend was Gladys's brother!), also rose to national leadership within the Latin American Council of Churches, but she too discovered the engrained patriarchy within the Methodist church and found that, because of her outspoken feminist views, she was boycotted for ordination. She and her family were forced into exile by the Garcia Mesa dictatorship in Bolivia in the 1980s, only to return to a church run by native Aymara pastors who ruled with an iron hand—an example of the patriarchal use of "power over" that even the indigenous are capable of repeating.

Both Coca Trillini and Graciela Pujol were active in the leftist insurgency movements in their countries in the 1970s. Coca tells about her work in consciousness-raising among the rural poor (like Coca, many of the interviewees have been deeply influenced by the methodology of Brazilian educator Paulo Freire). She describes the rise of the Montoneros, the guerilla movement that arose in Argentina in those years, and how many were motivated by a revolutionary understanding of Christianity to take up arms to create a more equitable Argentina. Coca recounts her history of mentoring the Christian base community movement for years; how she became an expert in both biblical and theological themes—and yet, how she could never be "taken seriously" by her male clerical colleagues, because she simply wasn't one of them. The story of her own evolution in feminist consciousness within Argentine's Catholic liberation circles is sober reading. Graciela, whose history coincides with the same time period as that of Coca, tells of her ultra conservative Catholic upbringing—and how, in breaking away, she rises to become a leader in the Tupamaro National Liberation Movement and the national director of its student cadre. The Tupamaros were the prime targets of the subsequent Uruguayan dictatorship, and Graciela found herself having to go underground to avoid arrest (and certain torture) and eventually having to go into exile in Argentina. Her story of both avoiding arrest and of life in exile in Argentina—trying to raise a family, be faithful to the option for the poor, water her spirituality by belonging through thick and thin to a Christian Base community—make for riveting reading. Her battles with her rigid Catholic sexual upbringing and her gradual liberation parallels her rise in feminist and ecofeminist consciousness.

Agamedilza's story of her sexuality and its relationship to the symbol of God first as a kind father (childhood) with Mother Mary always so near, and then the abrupt switch in symbols to an all powerful, punishing God taught by the nuns all thorough her school years is unfortunately common enough. However, her story of reading the biblical texts with a marvelous priest friend who empowered her to see through the patriarchal veil and bring a feminist perspective to each text is a story of liberation. Aga's enthusiasm for re-creating myth and ritual in a feminist key is indeed catching.

Several of the interviewees come from backgrounds of extreme poverty. Alcria Agreda is an indigenous campesina from the jungle region of Bolivia. At the age of thirteen she was beaten by her father and ran away from home, promising herself that she would never again suffer such abuse from a man. Alcida's is a story of determined willpower to pull herself up by her own bootstraps while at the same time serving her people—the poorest of the poor. Her story of searching for wholeness in the Catholic Charismatic movement, and then in liberation theology—especially in the life and example of Jesuit priest Luis Espinal who was assassinated by the Bolivian dictatorship in 1980—is as moving as any "lives of the saints". She tells of her experiences with the miners of Siglo XX in Oruro and of becoming friends with Domitila Chungara, the author of the classic *Si me permites hablar.* She also describes her 10-year experience in forming a new kind of religious community of women to live and work among the poor, her efforts to study theology and biblical studies as a poor woman—and finally her bout with cancer and how she discovered the "ecology of the body" through this experience—and how she healed.

Sandra Raquew was born and raised in a small village in the interior of Brazil's impoverished, draught-ridden Northeast. She describes both the conservative mores as well as the close-knit ties of the region and how strict her parents were with the children. For both her parents, this was a second marriage and Sandra's mother, at one point in her life, worked as a sex worker to survive. Sandra's father left the family when she was 10, and so she felt that the family had to be extra-exemplary to win the approval of the town. Sandra tells of her conversion to evangelism within the Baptist church and how good it felt to "belong" and to have a personal relationship with Jesus, and to express that relationship creatively through art, dance and song. However, when Sandra decided she wanted to study journalism, church members predicted that she would lose her faith—and that "there are homosexuals in the school of journalism". Today Sandra is a young professional journalist, an active member of the *Partido de Trabajadores*, an expectant mother—and a firm believer in both her roots and in the impossibility of belonging to any religious institution. She is nourished by her small community of feminist theologians where she can go to water her spirit.

Doris Muñoz also comes from campesina roots and has never minded proclaiming that she is a *pobladora* (a shantytown dweller). Two decades after a local parish priest saw in Gladys a future leader for the church, so in Doris' case a missionary priest from Maryknoll saw that this young woman had remarkable leadership talent to quickly capture liberation theology's most sophisticated points and translate them into language that the poor could understand. Thus from a very early age, Doris became a "popular educator" of liberation theology, social analysis and biblical history. However, as Doris tells her story, it was not until two events coincided—the arrival of Capacitar founder Pat Cane and of Ivone Gebara, both in 1993—that the ground collapsed and a new way of both doing theology and of teaching meaning emerged. In language filled with images, Doris tells how she discovered the centrality of the body and taking care of the body—one's own, that of one's neighbor, and that of the earth itself—as key to any feminist or ecofeminist understanding of theology and spirituality.

Silvia Regina de Lima hails from a working class family in a small suburb of Rio. She is black—and this marks her entire experience of being a Catholic. At a young age, she entered a Franciscan congregation, a German teaching order of nuns. She recounts both the joys of serving the people in those years—but also her growing discontent with the congregation's lack of commitment to the poor. She describes her eventual break with the congregation and her determination to found another religious community—they were three blacks, two young men and Silvia—to live and work among the poor. She tells us that one of the greatest joys of her life was living in that community of solidarity and love. However, she also tells us of her desire to study, which leads to a scholarship at the *Universidad Biblica Latinoamericana* in Costa Rica— and how, while there, she falls in love with a young Mennonite professor—and how they marry and now have a young son, Tomasito, the joy of her life. Silvia also tells us of her recent bout with breast cancer—and how she wanted to live at all costs.

It is from Clara Luz Ajo that we have an intimate glimpse of what it was like to live in Cuba in the early years of Castro's overthrow of the Batista government. Clara comes from Quaker roots—her father was a pastor and she grew up "in church" singing, playing the piano, and dancing. She describes the uneasy relationship the churches had with the new revolutionary government and how, at each step, she and her partner, an Anglican priest, had to prove that they were not reactionaries. One tastes the ordinary lives of Cubans throughout Clara's interview. She also describes her decision to go to Brazil to study feminist theology—and her amazing relationship with Brazil's Condomblé religion. Her study and eventual "initiation" into Santaria is an enlightening peak into a cosmovisión that is still deeply embedded in Cuba today.

Sandra Duarte and Marica Moya, who along with Sandra Raquew, are the youngest of the interviewees, both have had opportunities to study feminist theology formally. Sandra has recently obtained her doctorate writing her thesis on ecofeminist theology and Marcia is also clearly on an academic track. However, both women have strong connections to their countries' indigenous peoples. Sandra has spent large segments of time living and working with Guarani tribes in Brazil, observing gender relationships and participating in their rituals as well as in their ordinary lives—so much so that she has been given a "name"—a sign of belonging to the tribe. Marcia is engaged in her own identity process where she tries to recognize herself as a mestiza, a mixture of both European and indigenous blood. Marcia's research has taken her in the direction of searching out pre-Christian myths and cosmovisions that can once again empower. Both women are combining feminist theological insights with anthropological and psychological tools to reconstruct Latin American identities in these post-modern times. Sandra is also doing fascinating work on what she sees as the phenomenon of "religious shopping around". She finds that many Brazilians, especially women, are developing a "pick and choose" attitude when it comes to religious affiliation. They might say they are Catholic, but at the same time consult the Tarot cards, their astrology charts, crystals and runes to know the future, they might be practitioners of an oriental spiritual discipline such as Yoga, Reiki, Tai Chi, etc. They might also be studying Buddhism, Hinduism or Sufism. But the amazing fact is, as Sandra points out, that no one is feeling the least bit guilty about this "mixing" of beliefs. Indeed, just as one consumes products by selecting from the market what suites one, so too can one put together her own "package" of sources of meaning. Marcia, on the other hand, is having to battle conservative waves in Ecuador that find her classes in feminist theology too "unorthodox."

    An observer at the Second Vatican council; two founders of religious congregations (the same two, who interestingly have had to battle cancers); two women with doctorates in feminist theology and one almost finished; women who have founded grassroots feminist organizations, written books, held and then frequently lost positions of authority in their churches because of their feminist views; women who compose their own "Masses" and their own rituals; women who are poets, artists, dancers, body therapists—magicians all, they tell their stories in this rich tapestry of deep hues and shades that emerges in *Lluvia para florecer.*

    Below, I summarize their reflections on the five great themes. (All quotations are taken from the original interviews, which were conducted in Spanish. The translations are mine).

1. Definition of the human; "who am I?" at this juncture of my history

- "In the natural world, we are all brothers and sisters. It has fallen to humans, because of our kind of intelligence, to care for life, to watch out for the well being of the community of life and the planet's harmony. Sometimes I am saddened, even ashamed of us humans. On the other hand, when I see the struggles for life, for education marked by love, the exercise of citizen's rights, the way thousands of people strive to make life more abundant for others, I feel alive. Sometimes I feel alone in what I believe. I know that others exist who think like I do, who have doubts, but they are hard to find because there is a certain fear of open dialogue. But then there are always books to keep me company!" (Aga)

- "Since my childhood, I have been close to Nature—mostly through poetry where I could identify with the sea, the mountains, with the flight of the birds, with the dawn, the moon, etc. But this identification was more intellectual. It was only later that I developed a perception of Nature through my body. These sensations and vibrations appeared when I began to identify myself as part of the larger Cosmic body. I am the culmination of both created energy and reciprocal energy. Let me refer to Genesis where the human is God's created word. I was conceived through the exchange of my parent's energy—energy that we call love, affection, desire, passion. Throughout my life, I have continually felt an energy that has sustained me, which comes from those who surround me. This experience has kept me going, has kept me moving. I am very perceptive to life's processes, which makes it possible for me to be constantly changing and transformed. It took me a long time to discover that the human is not superior to other species. Because we have the ability to talk and to reason we think this makes us superior, but one only has to see a National Geographic TV program to realize how limited we are compared with other animals. The human is different as the birds are different from tigers; each has its place in the Cosmos and each must live in harmony with other species. In our own case, we know that we cannot dominate or exploit without Nature itself going against us. The abuse of the Earth being brought about by huge sectors of humanity enslaved by power and greed is based on this mistaken belief that we are superior. It is impossible to see the divine revealed in the human in an individualistic society where a culture of violence is the norm. We need to realize that a person is both divine and human at the same time—these are not two separate entities. This revelation of the divine in every human offers a new way of relationship: dialogue, friendship, solidarity, searching together for alternatives all help to improve our shared lives—and at the same time reveal ourselves to ourselves. We must remember that we are one of a great diversity of species, and that within our own species there is great diversity. We must respect that diversity while at the same time assure that our own diversity is respected. (Marcia)

- "We humans are no more and no less than the other beings on this planet; we are governed by the same rules that guide the plants and animals. It is just that we are self-reflective." (Coca)

- "We humans are always constructing and reconstructing ourselves, inventing and reinventing ourselves. I think we are persons who are constantly changing, which is why I believe that we cannot limit ourselves to anything—be it a religion, a tradition, a paradigm, yes even a paradigm. This is difficult, but we are beings in transition; at each moment we are building our affective relationships, we are building our relationship with the Sacred, with our work, with our thought—we are continually changing our ideas…So I conclude that we are change-oriented beings, we are beings in transition, and there is no final product, which is a problem, because we are always looking for "the final product." In my study on how Brazilians are constantly "in transit" as they look for religious experiences that satisfy them, I have heard it said that we are more individualistic than ever before and that religion is more and more individualistic. Not true! There is a growing process of individualization of religion, not of individualism. (Sandra is using the term "individualization" as understood by Jung.) There is a collective process taking place, but while before it was the priest or the pastor or another religious leader who told us what our religious symbol system should be, now we ourselves decide what our symbol system should be. We live this collectively; therefore it is not just an individual thing. There is an individualization of the Sacred in the sense that we are building our own symbol system. I also observe that people are looking for symbolic anchors of the most diverse kind. From the outside, it might seem really awful that a person has faith in Catholic saints and at the same time faith in the orixas of the Afro-Brazilian condomblé, while at the same time participating in a ritual to the Pachamama. But it is precisely through these devotions that a person constructs a particular symbol system that is always in process. Those who have problems with this are from our religious institutions because they are in charge of offering a specific "package" of symbols. If people begin to take what they want from the package and leave the rest, it clearly weakens these institutions. Today we have a veritable market of symbolic goods from which to choose. I don't see this as negative. People have more options and are therefore less able to be manipulated." (Sandra Duarte)

- "We humans construct definitions of ourselves from our own contexts. Within the Andean context, there are two ways to answer the question of who we are as humans. The first, present in both the Aymara and Quechua cultures, sees the human couple as the center of their cosmology and anthropology. Andean cosmology is cosmo-centered, while that of the Christian tradition is anthropocentric. In Andean culture everything has its sex—and just as there is a male body and a female body, so too everything is dialectically symmetrical, where balance is found in the complementarity of opposites. Thus man and woman complement each other and establish equilibrium in their coming together, which engenders new life, which is initiated and repeated. Those who remain single never really becomes a person in this cosmology; he or she is considered immature. One only becomes a person when one marries. However, in this complementarity of opposites, the masculine, the right side of things, is the stronger and dominates the other pole, which is feminine, weak and docile. Even the images of the Sacred reflect this dichotomy. The Pachamama (Earth Mother), which represents the feminine pole, is dependant on superior powers. We are confronted here with a cosmology and an anthropology which are hierarchical and androcentric—in short, patriarchal. Nevertheless, the Pachamama is a powerful force in this cosmology and over time has gained ascendance over the far away Sun god. Here there is a real richness to support an ecological awareness, because devotion to the Pachamama implies love and reverence for the Earth as that which sustains human life. However, migration to urban centers often weakens these cultural beliefs. My own view of the human is that we are incomplete beings. We form part of a process of ongoing creation by a wise and ever-present transcendent energy. In its human form, this energy always seeks life that is more abundant, full, harmonious and just. We form part of a planetary ecosystem that is dynamically interrelated. The natural world is a gift of infinite variety of loveliness and bounty for life itself, which graces and heals the human spirit. When everything seems hopeless at the human level, there are the green fields, the majestic mountains, the glorious colors of the sky, the movement of the clouds, the variety of texture and scent of the flowers, that speak out loud of a vital energy that struggles to augment the weave of life at all times—often despite the human. To plant a rose bush or a tree, to place seeds in a pot—these are creative acts that form and nourish both human life and the life of the planet, our only home. We humans are part of all this, not to utilize and then destroy, but to assume our responsibility for life itself and augment the creative process that is ours to carry out—and which we have unfortunately divided and compartmentalized into peoples, institutions, classes, churches and genders where some are forced to submit to the denomination of others, thus violating the primordial equilibrium of that energy that we call God. This God created and charged us with continuing to build and to create in that image." (Fanny)

- "I am a flower of Brazil's Northeast; I come from a tiny village in the interior. I feel I am very marked by being a woman born in this place, by this small space. We have a very strong sense of the presence of the Sacred, a profound respect for the forces of Nature—and this for me defines my sense of ancestral belonging...this sacred space that strengthens you, finds you, is revealed to you, affirms you. It is having a dimension of life where our relationship to Nature is valued as are relationships with others.... I see myself as a human-divine person with all the complexity of Mystery that is revealed in time. I have always thought of myself as a space of both corporality and eternity. I perceive myself as part of the same material of the Cosmos. It is this material that makes me see myself as in a mirror—that makes me feel things, sensations in my body, pain and pleasure, desire—all that I experience. My body, understood in this way, has incredible value and can do the most incredible things, because it is of the very material of the Cosmos.... This question also makes me reflect on my sense of ancestral belonging. For instance, my life has eternity in that it is connected with the lives of my mother, my father, my village where I lived for many years, and I will be connected to those who come after me. And what will I offer to them? Nothing perfect—I don't seek perfection. I am what I am: Sandra, woman, worker, journalist, militant feminist who belongs to a great feminist theological group. I am so many things at the same time!" (Sandra Raquew)

- "I feel I am a totality: I am a body and at the same time I am a spirit." (Graciela)

- "For a long time I could not describe who I was because of a false sense of humility. I could only describe my existence—who I am—with clarity once I began to reconstruct my roots as a woman and as a campesina. I discovered that I am unique and whole, both for myself and for others. I have my abilities and my limitations, but have innate value as a person and thus can engage in the process of learning and unlearning that life offers in all its intimacy and everyday-ness. All this I am, in relationship and solidarity with others, with the Earth and with Divine Energy. What I am saying is hard for me; it is the result of long experience of searching in the deepest level of my woman-being. For me, to say who I am has to do with the quality of life in all its dimensions, with my spirituality, with my dreams and my work. In the end, it is the full realization of myself as a person, which every person everywhere merits as well. At the same time, I find that the cosmology of indigenous peoples offers a more holistic, integral vision of what it means to be a person. The indigenous speak of the physical body, the emotional body, the mental body and Vital Energy, as all interrelated. This is a very ancient vision. I have also discovered that I live within an ecosystem and that I am not in any way superior to other beings. Of course I was taught that humanity was the center of creation and superior to other beings. This vision has generated domination, violence and destruction both of the planet's ecosystems and of the human. This has led me to open my vision to discover my own internal ecosystem, which is in communion with the ecosystem that surrounds me externally. I became more aware of this connection of who we are and who I am when I began to pay attention to what I was eating. (In order to save herself from her cancer, Alcira decided to change her diet.) It was here that I discovered who I was and what was "the other." By caring for, nourishing and protecting my internal ecology, I was also able to care for, nourish and protect the external ecosystem. This confirmed for me that to be a coherent person, we must realize that our essence is both internal and external. It is as if we persons depend on creation and creation depends on persons. Thus the potato, rice, vegetables depend on me and I on them. We live in a relation of constant reciprocity. In conclusion, I am a human person in deep relationship with my integrity. I exist in relation to myself, to others and am in communion and in reciprocal solidarity with the entire ecosystem. This sensibility allows me to be more sincere, honest and respectful of others and of the planet." (Alcira)

- "I feel part of a sacred enveloping." (Clara Luz)

- "When I discovered that I was an embodied human being, my world changed. It was a revolution for me, daughter of rationality that I was. The body simply had no value for me. But since then, I have come to understand that my body is who I am and what I have. My body contains my spirit, my conscience, my affections, my memories. Reclaiming my body was the first great step. Second, to rediscover the sense of body as energy—an integral energy. I discovered that everything that came through my senses, my thoughts, my relationships affected my body. My relationship to power went right to my stomach; my resentments went right to my breasts, etc. I realized I got sick when I was not able to channel my emotions in a holistic way, because I was blocking the normal flow of energy in my body. Everything that happens to the earth also happens to me, it passes through my body. All the elements affect me, water, air, soil, fire. That is why clean air is so important and why I am deeply anguished by the smog that sits over Santiago as a menacing cloud. That is why my understanding of ourselves as humans has to do with interconnection, with mutual dependency. And when I understand who we are in this new way, my understanding of the Sacred is also changed." (Doris)

- "I have my doubts about whether we are different and superior. Western civilization taught us to dominate the Earth, and this has ended in the destruction of the planet we are now witnessing with increasing anxiety and anguish." (Gladys)

- "Today I understand myself to be a person, a woman in the process of being constructed. The experience I have lived through in these past months with my cancer forced me to review my whole life. The experience was one of being born again. In the hospital, where I was going through chemotherapy, I met people who were going through the same treatment as I was, people who each month got worse. I began to ask myself, what is life, why can I live while others won't. And when I try to answer that question I find it is because I want to live and have discovered this source of life within myself. And I continue to be nourished by that source. I have been reading books on cancer and a general rule is that people overcome cancer because they want to live, because they decide to activate all the healthy cells in their body and because these cells are capable of eliminating or healing those cells that are diseased. Since I love symbols and believe in them, I asked myself how I could relate to my cancer at the symbolic level. I can't believe that this is the devil's work, as some churches teach. I realized that I had to activate all those healthy cells within my body to be in solidarity with my sick cells and help the part that is sick to heal. At many moments before the cancer struck, my body told me that all was not well, that I should change my rhythm of life, do things in another way, but I didn't listen. So this cancer was a huge shout to me to reorient my way of dealing with my body. I think this cancer happened because we are in such disequilibrium not only with our individual bodies, but also with the entire cosmos. So much violence is the proof of this, so much neo-liberalism. It is as if evil were the fruit of disharmony, of a lack of growth in communion. Neo-liberalism is all that is not life, not harmony. I believe that our bodies are also part of this. I know that one of the causes of cancer is the pollution in the environment. My sick body is also related to the Earth's being devastated and sick, and so from this experience I am now committed to care for the Earth. My recovery is related to the reduction of the number of buses that emit gases that are polluting San Jose. That is why, for me, the human is that totality that is in communion with other humans and with the entire universe. We are this totality of energy and power and in the measure that we are able to be in communion with other powers in the universe we will renew our own lives and the life of the rest of the ecosystem. (Silvia)

What is evident in these testimonies is a shift from the sense of the human as an individual to a larger sense of self, linked to the energy of the earth community and to the Cosmos itself. There is, I conclude, a change in the anthropological basis of what constitutes the human.

2. Images/names to describe Ultimate Mystery (the Divine, God/Goddess)

- "In my childhood, we always prayed to the kind father in heaven to protect us, but when I went to study with the nuns, I met a very severe God the father who punished, who sent his daughters to hell. Such an image was repugnant to me and I never accepted this father. I continued to search for the God my mother taught me about, which included such a strong presence of Mary. So when I discovered the Goddess, it was like rediscovering that lost feminine presence I had in my childhood. I especially needed a Mother divinity when I reached puberty. The absence of the feminine in the divinity was especially vivid: who to pray to, to confide in about my desires, my changing body, my fears, my conflicts, my first sexual relationships? To God? But God was male, what would he know about my life as a woman? The only way out was through Mary. But Mary was Jesus' mother, a virgin, pure, who did not know man. How to talk to her about my sexual desires? And so, little by little, I became a woman who discovered the Sacred in other persons and in Nature." (Aga)

- "My search is still continuing but for me right now God is life that is constantly renewing and transforming itself, surviving despite wars, pollution and every sort of violence. It is that life that seems to be born with ever-greater strength, regardless of threatening situations. For me, God is not all-powerful, but rather something that goes beyond the imaginable, something that needs to be discovered at every moment of our existence; it is there where the human-divine mystery is found, because both are, in the end, "mystery". God is the impulse for my body, the strength of my thoughts, the container for my feelings, the energy behind all that I am creating. God is all the vitality I find in both people and in Nature." (Marcia)

- "I have a deep respect, reverence, admiration, relation—but I don't know if I would describe it as energy, God, Goddess, a star…I notice that when I write articles on these themes, I'm forever putting more and more names to describe this relationship. Contact with Nature just as contact with other people, contact with tenderness as well as with pain—these speak to me of a Superior Existence, of a Different Existence, of an Existence that encircles us and at the same time has something to do with fluidity. As yet I haven't been able to write about this, because it is not yet clear for me. Despite the ability I have to work with images, I have not yet been able to give shape to the Sacred...I am pantheistic right now, with God in may places...right now, in the sunset, at another moment in a relationship, in the confidence someone has in you, or in someone in pain..." (Coca)

- "Memory. I believe that what I end up with is memory. Today there is a terrible loss of collective memory and I believe that because of this, we lose much of life itself. For me, memory is very powerful in my life because of the link with my mother (recently deceased). What is in me of her is the memory of a happy childhood, a happy life and this is very important for me, something sacred. It is more than simply remembering. How does one arrive at the Sacred? Through your questions, your desires. So when I sit down here in my small living room, drink a glass of wine, light candles and listen to music, I feel that this is a truly sacred moment because in this moment I am with my memories and I feel it is a moment when I find what I am looking for. It is a moment when I allow myself to feel whole. Not only in the present, but in the fullness of all." (Sandra Duarte)

- "I believe that God is a constant presence in my life. Many times, in key moments, something happens that speaks to me once again of a wise presence, a protecting spirit and counsclor who nourishes and augments life, showing us that the horizon is always broad and wide. It is like a spiral, like feminist hermeneutics of liberation, centered in an energy, a wisdom and loving presence that is always open and transforming. It is security, confidence, and impulse to be part of this spiral of energy.... A metaphor for God that I love is that of matrix or womb, because that is where life is gestating, taking form, being nourished, developing and maturing, where there is protection, warmth but at the same time there is no possession or obsession with keeping you there. The moment arrives when you must be born and free yourself to continue on your own journey. I love this metaphor for God and for the faith community. The matrix or womb nourishes life, but a womb that is not whole provokes abortions and death. Are not our churches like this? Also, the experiences of women show us how many times they are cut down, violated and even killed because they have a womb. Their pain can be such that they curse the day they were born women and have this organ that in Biblical terms is the home of divine energy. In Andean cosmology as well as in biblical texts, God is the great matrix, fount of compassion." (Fanny)

- "The Ecofeminist School on "Myths and their Power over us" (sponsored by Con-spirando in January, 2000) had a tremendous effect on me. We discovered how we women were creating our own symbols—symbols of friendship, love of the Earth, love of our own bodies, our own perception of justice and of relationships. All those symbols profoundly influenced me. I no longer see God as Father-God. Today I understand God as someone who goes beyond, who is defined by complementarity, where dimensions are revealed that pertain to us and touch us deeply. It is that intuitive space that is manifested day by day. God is no longer individualized or subjectivized. God is very present in collective experiences; it is something big. I often think of the women burned as witches in the Middle Ages. I suspect that they, like us, had collective experiences of the Sacred where they tasted the power of Mystery. In the end, is that power which gives me my existence." (Sandra Raquew)

- "I continue to believe in a superior being, in a God who with each passing day has fewer faces. The Holy Spirit continues to be a valid image of the Sacred for me, as breath of life. Even images of God as father or mother as symbols of unconditional love are valid for me because of my own personal experience, although they are not legitimate for others. I find myself reflecting and weaving my faith without many religious images. I simply believe in life in all its fullness. That is my passion. At the same time, I am getting to know other religious experiences from the Orient and I participate in a meditation group. I thoroughly enjoy finding those moments of encounter with other religions. I feel God very close. I say "God" to use a word, but this God, or this greater reality that is here and now is a very powerful presence. I feel this within me and in the encounter with others, in the relationship. And I feel this presence very strongly in our collective celebrations." (Graciela)

- "Before it was easy for me to speak of God as Father or as Lord. To name God as Mother, Friend, Lover seems more intimate and real. But I am most comfortable and honest when I name the Sacred as fountain of life, energy, wisdom, tenderness, which is within and breaks forth from each person. I find all this in friendship, sharing, giving service in solidarity, in celebrations, in the trees, in water, in food, in the daily struggles for justice. I like to understand and feel the Sacred as an experience of energy, which is a more open image. It is an energy that is here, in me, in the trees, the animals, in relationship, in the ways we love, the way we live out our commitments. This energy is Sacred, you find it and experience it through many symbols and names, rituals and myths, in relation with others. This energy, which I call Divine or Sacred Energy, is circular. It is like a current that flows and infuses life: this energy makes all life blossom forth and grow, not just human life but the entire ecosystem." (Alcira)

- "I think that that which we call the sacred or the divine is in all of us and at the same time is in all that is; it surrounds us, penetrates us, swaddles us as a loving mother. We are part of this sacred, divine swaddling that is also within us. My images are connected to the natural world—the sea, the flowers, the birds. Sometimes human images emerge as well because they are so engrained that it is difficult to easily let them go; therefore masculine and feminine images often intertwine. At the same time, images of love, friendship and solidarity are feelings that when they flower forth in the life and struggles of my people, I feel the presence of divine mystery very powerfully. I believe these powerful experiences make the Sacred present to us in our daily lives, in all that surrounds us. I think that the cosmology I have been evolving over the years has helped me understand the experiences of the religious expressions of African origin and at the same time, these expressions have opened me to a whole new perception of the Sacred that has been as powerful as it has been profound and has far surpassed any dogma or definition of the divine. With my studies and experiences with Cuban Santaria and Brazil's Condomblé, I have been able to break with rigid definitions and connect with the Sacred in Nature, but at the same time realize that I can't reduce Holy Mystery to static concepts or images." (Clara Luz)

- "My first image of God was of a Father God who was a magician. That imaged change with Jesus, but a militant Jesus whose kingdom would be established in justice. My idea of God also had to do with the humble, the small and insignificant...the widow's mite, the breadcrumbs under the table. God was never associated with the powerful. A second moment in my development of God images came when I began to relate God to the marvels of nature, majestic mountains, the stars, but also with the seasonal cycles and of giving birth. However, while I considered my giving birth a sacred moment, I never associated it with God. My cosmology changed when I became familiar with the thought of physicist Brian Swimme and the marvelous way he communicated an understanding of the cosmos as a sacred experience. This was my first hunch that the images we had of God might be only one dimension of that Great Sacred Mystery we call God. Today I cannot speak of my experience of God, of the Sacred, without talking about my own human experience, my experiences of affection, of sexuality, of my spirituality in relation to the Cosmos. I think my experience of the Sacred has broadened to include the most intimate things related to my body to the farthest outreaches of the Cosmos, but I am also discovering that all is related. I identify completely with the idea of pan-en-theism, that all is in God, all is sacred and that all our experiences of God are partial and within a specific context. Here I am influenced by Ivone: She says that all is God, she helps us understand that we are not the owners of God and that the Sacred is not imprisoned in a church or a book, no matter how sacred it may be deemed to be. If we think and live with this attitude, no reality is outside sacred space. There is no outside/inside or up/down—all is part of the Sacred. Thus life is sacred, our bodies are sacred—that is why we must struggle to end torture, violence against women and children, hunger and cold for the millions of marginalized people. All are in God, all are sacred—as are the rivers, which are the Earth's bloodstream and if they are contaminated, death will circulate throughout the whole body. So I don't believe that there is any divine reality outside. I think Jesus was the first to question that God dwelt in the temple and was shown to the people by the priests and Pharisees. He preferred to pray in the garden and on the mountainside, and said the temple was a den of thieves. He changed the sense of the Sacred because he lifted up the experience of compassion for bodies that were sick and rejected. That was the beginning of the reign of God. So today, for me God still exists but the concept I had does not. First, God the Father doesn't exist. What does exist is a Force, an Energy, a Spirit that develops and evolves with perfect precision. You can see this in the perfection of the flowers, our bodies, the Cosmos. This is just what we humans can observe, but God is much, much more that this, it is Great Mystery—and all my descriptions are just mere sputterings that reflect my own limited history and experience. We have no certainties, but we know we live and move in this Great Mystery. We humans have always tried to name "This" which we can never know totally but do indeed experience. (Doris)

- "The God I was introduced to as a child—the old man with a beard—strikes me as an aberration. I imagined God to be so superior, so indefinable, so powerful! And yet, as well we know, all the cosmologies of the world speak of the Creatrix of the world as feminine, or as paired. Making God over only in masculine form has subordinated and devalued the feminine." (Gladys)

- "Perhaps it is easier to say what God isn't than to say what God is. Based on my own experience, I can't believe in an all-powerful God that has power over life and death. At the same time, I can't believe in a God that is always testing me to see if I love "him" and remain faithful to him—or that I was sent this cancer to see if I really did have enough faith. Because I am a mother, I know that I would never make my son Tomás prove he loved me by threatening his life. No, I cannot believe in such a God. Rather, I have discovered that God is someone who is deeply in my being, that loves me, but at the same time is beyond me, or isn't limited to me. This God is life, goodness, positive energy that is present in others, in Nature and in history. I don't want to contradict Christianity, which is a history of God's manifestation. But there can be many histories of salvation, not just one. I have discovered a many faceted God: in difficult moments God is crying with me, feels with me, laments with me. At the same time, this God is present in community experiences—this is where I experience this presence very, very strongly. This God has a huge shoulder and a huge hand to hug me and where I can rest and cry. She is the faithful friend. I also have the experiences of the Afro-Brazilian religions where I have learned to contemplate and celebrate God in Nature. In these religions the orixas manifest themselves in Nature. So the river is not simply a river; it is also where energy and strength are stored. I am aware that speaking in these terms is considered dangerous from the point of view of the Christian world. Even so, I am very attracted to these religions and firmly believe in this form of God's presence. I hope it is possible to restructure my life so that I can have a more intimate relationship with the natural world—not in any romantic sense, but with a sense of mutual care. I am beginning to relate through herbs, teas, certain baths—this is not some sort of magic or spell; we really can enter into contact with the powers present in the natural world." (Silvia)

The God-images of the interviewees are shifting from a deity somehow outside and above the created universe, to a sense of something within yet beyond; relationship that holds everything together. Images most used are: Energy, Presence, Wisdom, Matrix, Complementarity, Memory, Intuitive Space, Greater Reality, Swaddling, Fountain of life. All talked of *experiencing* this energy rather than being able to define it. Here, I conclude, we are witnessing a change in cosmology.

3. Beliefs about death and afterlife

- "When I was still searching for images of the Sacred, I was afraid of death because it was such a mystery. But as I discovered the sacred in my own body, in that of others and in the universe itself, I lost my fear of death. Sometimes I am enthralled by death because I feel I will find some great desire fulfilled. Those who have died are with us still; they circulate among us. At times I feel this connection. I don't know how it will be, but I am not anxious about death. I always invoke those great women who have gone before us to accompany us by sending us their energy and wisdom. I'm not sure what will happen to me when I die, but I hope to form part of that energy and to somehow be present to those women and men who will come after me." (Aga)

- "Before the death of my father, I feared death, but now that fear no longer exists because I was able to experience that death is not the end. My father's existence is transformed into a different dimension, where I too will be someday. I experienced his resurrection in my life: this was possible because I remember all those events and positive experiences that I shared with him. I also overcame my fear of death when I understood that I had lived a human-divine experience with my father while he lived because I am part of his very essence and both of us come from that essence from which we have our image and likeness "that is God". Death, then, is a transition of space, time and place. More than a physical place, it is where we can live intensely that which we hope for; we enter into a dimension that is without limits or borders, without laws and rules. We will be in those persons with whom we have experienced God. I will live on in the memory of those who have known and loved me, just as my father lives on in me. Death, then, is not the end. We are transformed; we become part of the energy of the Cosmos." (Marcia)

- "I believe that with death we return to where we have come from and are transformed into something else. I've engaged in long discussions about what is death and what is resurrection with a dear priest friend who helped me immensely when he said, "Resurrection isn't resuscitation, always remember that!" What happened to us that we developed a fear of death? We must find a reason for this fear. And while I fear death, but together with this fear I am now totally convinced, sure, certain that it is a process of transformation that is permanent." (Coca)

- "I know what the feminist theologians say, I know what the ecofeminists say, I know what Christian theology says, I know what condomblé says, and what the indigenous say about death—but I don't identify with any of them. Again, the answer for me is memory. I am not interested in knowing if my mother is in heaven, or part of a tree, or whatever. I feel her presence through my memories. I don't have a theological position on death, perhaps because the death of my mother was an experience so hard and the pain so strong, that I refused to think about or talk about death. Nevertheless, my memories are sacred and this allows my mother to come to life every day. I dream of my mother everyday and this makes me feel good. I recently mentioned this to someone who said that I had better go for some therapy. No way! This is no aberration; it is quite marvelous having her with me each night. I enjoy this as much as I can and am very content." (Sandra Duarte)

- "In front of me are a collection of photos of my family, many of whom are dead. In them I see my children and myself. Yes, we die, at least physically. Indeed, our lives are but a sigh, a second in universal time, despite the fact that our earthly life is tough and there are some moments that seem to last an eternity and others where we will never forget for their intensity, tenderness, beauty or pain which seems like heaven or like hell. Our bodies, at death, can still feed life on earth, both animal and plant life, as the latest discoveries about DNA reveal. Our bodies consist of life that decomposes. These concepts are also present in Andean cosmology, in that the time and space of someone from these cultures continues in life and in death. Even after someone dies, he or she lives on in the memories of the family, the community, in the hills and in the Pachamama herself. I believe that life and death are intimately connected. Although a specific individual event, death is also a communitarian and global event. What I am is something that transcends my ancestors not only in my physical DNA, but also in the comings and goings of the history of my family. My ancestors rise in me, as I will in my descendants. Life and death are interactive, continuous parts of the great matrix of oikoumene, where individual life is only a cell in the universe." (Fanny)

- I don't see death as the end of life. Death brings my separation from time—and for me, time is sacred. Death is that transition moment to eternity, a return to that materiality form which we have come." (Sandra Raquew)

- "Perhaps one of my strongest original beliefs was life after death. If you ask me what sort of life, I cannot say, but I have always believed in a transcendence, an integration into the whole, into this greater reality. I think our mistake lies in always thinking that life after death is something individual. I continue to believe in some kind of fullness of life after death. I have no images, nor the ability to think how this integration into wholeness could be, but I do believe in transcendence. I like thinking about life after death from the image of God as relationality, to use Ivone's concept. This God who weaves relationship among all the beings of the universe." (Graciela)

- "I look at death from the experience of my mother's death. When she died, I found that traditional theology didn't water my faith. So I returned to our indigenous people's beliefs. Here life and death are not separate. Those who die continue to live among us. They live on in their teachings, their example, their counsel and witness—and in the very atmosphere that surrounds us. They remain in the things they liked: music, food, plants, candles, flowers and in their gestures of kindness. At the same time, we know that they are not with us physically; they have gone and are now enveloped in Divine Energy. So the experience I have had with my mother is that while she is no longer here physically, she continues to be my companion and confidant. She is alive in all those kind ways she marked my life. It is based on this experience that I can say that I have felt resurrection in life. Our loved ones live on and accompany us for the rest of our lives. They are present in their words, advice, in a garden they planted, etc. I feel that the dead give us strength to continue on living. On another note, I think it is just horrible to think that our bodies stay in the cemetery while our souls go off to heaven. No, the dead stay with us. That is why, for the indigenous, rituals surrounding death are so important." (Alcira)

- " I believe simply and sincerely that death and life are processes that one cannot separate, just as we really cannot separate good and evil. They are dialectical processes that are constants in our lives. I don't think death is opposed to life nor is death the end of life. As part of this envelopment in which we exist, which is sacred, we are born and we die. When I die I am going to return to the Earth, which is part of this divine envelopment and she will embrace me as a loving mother. Then I will live on in another form, perhaps as a tree, perhaps as a flower, I don't know. But now I don't worry about my death. I've told my children that when I die, they are not to bury me in some cold tomb or mausoleum. I want to be buried in the earth with trees above me so that I have the chance to become organic matter through which I will continue to be life and produce life. I'd like it if they planted flowers or a tree above my remains. Perhaps there are other levels of existence, I don't know, but I would be content if this were the level of existence of us earthlings, and that this was our lot. I like the idea of becoming part of the earth, a seed that flowers in another form, that can give life to others, that might become a tree, a flower, who knows? I love the natural world and if I come to form part of the cycles of this marvelous earth that produces so much life, well—I will be very happy indeed. These reflections are part of a long process where I have created my own synthesis, where my own stages of life have been fresh breezes to urge me to open new paths, to hear new sounds—sounds that are joyous and marvelous and invite me to dance. And I find myself in a dance where suddenly in the circle there are many bodies intertwined, loving each other, giving each other life. It is the infinite dance of the Sacred that envelops us and of which all of us are part". (Clara Luz)

- "My concern about death and life after death has changed with my new understandings of the human and the Sacred. I am now free of the concepts of heaven, hell and purgatory and can now live and die in a different manner. It is as if we are inside a huge time-space reality where we have the possibility to affirm life or reject it. I suspect that we will live on in the memory of those we leave behind, in their remembering us in those times when we were able to leave our own small selves behind and love and open ourselves to all that surrounded us. What I will miss is being able to hug and kiss those I love." (Doris)

- "We don't talk much about death because we fear it. I have never been afraid of death, however. Perhaps it might seem strange, but death has never worried me because it seems as natural to me as life. Nor do I worry about the future because I have always believed that my future is created in each of my actions. Death is part of the future—the difference being that it is the only thing we can be sure of. Just as my life is, so too my death with be the result of how I live. I believe that all is Sacred, all is energy, which is why I have such great respect for all life on Earth, because we too are part of this. So, when I die, my spirit will return to its place of origin and I confide in that original goodness. Those who believed in the Pachamama, or the goddess of the lake or of the mountain, did so because they depended on these presences and loved them dearly. We believe in gods and goddesses because we are weak and insecure. That is why some have created one patriarchal god who has power over all. But such a god crushes the human spirit, destroys horizontal relationships with the community of life. That is why I reject the notion of a patriarchal God and prefer to speak instead of the goddess to whom I give thanks daily for being alive to breathe this air, see this light, feel this heat. I believe in this energy." (Gladys)

- "The Brazilian-Afro religions have this dimension of community—that we are more than what we are now in our bodies. Those of us who are here form a community, but those who have gone on are also members of this community. We are not speaking here of reincarnation, but of bodies that are now enjoying themselves, who enjoy others ways of being that are not the same as what we experience here. When they are here, they enjoy our world. This is another way of explaining the ancestors, I think—and gives me much joy. So those who die become ancestors and communicate energy to us. That is what ancestrality means to me: the continuation of a life, of a mission. Positive energy and power never die. These ancestors will continue in nature as rocks or rivers, etc. For Afro religions these people really do become immortal in that they become a permanent presence in a place in nature, which are symbolic of the life of the person. Thus their histories stay with us forever. I like this perspective because the person is more present than absent. Of course, I am still afraid to talk about my death because I am so near to recovering from cancer. For me death as a human phenomenon means the end of a bodied life that frightens me. I love to hug and kiss people and to loose the ability to enjoy my body scares me. I am also afraid of the suffering one has to endure in order to journey to the other side. I guess I have to work a bit more on the physicality of death." (Silvia)

The interviewees' shifting cosmology is revealed in their reflections on death. The majority view death and life as not separate, but as part of the same cycle. They speak of returning to that primal energy, that original goodness from which they have come. Some speak of going into a different dimension, of being transformed. Others speak of memory—how loved ones are present in the memories we have of them and how they will be present as well in those who remember them. For some, the concept of ancestors is key, a concept

shared with indigenous and African communities. Several spoke of a fear of death that changed when they experienced the death of a loved one, or when their images of God changed and they saw everything as related.

4. Ethics and ethical practices (especially in the area of sexuality/reproductive rights)

- "I believe that we must always start from the body, from respect for each person, for her right to decide how she wants to live—always with the understanding that human rights must be secured for all. I don't much like laws and rules, but we do need norms with which to guide our daily lives. For me, it through my daily living with people, with the Earth and with my own body that I construct my ethics." (Aga)

- "We must differentiate between morality and ethics. Morality establishes an ideology of correct and incorrect ways of acting which respond to pre-established codes, in our case set up by a patriarchal, capitalistic society. A characteristic of this morality is that it always prohibits and judges what is right and wrong and usually does not allow a person to grow in responsibility. Women's bodies—especially in the areas of sexuality and genitality—have always been seen as immoral, sinful, negative. In our modern societies, those who follow accepted moral codes are considered good, but often this reveals conformity, hypocrisy and an inability to establish one's own moral principles. Ethics, on the other hand, hold that life itself demands respect and responsibility from each and from all. For me, ethics must be accompanied by a spirituality that expresses our ordinary attitudes. This has everything to do with our cosmovisions and the way in which we perceive all of life. Ethics, in the end, does not depend on ideologies or religions or codes of law, but rather on how we responsibly assume our location in the Cosmos—a stance that is prior to either ethics or morality. From an ecofeminist perspective, humanity is not separate from the rest of the Cosmos—this separation that the human is superior from other species, that the male is superior to the female, that the white race is superior to other races, has led us to our current crisis. It would be a great move forward if we could see that women's bodies were an integral part of Nature, and from this life-giving space that creates, defends, resists, celebrates, and finally rescues the bodies not only of women but also of men and the Earth from the patriarchal mindset. Ecofeminism is searching for, defending and creating new alternatives that will enhance life's evolution. Ecofeminism holds up an equality between humans and the rest of the community of life. Ecofeminism calls us to recreate ourselves in a new spirituality that instead of "should nots," invites each to contribute from its own diversity to the whole. This is an exciting process of seeking, learning and trying out new possibilities. Morality has made us passive beings." (Marcia)

- "There are two key concepts in the construction of a different ethics. One has to do with the body, which for me is fundamental. Our starting point for any ethics must be from the experience of the body and the memories stored there. The body speaks, right? The second is that we make our ethical decisions based on the experiences of our body. Nevertheless, often a decision that for me might be a very good one, for you it would be the worst possible decision. Thus this position is almost always labeled "relativism". But I am convinced that we women are capable of making our own ethical decisions about our own lives and that we have the right to make these ethical decisions that involve the history, the results, the longings and the values of each woman. We cannot universalize laws; we cannot once and for all establish absolute norms for everyone equally. Furthermore, one of the very difficult themes in terms of trying to systematize ecofeminist ethics is that we are expected to come up with definitive, justifiable definitions and scales of values—and that is just what we don't want to do." (Coca)

- "For me, ethical religions are in error precisely because today people are looking for meaning and not for an ethics. They are seeking those symbolic elements that will give them answers for immediate needs. Ethical questions always come later. I sense that currently we are at a moment when we need new ethical constructions—a new global ethics. We need to search for ways to build an ethics that evolves with people's aspirations. For instance, I am here with my experiences and symbols of meaning, but when I go there, what is it that I can offer that is more than just my own ecstatic experience of say, the goddess? This ecstatic experience is important for me, it offers me key symbolic meaning, but I must also bring something else to the table, something like an ethics, something that conveys how I am committed to act within the world. I don't quite know how to elaborate all this but we need to develop a solid ethic that attracts people." (Sandra Duarte)

- "I think that from my centuries-old ethnic and religious roots, I will always defend life, struggle for justice and equality, for freedom and solidarity with the most oppressed and marginalized. At the same time, something is changing in me. For most of my life, God was masculine and Father. I was a person who remained quiet and humble, not having much confidence in myself. But now I feel that I have different views that are valuable and worthwhile to be considered." (Fanny)

- "I remember that the very first topic we considered in my feminist theology group was abortion. Looking back, I see that the only way to really understand this issue was by listening to the experience and the wisdom of this group. It wasn't the school, or the church, or the university or the workplace that offered this space to discuss abortion honestly and openly. This has convinced me that ethics must be built in a common space; it is a collective exercise. Personally, I want to hold on to the liberating ethics of Christ. It is also important to me to incorporate those values I learned from my home, my mother, my grandmother, my father, my brothers and sisters. At the same time, with the help of my group, I can see the errors of my family's ethics. That is why I insist that the construction of any system of values or ethics must be a collective experience. Together we can study cases, and weigh social factors. We can weigh each particular situation of each woman and of all women, without neglecting to see her past and the historical context so that we can have a more mature understanding of how we make our choices. I am convinced that we live in post-Christian times because post-modern times are post-Christian. At the same time, my post-Christianity speaks to me of a world that is going through deep change and many see that the values that they once held must now adapt to a different world. The values might stay the same but we will live them out in other ways." (Sandra Raquaw)

- "For me, ethics is fundamental because it touches the key point in traditional theology which is freedom. Dogmatic religiosity has been key for maintaining oppression—especially in the case of women—by denying our ability to make ethical decisions. I underline the importance for an ethics where the meaning of freedom is embraced to be able to break with a theology of guilt and sin. From here we see the need to create a new ethics from the experience of women, for it is women who have experienced this oppression for centuries and therefore it is women who are able to elaborate something new. Resituating freedom—not in the liberal definition of freedom of autonomous subjects—but from the creation of new relationships. I think we are doing this slowly but surely, without doing violence to anyone. This is where I am working and I think I have the gift to be able to analyze, critique and denounce certain forms of oppression, especially in the religious field, as well as the ability to build something new. This is what I sense other women want from me. To be able to deconstruct it is essential to start from a critique of Christian morality and then move to rethink the meaning of freedom. It is within this new view of freedom that we can embrace pluralism, diversity—always based on experience. Ethics, then, is built from our contextualized experience. We must ask ourselves what experience is behind each ethical affirmation. Each person is a different expression of freedom, which is why it is necessary to reaffirm an holistic sense of what the human is in relation to the Cosmos." (Graciela)

- Ethics has to do with life in all its dimensions, in the ways we relate, the way we are, the way we act, our attitudes, our stance on justice, on ecology, on the way we live at home, in our communities, and in society. I feel that I am quite capable of deciding for myself and take responsibility for the decisions I make, according to my conscience, my abilities, my commitments, my options and my creativity and solidarity with all of humanity. Ethics lived from this perspective makes me more human, more dignified, more honest and coherent, more whole. I believe that ethics is not static, but always dynamic and as such, can always be revised, rethought, questioned and reformulated according to new lights in the way we are living and feeling and acting. And from this position we are able to question those norms, institutions and societies that speak of an ethics that is not incarnated, that is far from the lived reality of the majorities and that makes the body a prison of guilt. I feel that ethics is a key area where women's bodies have been the focus. Until very recently, official ethics have defined the way women must behave in relation to their bodies. We have been confronted with an androcentric and patriarchal ethical code that exercised strict control over our bodies. This is an ethics that punishes and imposes; it represses women's sexuality, our affectivity and our ability to be in charge of our own bodies and our own feelings. It has not allowed us to decide for ourselves. To live by an ethical code that flows from our bodies will allow us to once again value our bodies as sacred. The ethics imposed by our institutions has battered women's bodies with a morality that is morose, built on guilt, is leveled from on high and is dualistic in that it determines what is good or bad, pure or impure. This is why it becomes imperative to resituate ethical conduct based on our own perspectives and from our own bodily experiences. We are the owners of our own bodies, of our sexuality, of our decisions and options. This way of thinking will give us autonomy as dignified adults able to orient our lives according to the lights of our own conscience and experience of the Sacred. This was the ethics Jesus proposed." (Alcira)

- "I believe that ethics are part of a process whereby we must open ourselves to a new understanding of who we are as humans, who we are as women, how we understand ourselves in relation to our world, to those people who surround us, to the animals and the plants, to the whole with which we share an intimate relationship. For me, ethics consists of a relational attitude toward life, in the measure that we manage to understand ourselves as part of a relationship of communion, respect, justice and love; in the measure that we understand that our bodies continue in others; in the measure that we can feel part of a greater body. I hope that we will come to understand that we humans are not superior to other species. I hope we rise to the challenge to become ever more "humanized" by deeper and deeper relationships. It is from there that we can build a viable ethics that liberates. If we build communitarian relationships based on mutual respect and reciprocity with all the life community, we will be able to transform power relationships that dominate, repress and kill in favor of a dialogical power that defends and empowers the weakest. To defend and give back life is a process that heals our life and that of the entire cosmos… A word about abortion, which is legal in Cuba. After the revolution, many young women began to use abortion as a form a birth control. I have lived through this process with many young women who have gotten pregnant and were ashamed to tell their parents, so they had an abortion without their parents knowing it. Many doctors began to worry that there was a growing tendency to use abortion as the birth control method of choice. However, it is absolutely true that young Cuban women have broken with those traditional patterns of sexuality and are challenging their parents about sexual taboos that were the norm in pre-revolutionary Cuba. The present generation of young people have no qualms about sexuality or any sense of guilt or sin about having sexual experiences—no, absolutely not. " (Clara Luz)

- "For me, the challenge is to recover power and autonomy for women and for all people so that we can make our own decisions, and that these decisions are made in a more integral context. More and more we are realizing that everything is related—not just to other people, but to one's entire surroundings and that decisions made at every level affect everyone and everything else. The challenge coming from ecofeminism is precisely to promote a more integrated view of life, so that every decision is made with the focus of promoting more equitable relations that do not continue to crystallize domination over the weak and voiceless, including the entire life community and the Earth itself. It is within this integrity, where I believe we can pay attention to what our bodies are saying and can hold conversations with those we trust to get advice about a pending decision. Here the question of power is key. I am talking about "power with", not "power over" or outside me. If I am going to make a decision or share my deepest experiences, I'm not going to go to persons that I don't even know or are going to ask me very intimate questions and perhaps "condemn" me apriori. No, I'm going to go to a friend or group of friends who listen to me, ask questions to help me clarify things, but in the end, it is I who make the decision, because I am the only one who knows how this decision is going to affect my history, my body. That is why the challenge is to create spaces where we women can share our power and help each other to make decisions, but not make them for the other. If we are able to return to people their power to decide according to their own conscience, this will transform ethics and give us back responsibility over our lives as adults. From an ecofeminist point of view, we must remember that every decision has repercussions about how and what I eat, where I live, how I get around—decisions as simple as what detergent I use, what clothing, what energy source. I am convinced that we are living in a moment of deep connection with ourselves, our larger ecosystem and it is a time of letting go, of breaking with certain needs and practices." (Doris)

- "Clearly the human body is sacred. That is the main reason why we must take care of ourselves, respect and love ourselves. And from there comes my anguish, which is shared by all feminists, in the face of the devaluing and the violence that patriarchal culture levels against the female body. It is also that violence that sees women only as reproducers of the species, as wombs—and does not see us in our fullness—our hands that create, our minds that think, our spirits that soar. The quality of the body's sacredness is directly related to how we respect, love and commune with others." (Gladys)

- "I am guided by happiness. I believe that humans were created to be happy, to be fulfilled. Now, along with my own happiness, I place the happiness and fullness of life of others on the same scale. That is why my criterion is to search for happiness, but my happiness can never, ever mean the death or the unhappiness of others. It is in this space where we negotiate through laws and precepts how we are to go about creating happiness for all. That is why we say: "thou shall not kill" in every sense: don't kill dreams, don't kill through hunger, don't kill through violence, and don't kill by not doing what you have to do. I believe that from here we can create an ethics for life. I think that all the laws and principles should be a result of accords made from the basic principles of life—do not kill, be happy. What do I mean by happiness? I could interpret it as something very individualistic, but we must put happiness in a larger context and say that happiness is a right to life that all people have, that all life, Nature, the universe—that everything has. I am certain, in contrast to other theologians, that happiness can take un toward a new paradigm that will take us much farther than all the prohibitions and negations surrounding the body that now exist. " (Silvia)

The interviewees call for a new ethics beginning with the experiences of our own bodies, our own histories, our own longings. Starting from the body, then, is essential. This is especially true if we are going to challenge the patriarchal mindset that construed morality largely on the negation of women's bodies, which were considered to be the sources of sin and evil. An ecofeminist ethics would involve calling forth respect and responsibility from each and from all—and seeing the human in relation to the rest of the life community and to the unfolding universe. We are part of a greater body and therefore must take account of repercussions to the whole in making ethical decisions. Emphasis is placed on those community spaces where listening to the experience and wisdom of the group becomes important to allow decisions to be made freely. This ethics is always contextualized, pluralistic and respects diversity; it cannot legislate universal "once and for all" laws. Such an ethics offers an expanded meaning of what it means to be human and is based on expanding our sense of happiness and care.

5. Spiritual practice/discipline that nourish belief

- "My difficulty now is that I just can't feel comfortable celebrating in church. They are celebrations that just don't relate to me. In our gatherings (of women), we celebrate our bodies and everything that surrounds us—we celebrate the elements, the lives of other women; we celebrate life with our women's bodies." (Aga)

- "I have come to realize that life must be lived intensely at every moment. Yes, I believe that life is made up of moments. In this moment I am here and I must live it intensely because it is non-repeatable and each moment is an opportunity to find deeper meanings to my everyday life. I am sustained by sharing what I know with those with whom I share dreams, small achievements… I am also sustained by contemplating the natural world and I never tire of discovering its hidden mysteries. I am fulfilled by my family and friends. I am supported by the women I work with, because I can express who I am, what I feel and think, what I am learning and discovering with them. With them, I try to create new possibilities to better our lives. All this is a profound expression of life. God is life. Right now, my passion is related to discovering the potential in the mestiza cultures where spirituality is found in dance, music, colors, rituals, myths, community celebrations, etc." (Marcia)

- "At this time in my life, I have three practices which, for me, are profoundly spiritual. First, I engage in bodywork, which helps me to move into a different time and space. Second, I love the rituals and celebrations we create with women—here I feel connected to the depths and heights, and they are very powerful moments. Third, being alone in Nature." (Coca)

- "I am continually having spiritual experiences. Whether I go to an esoteric circle, an indigenous ritual, a condomblé ceremony, I participate fully with everyone. I observe and participate at the same time. It is not just a way of getting close to people—I really enjoy myself. I don't feel guilty—guilt simply isn't a part of my life. But again, my own sacred moment is when I am in my apartment with a glass of wine, a candle and some good music. It is in those moments when I feel whole, totally alive." (Sandra Duarte)

- "The heron and I are one, in our brief time together, we breathe the same air and each in our own way feels the beauty and peace of the moment. She comes close o me—our relationship is sealed. Then my heron moves away, but we each still look at the other. We have formed some sort of sisterhood, friendship. We are silent partners in that scene that rings out God's glory…" (Fanny)

- "For me spirituality has nothing to do with belonging to a religious institution. My spirituality has to do with contact with color, art, poetry, taking photos—these are powerful moments of interiority. I also share a deep sense of community with my feminist theology collective Chimalman, which is a fundamental source of sustenance for me. Together we cultivate seeds of new beliefs and values for ourselves. This is our space, the place where we can feel accepted, where we can think, share and celebrate together. The Sacred for me takes place in sharing, in sharing our experiences with others who also share their life journeys. In these moments, I know I am not alone." (Sandra Raquew)

- "More and more there is a tendency to celebrate outside of church circles. Like others, I find myself celebrating in small groups where new expressions of spirituality are being born. First of all, we are breaking with being disassociated from our bodies. This is a fundamental change for us women who have been socialized as beings-for-others; our sexuality and our bodies have been expropriated for the service of others. That is why work with women must include this dimension as part of our conscious-raising process and our own transformation. Bodywork, while pleasurable and liberating, is often very painful because we must deal with so many hurts that are stored in our memories. But I feel that we are now able to begin to weave new relationships, and experience solidarity among ourselves as women, counting on tenderness to help each other to be what each is meant to be." (Graciela)

- I am sustained by those values that allow us to be fully human. I find these values expressed in those alternative spaces such as women's reflection groups, local CEBs, indigenous and black organizations. Also the witness of many theologians and biblicists who have dared to present alternative readings of theology and biblical texts that offer more integrity and honesty. I am helped greatly by the "hermeneutics of suspicion" and research that passes through my own skin, my body, my feelings as a woman. I am also sustained by contemplation, meditation and concrete reflection on my surroundings. I live next to a campesino market where I have the opportunity to do multiple readings on life based on the faces of so many people from all social strata. I am also watered by the rituals we do as women that are connected in some way to the Earth, and to healing rites for women, the Earth, the ecosystem. I love to dance ritually and to express through my body my dreams, hopes and desires. I try to keep contact with other women throughout Latin America who think as I do, so I don't feel alone—and to remember that we are many who dare to "suspect," intuit and search for new ways of living. That is why in my biblical work I include alternative health work, self-esteem work, gender studies, reflexology, aromo-therapy, etc. I also must admit that for a long time now I have stopped participating in the Eucharist because I can no longer tolerate just an empty patriarchal, androcentric ritual where

I have no chance to express what I think and feel. Instead, I visit the trees. One of my favorite personal rituals is to go to the park in Santa Cruz before taking a trip and sit for a while under one of the trees. I greet each tree and ask them to orient me and accompany me with their wisdom and strength so that I may do what I am meant to do where I am going. I feel a deep bond with these trees, a communion and solidarity. When I return, I go to thank them. This is a ritual that fills me with energy; it is where I find the Sacred. The trees are part of me and I am part of them. I follow their cycles throughout the year. Their closeness inspires me to be creative, more sensitive to people. They are my confidants" (Alcira)

- " I connect with the deep in many different ways. Through strong feelings related to friendship, love, passion, joy, anger, impotence. Through those pleasurable movements of my body when I dance, when I hug someone, when I caress, when I make love. Through contact with Nature—the perfume of the flowers, the smell of the sea, the sound of the rain on my windowpane, the sound of the breeze at sunset. When I do Tai Chi, when I swim in the sea, when I meditate in my favorite corner surrounded by trees and flowers, when I can contemplate the sea or the river from afar. I also connect with the deep in the warmth of the company of my children, through the laughter and pure gaze of my granddaughter, through the love of my husband and of my parents. Through the friendship and warmth of friends, or when I hear a lovely melody or taste a rich cup of chocolate or enjoy a tasty meal; when I can extend a helping hand to someone in need, or when someone gives me a hand in tough moments; when I experience deeply the sufferings of others as a result of injustice and impotence that I want to sob with rage; when I hurt with the cry of the children and all victims of the disorders of our world; when I am able to perceive the pain of others as my own pain. (Clara Luz)

- "My spiritual practice has to do with a constant remembering to be in contact with myself. For a long time, my spirituality was centered on external practices—marches, protests, via cruces, which had to do with the context in which we were living. But today I have other practices and they always begin from me, are a response to my own core, my own need for contemplation. I practice Tai Chi, I love to meditate in Nature as well as to participate in the rituals we women are creating. I love to have deep conversations with friends, share dreams, dance and sing and chant—these things give meaning to my life. The spirituality I live today has to do with movement, with sacred dance, with being in community, in a circle. It is my whole being that celebrates now, not just my spirit." (Doris)

- "For how many years did I go to Mass and say the rosary at funerals! For me, my spirituality consists in how I relate to all I meet along my path—with you who I love, as well as other friends, with those I meet for the first time, a little girl, a little boy, a vagabond, a dirty beggar who asks me for food. My spirituality, my peace rests in how I relate to all of life. I also meditate each day, which is a practice I engage in for my health so that my mind is clear of all thought and I can center myself. I also have the spiritual practice of climbing Mount Avila every day, which is right here on the outskirts of Caracas. To walk for a few hours in the midst of such beauty, enjoy the harmony of the forest, the birds, the butterflies—all this gives me a great sense of harmony." (Gladys)

- "For me the celebratory and symbolic aspects of life are absolutely indispensable. I enjoy being in a space where I can animate the people to celebrate, a space where I too can celebrate, where I can make the liturgy alive—much of my life has been dedicated to this, to making liturgies real celebrations of life. I am Brazilian, and in Brazil we celebrate everything. It is a way to circulate energy, to circulate and radiate more life. However, during the last few years

I have felt very dry... your question, where do I find my strength? My black community had been a real source of energy for me, and now that I am no longer in my country, and far from my family of origin, I feel like I am drying up. At the same time, I am discovering that one "is with" "is in" a community or a group. I can recharge by participating in the liturgies of the Mennonites or in a Catholic Mass. Perhaps I am becoming too relativistic, but I find spaces to water my spirituality all over—in a celebration of Condomblé in Brazil, with the gay community here in Costa Rica. Lately I have been nourished in many forms." (Silvia)

The interviewees nurture their spirituality by celebrating with their bodies, wholly and freely. Many engage in bodywork, body movement, dance and ritual. Their spirituality is also nurtured in contemplating and celebrating Nature—from talking with the trees, to walking mountain trails, to celebrating the elements. A third source of spirituality is sharing deeply in women's circles and through friendship. Contact with sensuality—poetry, color, music—as well as with pain, is essential to this evolving spirituality. Few still find nourishment in the liturgies of their churches.

Although not part of the five great themes, I sometimes asked the women about Jesus and his role in their lives. And because I wanted to find out about how they saw their relationship to both liberation theology and ecofeminism, I included questions about both in the interviews. Not all the women answered these questions. A summary of their responses follows:

Understanding of Jesus

- "I don't believe in God the Father, God the Son or God the Holy Spirit. I can't. I believe in something Sacred that makes it possible to be born, evolve, transform. One only has to look at the perfection and harmony with which the community of life functions to know this marvelous mystery. Jesus was a very special person who, like many others, lived and fought against the Temple Laws that excluded the poor, the sick and women. I admire the courage he showed in his time—a time when women were forbidden to read the Torah and yet he founded a movement where women were allowed to assume leadership such as Magdalene, Prisca and many others. There are many passages in the Gospels that I love...the multiplication of the loaves and fishes, the image of God as a farmer, for instance. But I certainly don't accept the idea of Jesus' resurrection that we were taught in religion class. I believe that Jesus is with those who have died. He is in that great energy which forms the essence of the web of life." (Aga)

- "Jesus wanted to raise up humanity to our most authentic dimension, free of political, economic or religious interests. He was inspired by his ancestors, who tried to live in harmony with the Earth. That is why Jesus was different than most humans of his time. He had another goal, which was to critically assess power and religion. He became conscious of this gradually and began to act responsibly. But not as a great leader or as one sent by God. I don't think Jesus ever thought of himself as having certain "god-like" traits. It was only after his death that his followers discovered that his way of being a human was so authentic that it revealed the Divine. In this sense we recognize Jesus as "son of God" par excelance. In his life's project, Jesus offers three proposals to humans: first, each of us can relate directly to God as son or daughter; second, this means that a relationship of equality and solidarity exists among us; and third, the first two proposals demand that we live a relationship of respect and harmony between our species and the Earth." (Marcia)

- For a long time now, Jesus is no longer the only begotten Son of God who came to save the world from sin. He is, for me, another prophet, a person who achieved great wisdom in his day, but there were other wisdom people then as there are now. I believe that there is much to learn from his teachings, that his message of love was one where no one was excluded. Jesus and Buddha are more or less of the same rank, of course with Jesus having more impact in my life." (Coca)

- "Jesus of Nazareth is a reference point, but not because he is or isn't the only Son of God. I like Umberto Eco's thought here: Eco, an atheist, says that the miracle of Jesus consists in that humanity had arrived at a moment in its history where we could take up the values Jesus proposed—love without exclusions, giving one's life for another. These are manifestations of God." (Graciela)

- "Jesus is the way, the source of life, a friend, a life's project, my guide. That is why I am passionate about Jesus' project and am committed to it as well. Jesus is so human and so divine at the same time. And if Jesus is human in all dimensions of what it means to be human, so then do all persons have the right to experiment all the dimensions of being human." (Alcira)

- "The person of Jesus is important to me, especially from that moment when I was able to get rid of the patriarchal, dogmatic structure that placed him on the side of the powerful and placed him again with the humble fisher folk, the Mary Magdalenes and the other Marys. For me, this Jesus is the humble carpenter, that simple man of the people who know how to circumvent the law that oppressed his brothers and sisters to demonstrate love and justice. Jesus broke with those religious, dogmatic structures of his times and preached a kingdom without kings, a Messiah who serves, the power of love and a new relationship between the divine and the human that goes beyond hierarchical relationships of denomination and subordination. For a long time now I have removed Jesus from these patriarchal relationships. I have taken him from the temple and put him back on the street among ordinary folks where he belongs as well as I." (Clara Luz)

- "For me, Jesus is an extraordinary person who has deeply moved, illuminated and excited me. His life has marked my own journey. His experiences have helped me in my own search for meaning and the searching of many people who have grown up in the Christian tradition that so marks Latin America. However, now I see Jesus as only one reference point toward understanding the Sacred. I believe that his experience enlightens me because it was a counter-cultural experience so huge that the patriarchal culture in which he lived could no longer tolerate him. Jesus' own way of acting and being were not based on power structures, which makes me feel comfortable in working with women to re-read Scripture from this counter-cultural perspective. What does anger me is how the churches and the hierarchies have appropriated the experience of Jesus as their own." (Doris)

- "Jesus is a human who is very credible—the way he had compassion on the woman taken in adultery. He was known for his attitudes of respect and fairness in his relationships with others; he didn't establish differences. He is the only male I know of who wasn't a macho. He must have been really a convincing, enlightened and charismatic figure. However, humanity has produced equally enlightened figures after Jesus such as Marie Curie, Albert Einstein, Gandhi. And because they are closer to us in time, we are able to know their faults as well" (Gladys)

- "I have always loved the mystery of the Incarnation, which was the subject of my thesis. I worked backwards, that is, I examined how we see Jesus today—in the Christian communities—and moved backward until I reached the time of Jesus of Nazareth. I have always been drawn, since my days as a religious, to the Incarnation of God in human flesh, that he became one of us and took on our history. It is simply my intuition, but when I developed this topic, to propose God made human in human culture gives an entirely different vision of Jesus as the Incarnate Son of God, a vision of God as one who takes on our flesh—this can overcome obstacles to inter-religious dialogue. (Silvia)

What appears clear is that Jesus is a major historical figure, a prophet and wisdom figure. He is counter-cultural, authentically human, inspired by his ancestors. He is with those who have died. He is a heroic figure, but one of many. He has inspired a whole civilization with his message.

Reflections on liberation theology

- "I drew close to liberation theology through reading many books and working with the scriptures, especially with the help of my great friend (now deceased) Italian priest Claudio Dalbon. But I missed women's participation as an active subject; women were in the texts just as helpers or ones who listened. I also became aware that women are not included in the reading of the Bible from the viewpoint of the poor; neither are they included in liberation theology. Neither helps women become liberated from the burdens of patriarchy and machismo. I miss women "inside" liberation theology; I miss the feminine "inside" the scriptures—where is the feminine in the Divine? I miss the Mother, the Creatrix! Never have I accepted the fact that a man, a male, even if he is God, can give birth... I think we were conceived just like everything else in creation. I don't accept these miracle stories. I suspect, doubt and often remain silent. However, reading feminist theologians I discovered the Great Mother, the Goddess, and I found peace and have never again felt alone." (Aga)

- "It seems that initially, the poor were spoken about in very general, theoretical terms by a certain elite, without bringing about deep changes. However, with the help of a grassroots reading of the Bible, the poor really began to feel as subjects of their own process and discovered their own faces in the struggle for liberation, which opened a new stage for liberation theology. The proposals of liberation theology have become more concrete and more identified with these faces who now are beginning to raise their own voices of liberation, because the theological task that we must take on now will be engaged in by this great web of men and women of different cultures, races and ethnic backgrounds.... Our peoples are "Christian" and half of them are women. I'm convinced that we women can find elements for our liberation through studying the Bible. At the same time, I recognize that the Bible was written by those responsible for patriarchy, but it still contains many traditions of poor people, men and women in search of dignity, equality and justice. To live out these values, we must engage in a process of deconstruction of stereotypes and build Good News for all. For us women, this process must necessarily pass through healing our bodies. If we say that the Gospel is generosity, love, service, then first of all we must heal ourselves." (Marcia)

- "It was because of liberation theology that I became deeply involved in politics. In fact, I think it would be correct to say that it also was the reason why later on I became involved in feminism. It was through liberation theology that I could see that classical theology wasn't the only theology, not THE theology. Despite the fact that liberation theology has received much criticism by feminists and others in recent years, the feminist theologians that I know here in Brazil have a history with liberation theology that was key in their evolution toward feminist theology. So, although I too have my criticisms of liberation theology, I think that these criticisms often neglect to mention the importance that liberation theology had in our lives. We now must work in the area of gender, but this does not mean that we are no longer liberation theologians. I want to be a feminist theologian of liberation always. That is why I don't like the idea of denying liberation theology, because it was our "cradle". We don't need to be always looking for an enemy as if we were in some sort of mortal danger by shaking a man's hand...or by sitting next to liberation theologians. We must admit liberation theology's influence on our theology. When we write the history of feminist theology, we must start with liberation theology." (Sandra Duarte)

- "I think that today it is women who are developing liberation theology. Actually liberation theology is no longer nourishing a lot of people and male theologians, even the most progressive, have some black holes in their theology. One of the limitations of liberation theology is that it has made an absolute out of one dimension of oppression while ignoring others that are just as fundamental, such as gender and sexual oppression." (Graciela)

- " In my opinion, liberation theology is in a period of stagnation and institutionalization. Many of its theologians who were once in the vanguard are now silent. Liberation theology was born out of the cry of the poor and is a response to the excluded of history. It gave me elements to confirm my own intuitions and theological questions and for a long time I identified with liberation theology. But liberation theology became sort of the "in thing" and phrases like "the preferential option for the poor" came to be slogans. I began to feel more and more uncomfortable with this theology, without denying its prophetic voice. However, I missed other actors—

women, blacks, indigenous; points of view from ecology, from a gender perspective, from daily life. I feel that the term "option for the poor" has been emptied of what it once contained. The poor have become those "outside" and not me. It is liberation theologians—not us on the "outside"—who define the poor. I am convinced that it is time for a radical revision of the basic constructs of liberation theology and little by little I have felt more and more uncomfortable with liberation theology. I feel more at home with ecofeminist theology, biblical studies from the perspective of women, blacks, indigenous." (Alcira)

- "We didn't have much relationship with liberation theology in the rest of Latin America. In Cuba we talked about Theology of Revolution, where slowly but surely women's voices began to be heard. But it was a slow and arduous process." (Clara Luz)

- "My greatest criticism of liberation theology is that I now realize that it is still situated within the constructs of traditional theology. This is particularly true in relation to liberation theology's symbolism, its spirituality, its concept of God, its sacred images." (Doris)

While most would recognize their debt to liberation theology, the interviewees express a certain frustration with liberation theology and feel it is "stagnating". Some would say that it is still caught in many traditional theological concepts that are anthropocentric as well as androcentric.

Commitment to ecofeminism

- "I was raised in close contact with Nature and do not consider myself somehow "outside" as a spectator. I am part of her and am enchanted by her. I relish contact with water, wind and earth. I love the birds, the flowers. I talk to the moon, the stars. I suffer in my own body the Earth's devastation. For me, here is where I find the Divine. The Divine is not a God outside. Both the feminine and masculine principles are present in the Divine because it cannot be different than what we find in Nature... I identify with ecofeminist theologians such as Ivone, Coca, Graciela. The world needs them, and so do I." (Aga)

- "Healing of women's bodies is totally connected to the healing of the Cosmos. Today women's bodies as well as Earth's body is fragmented by the idea of male superiority. The two processes of healing go together, because they have always been connected to our survival.... Contemplation of the natural world reveals that as persons, we are part of this world. In my own journey, I discovered that in order to heal myself, I must make myself uncomfortable. Sometimes material discomfort is easier than that feeling of discomfort demanded in giving up internalized mindsets, such as patriarchy. For instance, I must try to disconnect from the definition of myself as a "consumer" that this system tells me I must be. I must divest myself of trying to be what others consider "feminine" in order to be a feminist.... We should live every moment of our lives with intensity, because each is unique. To have greater contact with Nature, to conceive time in another way, to contemplate the day in another way—how often I am dismayed when folks comment how ugly the day is because it is raining. What I shame, I think, because I whole possibility of living a unique experience is lost. I believe so much in this, that we are one integral, reciprocal whole. We cannot exist without reciprocity.... I identify with many elements of ecofeminism, but as yet I can't say I am an ecofeminist because I haven't developed my own ecofeminist thought or posture. With my biblical work within Andean culture, I have discovered that our indigenous cosmology is clearly ecological, and for recovering women's cultural and religious values, ecofeminism offers a real possibility for recreating and re-dimensioning their own symbolism, rituals, celebrations, life cycles, etc—as well as the whole dimension of the Divine revealed in Nature." (Marcia)

- "First of all, I must admit that I am totally urban; I was born in the world of concrete, I am petrified of bugs, I think that any strong wind is an earthquake, etc. I experience my ecofeminism in my body. Contact with Nature, its rhythms, the rhythm of day and night. When I am able to really connect deeply to these rhythms and see other women doing the same, then I experience what I would call an ecofeminist stance. Also, ever since I began to read and study Ivone and ecofeminist theologies, I have found meaning in my life. Of course I admit that my ecological commitment is still small and must be developed. I plant my herbs and try to be more in harmony with the seasons; I try to use the car only if more than two people are going; and I try to teach these values to my grandson. But if I had to give you all sorts of reasons to theoretically tell you why I am an ecofeminist, I don't have them. I am convinced that ecofeminism is absolutely inclusive for both men and women, with the diversity of culture, class, race, age and all the other variables there are—and that we always must retain a critical posture. But we really must leave the mechanistic paradigm in which we find ourselves! The discoveries coming from quantum physics are very attractive to me and help me to see our larger context. Also, ecofeminism allows me to continue dialoguing with the theological world from another perspective." (Coca)

- "Because I was very involved with Brazil's feminist movement, I began to notice the importance of ritual for women. I was struck by this and began to study ecofeminism in the university in order to see why so many women in Brazil were participating in ecofeminist rituals—often without knowing what ecofeminism was. I am convinced that ecofeminism contains some very dangerous positions, one of which is its essentialism. There are many different tendencies in ecofeminist thought, but one central idea is that women will save the planet. I think this is very dangerous because it puts an immense responsibility on the shoulders of women. So I began to read ecofeminist theory, especially what is being written in Brazil and in other Latin American countries. In the ecofeminist rituals that I have witnessed, there are many elements related to Nature and having to do with shamanism. Originally, I thought I would concentrate more on these ritual practices, but I discovered I must first understand more fully the theory behind ecofeminism. That is why my thesis concentrates on ecofeminist discourse.[2] When I was writing, I could clearly distinguish between those ecofeminists who were essentialist and those who were more social-constructionists. But in actual practice, it is not so clear. When I participate in a ritual, I don't see the discourse, I see a women who is constructing her own symbol system and today she might have one question and tomorrow another. One constant in all of my research is the need to enter into greater contact with Nature." (Sandra Duarte)

- "I need to be more of an ecofeminist...it is small yet and it needs to grow. I see that there have been changes in my life in terms of a consciousness of my body, the awareness that this body is part of the earth, that is forms part of the history of life itself, of time, of gods and goddesses...Because of ecofeminism a new relationship between my life and the lives of other people is possible. Because of ecofeminism, I can enter a forest and know that this forest is sacred, and as such, also has rights." (Sandra Raquew)

- "I like to call myself an ecofeminist. Feminism has given me the ability to recognize that there are different ways of engaging in the struggle for justice against every kind of oppression. Currently I am working against gender oppression, but without loosing sight of class, race and other oppressions. These struggles are not mutually exclusive. For me, ecofeminism is all embracing. It offers a feminist and an ecological perspective that I feel is very broad and I want to deepen my understanding and commitment to ecofeminist theology. What I first discovered through ecofeminism were the tools to deconstruct all the dogmatic precepts that were oppressing me. I reached a point where I didn't know what I believed anymore, but this process was necessary to be able to re-construct what is important to me now." (Graciela)

- "It was Ivone Gebara who helped me express my suspicions and intuitions. One day I listened to some cassettes of her talks on ecofeminist theology and what she said gave form to many of my questions. I had observed and suffered in my own flesh the violence leveled against the ecosystems and against women, but I didn't know how to relate this violence. It was Ivone who gave my suspicions and intuitions a name: ecofeminism. Also, when I lived in the mining areas of Bolivia I reconnected with the Earth and was anguished by the erosion, the intoxication, the violence being leveled on that land. It was there in the Siglo XX mine that I made the connection between the body of women and the body of the earth and how both have been subjected to abuse of every sort. For me, to speak of the Earth as Body is to speak of my own women's body. As a woman, I need to make that connection if we are going to heal our ecosystems and ourselves. The Earth and we humans are one; I am part of her and she is part of me. The damage she receives, I also receive, and what I suffer, so does she. A deep, inseparable bond exists between us both. At the same time, my experience with cancer gave me another way to see and experience life. It was through this experience that I discovered how the internal ecosystem of each person is as important—and as violated—as our external ecosystems. As a woman I feel I cannot continue to re-enforce the ideology of the patriarchal, androcentric system present in both church and society. I am convinced that there is another way of being human possible that holistic ecofeminism offers." (Alcira)

- "In Cuba, the experience of dialoguing with the Santaria tradition was a real watershed. It was a chance to interiorize some of the concepts of ecofeminist discourse—once we got rid of the patriarchal images of God. In this sense, ecofeminist reflection responds to my own spiritual restlessness and searching. To feel and understand the Sacred in everything and in everyone is also to understand that I am part of this sacred enveloping and unfolding. When we are able to experience this, our perception of the world changes and we are able to feel a little bit that the body of the other is my own body. (Clara Luz)

- "Ecofeminism is what most defines where I am at this moment. Here I must give thanks to Ivone Gebara because it was she who helped me finally put together the pieces of the puzzle that were separated—ecology, feminism, poor women, the body. She was able to express our intuitions, our allurements and at the same time put her finger on our tiredness, our boredom with certain practices, our lack of a sense of direction. She offered a new cosmology and laid bare our anthropocentric mindset—which gave me the marvelous insight to understand how the domination of women and of the Earth have come from the same root, which is much deeper than either neo-liberalism or capitalism. It had to do with patriarchy, where everything is structured in pyramid fashion: political parties, the church, the family, the university; every kind of construction of knowledge, every kind of institutionalism is based on hierarchies and dualisms. In the same dualistic structure, we have God and humans, heaven and earth, the sacred and the profane, the spirit and the body—after Ivone's visit, things became very clear for me. I now define myself as an ecofeminist theologian because in this way of thinking I can understand my experience as a woman from the popular class. And I can also understand myself as part of this expanding Cosmos, part of this billion-year-old history." (Doris)

- "I try to teach ecofeminist theology because I believe that the human (read male) is not the center of the universe, indeed this attitude is responsible for our devastating androcentrism and anthropocentrism. Who invented monotheism? Why do we consider ourselves superior to animals—because we can laugh and talk? We must permanently combat androcentrism—not for reasons of altruism or justice—but to secure our own survival. Because if the Life that surrounds us no longer functions, neither will we. We humans are latecomers on the Earth, and we must recognize that we form part of the community of life and live in harmony with that community." (Gladys)

- "I find much echo in ecofeminism of what I think and feel. But I don't think I can define myself as an ecofeminist yet. I will have to work on some elements more thoroughly, especially in theology. However, I don't think of myself as outside ecofeminism. But I first have to struggle with my questions. For instance, here in Latin America we still must work in the areas of gender studies and feminism, and not pass too quickly to the next stage without having made the necessary examination of our own context. We must look at ecofeminism from our own realities of Latin America, and not ride roughshod over stages. (Silvia)

The interviewees' comments reflect their own ecofeminist convictions—as they themselves define ecofeminism. Some would not want to be labeled "ecofeminist" but are in dialogue with its evolution. Others embrace ecofeminism wholeheartedly, but are also defining it within the Latin American context.

Summary of Workshop

From April 7-11, 2002, I gathered these 12 women together here in Santiago, Chile for a workshop to reflect on the interviews. Ivone Gebara was also present throughout and played a key role in raising questions and offering input. Each woman had received the collected interviews beforehand. The task before us (as laid out in my original project) was to analyze these texts as a whole, note patterns, similarities and differences and offer theological reflection based on the interviews. My hope was to see if we might be able to describe the "theological moment" we found ourselves in at this point in history. However, the content of the workshop was purposely left open so that the participants themselves could decide what they wanted to talk about, as a result of reading the interviews.

I had a wonderful support team that helped in the planning and conduction of the workshop: Ute Seibert from the Con-spirando Collective, Victoria Martínez from Capacitar-Chile and Veronica Cordero from the Forum of Sexual and Reproductive Rights, who acted as secretary, directed the process. Ecological theologian David Molineaux was also part of the planning team. Maryknoll lay missioner Mary Jo Cummerford from Venezuela and Toni Ryan, an Irish volunteer working with Capacitar-Chile, also provided essential logistic support. Finally the Maryknoll community in Chile offered hospitality and financial support, without which I could not have held this gathering.

The workshop opened Sunday evening with a ritual of honoring our stories. The collection of interviews was placed in the center of our circle and we blessed them with the elements. Each woman had been asked to bring a picture of herself and her family of origin with her so that we might celebrate our roots more visually. These photos were placed around the book of interviews and we slowly circled them, asking these ancestors as well as others to be with us in these next days of sacred space and time together.

Monday, the first day of the workshop, was spent reflecting spontaneously on the texts. The summary that follows omits the names of the individual women who made the comments. We made a commitment to ourselves not to publish anything from the workshop with specific quotations from individuals, respecting our time together as a sacred space—and a safe one where privacy would be honored.

Impact of the interviews on those interviewed:

- "I was so impressed by the courage of the women interviewed, the difficult experiences they lived through, and often all alone."

- "Despite the differences in age and background, I found pieces of myself in these histories. These are not isolated stories."

- "I can identify with the stages each woman goes through; so many of us have the same reference points—Ivone Gebara, Paulo Freire, liberation theology. I found myself trying to see if the person was speaking from her head or from her gut-level feelings. I want to see if there is a change in our theological discourse which up to now has been so linked to church institutions."

- "I noticed how our images of the Sacred have evolved and that each of us has gone through the same process where we now find the Sacred in all that envelops us, in the faces of ordinary people."

- "We are reshaping the Sacred and this gives us greater autonomy and freedom. We are no longer so tied to structures that hold us down. We don't seem to be interested in spaces of power."

- "But there is a certain feeling of being alone, even though we know each other exists. I feel the need for a new kind of community. There is no doubt that all of us have experienced a break with our (ecclesial and theological) institutions. I feel a "social commitment" to each one of the interviewees because we are traveling the same road in relation to our images of the Sacred."

- "These texts really moved me deeply. The richness of the collection is that while there is much in common, there is also a great diversity. One of the things we all agree on is that there is no more All-powerful God! We could suppose that we are all ecofeminists, but we resist declaring ourselves as such, because we are tired of being labeled. However, reading the interviews, I felt part of something—and that what I believe isn't just some personal craziness."

- "It wasn't until I read these texts that I realized how ecofeminist I really am! I had been feeling frustrated with liberation theology for some time now, but didn't know why. These interviews were like connecting with myself again. I have also been so abused by the church."

- "The interviews show how all of us carry around the vestiges of abuse from our institutions in our bodies. In breaking with the institution we discover a way of surviving by giving new meaning to what it means to be human. Liberation theology has lost the ability to give new meaning; it is time to birth new understandings of meaning… I was also surprised by the presence of Jesus in the interviews. It wasn't the presence of a macho, but of a human-divine person."

- "A common element throughout is the great faith of the interviewees despite the lack of compassion from their churches, which I see as a great violence. Abuse of women has been going on for 6,000 years of patriarchal history. We need to unite together to struggle against patriarchy, its power and influence."

- "In any conversation about the sacred, speaking about the body, about sexuality in not allowed; they are intentionally left out. A real change in theological discourse would be to change sacred space, where celebration of the body becomes sacred. We women can attest to the fact that aspects so important to us, such as our bodies and our sexuality, are simply left out of any religious discourse. Our experiences related to the ordinary, to the affective are simply not valued—this is true of liberation theology as well."

- "Sensuality has no place in religious practice. Men have become producers of theories; they have internalized dualism. We women have not been able to change this."

- "Men have not understood that our experiences are also theological. They say there are no facts (for example, in Scripture). This is part of our history of abuse in the churches."

- "I was so happy after reading the interviews to know that there were women who thought as I did and that my intuitions are not crazy."

- "I share much of what we women say in the interviews and now that I know all of you, I embrace this text as a sign of my commitment to you. I see that there is something common in this "history of abuse" against women and it is that "we have found each other". Feminism has been a first step. All the stories are similar, but none are the same. Despite our doubts, it is fascinating to see who we are, what we feel, how we have made mistakes. We are free to allow ourselves to weave a tapestry."

- "I read the interviews in gulps and saw how we are transgressing our institutional restrictions. I offer a prophecy: if the church does not open up, it will loose the women. I also note that all of us speak from our bodies. Dualism is a masculine theory, which we women do not experience. To speak of body and soul is masculine language."

- "The place from which we do our theology is from our own life experiences, from our own corporal experiences. The sacred is seen as those life experiences where both the good and the bad are present. Although there is much diversity in the interviews, we all speak of experiences of freedom, of what we feel. And feelings, in traditional theology have always been considered "lower". We women have suffered from dualism; it has been a real cross for us. Yet we know that we cannot feel the world apart from our bodies. To recover this is vital. Also, we experience a fear to declare ourselves ecofeminists because we do not want to be boxed in by a concept; we don't want to be defined and classified by rigid categories."

- "We are also very careful in what we say. We have internalized a certain self-censorship because what I believe is so different that it will frighten people. So I suspect lots was left out of these interviews because we still need to protect our families, our jobs."

By the end of the first day, the group surfaced the following themes they would like to reflect upon:

- Body and healing
- Sexuality: how we live it out
- Power: how do we use power, and how does power affect us as women.
- Jesus: From Jesus as God to the Project of Jesus.
- Ecofeminism as a project for social change
- Spirituality: how to create spaces to cultivate new images of the Sacred.
- What still remains of Christianity that we can affirm.
- Death

At this point in the workshop, an unexpected shift took place. After discussing each of these themes, the group decided to concentrate on deepening its reflection on sexuality, because it appears as a great absence in the interviews, and yet it is present in the ethical posture of each woman interviewed. This was a major departure in what I had projected for the content of the workshop. But it became clear to all present that we needed to wrestle with sexuality theologically if we were to be faithful to our own sense of calling. For the next two days, then, through both tears and laughter, the group delved deeply into this subject in an absolutely unprecedented way.

While these conversations were confidential as well as sacred spaces for healing, a real leap in ttheological reflection took place. This leap is eloquently chronicled in Gebara's Preface to Lluvia para florecer, which I summarize here.[3] Working from both her own notes and from Veronica Cordero's notes, she offers the following synthesis, which I am convinced is absolutely groundbreaking.

From a category seldom talked about, women as genital bodies came to the foreground. It became possible to speak of God and female genitality, where these two asymmetric "subjects" could be compared historically both in terms of places of oppression and places of social power. At one point early on in our reflections, some began to feel uneasy about speaking of such an intimate, taboo subject and wondered if we were not being irresponsible in our commitments to the poor of our continent and to our task of transforming structures of oppression by talking about our genitality. Were we not diverting the "locus" of theology; were we not reflecting on our own intimate experiences without giving thought to our larger, supposedly more urgent, political and social contexts? However, as we continued to probe, we gradually discovered that we were breaking out of one of patriarchy's most entrenched rules—that which forbids us to speak truthfully about what is either banalized by pornography or described in medical or academic circles in "rational" and "objective" terms. While it is practically impossible to describe what actually took place among us, each of us acknowledged that we were genital subjects. We discovered that engendered-ness is related to genital oppression and is connected to other forms of oppression.

Gebara underlines the fact that our reflections concentrated on the "shadow side" of genitality as portrayed by patriarchy: that which has been labeled dirty, sinful, the result of temptation, the door of concupiscence, and a curse for the pains of childbirth. We didn't focus on the marvels of sexuality, or as sexuality as part of our identity—these aspects of sexuality are well known to us. But this shadow side, dominated by the world of patriarchy, is always portrayed as being a source of sin and therefore always meriting punishment. Never has it been seen as a space of freedom. Freedom, according to Christianity, is never present in these "lower areas" which are considered dirty, wet, bloody and foul smelling. On the contrary, freedom is equated with control and denial of this site of our animalism, of instinct, of the flesh which reminds us of the flesh of all living things and of the very "menstruating womb" of the earth. In many ways, freedom is the denial of this side of the human, especially when it is identified as feminine, subject to cycles, secretions, associated with the darkness of the caves and with secrets of a hidden and feared mystery.

Gebara reminds us that for millennia, the patriarchal God controlled both the political world of the empires and the bodies that built those empires. He divided bodies into classes, colors, genders, and between nobler and less noble parts. The head dominated, as did the masculine gender. Male genitality reigned. Patriarchal tradition lifted up the grandeur of rational thought and the insignificance of sex, the sordidness of genitality, especially female genitality. And the more this grandeur was elevated and the spirit hailed as supreme, the more the other became the object of forbidden desire, the object of lust, war and rape. In its attempts to deny and hide genitality, patriarchy allowed this repressed energy to rear its head only as sin, which then had to be punished with increasing rigor.

Female genitality is the place where the macho is king, where the war between the sexes is allowed. *But it is never recognized in its own right*. It is the "resting place of the warrior" and as the place of "feminine silence". It is here that all the force of social and religious repression of the female body lies. And it is from here that the other forms of social, cultural and religious oppression spring. Gebara points out that it was absolutely necessary for patriarchy to establish a constituent dualism dividing body from spirit, so that our genital bodies could be dominated, hurt, broken, violated—all this while we also built civilizations. Our dominated "Eros" thus became the ground over which a civilization of repression was built. We became capable of believing the illusion that we lived in freedom, in more or less complicity with other forms of oppression.

Gebara reflects that during our days together in Santiago, or collective corporal memory was awakened in a very real way. Our grandmothers, mothers, and friends were very present to us. Their tears watered our memories and flowed through our eyes. The knife's edge of their oppression took place in their genital bodies, just as it has in ours. Can such suffering be salvaged and learned from? Gebara asks. Will the emerging planetary counterculture, with its feminist sensibilities, be capable of offering a sexuality and a genitality that is more pleasurable and more responsible for all of us? We did not look for immediate answers because we knew it would take time to process these discoveries.

However, Gebara notes that the group quickly realized that sexuality—and explicitly genitality—had always been present in patriarchal religious discourse in the form of a repressive silence. All of us saw clearly that the denial of genitality as a human attribute capable of beauty and freedom is clearly linked to an asexual image of the divine and is grounded in a dualistic understanding of life. The patriarchal God of the Bible seems to take a stand against genitality, especially feminine genitality. He exerts power over women and condemns our genitality as if it were the place of absolute transgression, of ultimate disobedience and that space where women competed with Him. Throughout the biblical tradition, the only *locus* for prostitution was when, symbolically, the feminine went against masculine law. Neither is female genitality a place where the Christian God dwells. Christ is conceived in the womb of a virgin and is born of her in a totally miraculous way. In Christian symbolism, Gebara reminds us, sexuality appears mysteriously by the power of a patriarchal God capable of "birthing sons of Abraham from the rocks" and by sending his all-powerful Holy Spirit to engender his only son. And we, poor descendents of Eve, after all these centuries still have not been able to understand and assimilate the transcendent sexuality of Mary! We continue to be condemned. As we have for thousands of years, we continue to feel guilty and hide under the weight of our sin, of our pleasure or our repression of pleasure.

That is why, as Gebara points out, we must allow ourselves to rescue our genitality through our collective reflection. This can be a major step in the process of healing and of moving beyond our current patriarchal culture, a step toward redeeming our own values, our libidos and our self-esteem. Other interpretations and other myths can now inhabit our imaginations and help us to take further steps toward freedom. The patriarchal spell has been shattered. We were able to look it in the eye and challenge its power over us by affirming our own autonomy and loving our own bodies—and being grateful for all that life has given us.

For Gebara, another major point of our time together was being open to a different perception of the place of the Sacred in our lives. We are leaving the patriarchal sacred space, which is often limited to our religious institutions, and are entering the sacred space where values related to our own human situation can be celebrated. From an ecofeminist perspective, the sacred is in a kind of quality of life, an attitude through which we connect to the whole in a very special way. The sacred is not "something" in itself, but a situation, a relation, a value of life that takes us beyond ourselves; it invites us to silence, to laughter, to tears as expressions of both the nearness and the larger presence of Great Mystery. And reciprocally, the sacred is born in us and pushes us beyond ourselves at the same time. The sacred includes beauty and grandeur, esthetics and ethics—like notes in the same piece of music. Thus, in these days together we found ourselves redesigning our sacred maps as we searched for experiences of dignity, freedom and fullness through uncharted waters. We are leaving behind those experiences of the sacred marked by a masculine institutionality, although many of us still live with the duplicity of these experiences and allegiances. At this time, it cannot be otherwise.

And so, despite our insecurity and limitations, we began to design other maps, to offer other sacred blueprints, propose other rituals because we are starting to write other sacred texts and suspect that are own lives are also sacred. And so it is that we find ourselves at the beginning of a whole new common creation.

The question of "limits" also engaged us. Gebara reminded us that in patriarchal society, limits to behavior are established by outside authorities, usually male. It is they who decide what is orthodox and what is orthopraxis. It is they who decide what is allowed and forbidden. To criticize the patriarchal system implies a new ethics. But how do we establish limits to this new ethics? What criteria can be established to govern the ethics of our action and desire? We cannot annihilate the past or deny the values of the present, or say that efforts toward justice in the past are void of value. We do not pretend to be more ethical or moral than other periods of history. We don't believe that we can bring about an earth without evil. No. We are a mixture of many things, of many currents of thought, which are often contradictory. But it precisely from this "mix" that we must find ways to live with justice and dignity, where we find utopias and dreams, where a new historical time seems possible. In this way we remember that we ourselves find value in the Christian experience, in the values of the movement of Jesus, although we are critical of the patriarchal way these values have been communicated to us throughout history.

These reflections left the group somewhat stunned by its own audacity. I sensed that some felt that perhaps they had let me down somewhat by not reflecting more at length on my five great questions or by wrestling with ecofeminism and what an ecofeminist vision might offer the planet at this point in history. And while I agree that I was as surprised by this turn of events as they were, I reminded them (and myself!)

that the objective of this gathering was to go where we felt we must go in our theological reflection—and "by god/goddess/great mystery"—that is just what we did! I predict that these reflections will be a small but essential page in the history of Latin American eco/feminist theological reflection.

We ended our time together by sharing our utopian dreams for a different tomorrow. These included everything from establishing feminist communities in the countryside with "ecofeminist libraries", to having banquets where everyone in all the planet's diversity was welcome and where food was plentiful and free of toxic poisons, to dancing naked under a clean sky where all kinds of tender relationships were possible. These visions poignantly reflected the women's longing for both a more ecologically sound world and a world of peace, harmony and pleasure.

I conclude this Chapter by admitting that my dissertation work of conducting these interviews, publishing them and reflecting together on their meaning turned out to be a much more communitarian project than I could have ever anticipated. I have been deeply moved by what has happened in the process and am profoundly grateful.

---

[1] Madonna Kolbenschlag, *Diosas y Arquetipos: en memoria de Madonna Kolbenschlag.* Colectivo Con-spirando, Santiago: 2000, p. 2.

[2] Sandra Duarte da Souza. *Ecofeminist Theory, Ethics and Spirituality: An Analysis of theDdiscourse.* (Doctoral Dissertation) in Portuguese. Sao Bernardo do Campo, Universidade Metodista de Sao Paulo, Brasil, 1999.

[3] Ivone Gebara, *Presentación*, in *Lluvia para Florecer: Entrevistas sobre el ecofeminismo en América Latina.* Santiago: Colectivo Con-spirando, 2002, pp. 9-17. What follows is a summary of this Preface, which I am translating from Spanish.

The continent of the Unconscious
turned upside down
And out flew spirits of the dreamtime
A rainbow serpent coiled itself
Into a brain
(The color of dried blood)
We are children of the rock
—Madonna Kolbenschlag[1]

Chapter V

Clues for Transformation:

Reflections, Conclusions and Challenges for the Future

As I conclude this research, I find myself and those who have shared their lives so profoundly with me on the threshold of a whole new venture. We find ourselves at the beginning of a new common creation that is both exciting and daunting. As we embark on the long psychic journey of ridding ourselves and our world of a patriarchal mindset so imbedded in us that it seems as normal as the air we breathe, we have only faint glimmers of what a post-patriarchal world might look like. Only intuitions, dreams, hunches. AND a growing circle of like-minded seekers, each of whom now knows that she is not alone in her search.

That we are leaving behind patriarchal constructs and pushing toward something new—yet something that we only intuit and cannot yet define—is clearly evident in the interviews with the 12 women and in their joint reflections during the workshop. While there is a certain skittishness at this point about calling themselves ecofeminist or of embracing ecofeminism wholeheartedly "because we are tired of being labeled or put in boxes and categories," there is agreement that they feel "part of something larger…that what I believe isn't just some personal craziness."

At this point in their history, very few of the women would fervently insist that their evolving theological, spiritual and ethical insights be called "ecofeminist". But that there is a paradigm shift, that their intuitions are changing and mark a whole new way of understanding the human and the divine, is beyond dispute. We apparently still lack a more adequate metaphor, a more poetic yet accurate way of describing the constructs of meaning we are feeling and describing. At the same time, what Ivone Gebara describes as "holistic ecofeminism" has struck a deep cord in the hearts of these women. ("She was able to give words to what I had been feeling...")

I conclude, then, that the term "ecofeminism" is not as important as what is happening in terms of the shift in consciousness taking place, which evidently needs more than one term to describe it. **But what can be tracked is the shift.** This shift is manifested in the evolution of the interviewees' anthropology (the way they now define the human), cosmology (their understanding of origins, which in turn has altered their images of the Sacred) and their epistemology (the sources for their knowledge). This shift is affecting their ethical postures and their spiritual practices.

Shifting anthropology

The women interviewed express in a variety of ways a shift in their understanding of who we are as humans, as *anthropos*. Their sense of themselves as an individual, separate ego is evolving toward a larger sense of self—what Joanna Macy would call the "ecological self". This shift in identity from an isolated entity to identification with the larger cosmic body is evident throughout the interviews. We humans are not superior to the rest of the life community; we are part of the natural world, part of the materiality of the universe—or as Aga reminds us, "we are brothers and sisters of Nature." Because of our particular kind of intelligence, we are meant to be the Earth's caretakers and to assure its well being. "Everything that happens to the earth, happens to me, " reflects Silvia, paraphrasing Chief Seattle' well-known prophecy: "What happens to the Earth will also happen to the children of the Earth." Referring to her own recent struggle with breast cancer, she says: "My sick body is also related to the Earth's devastation." Alcira speaks of her own internal ecosystem as a mirror image of the external ecosystem where she lives, and knows that she must live in reciprocity with both because each depends on the other. Some of the women spoke of themselves as "beings in process," as incomplete in themselves yet linked to all those who have gone before them and to all those who will come after. This is especially true of Alcira, Fanny and Sandra Duarte who have been deeply influenced by indigenous cultures. We are, it seems, the collective memory of all that has gone before—the very elements in our bodies were present in the primordial fireball—and we can count on the probability that in some recycled form we will be present in the community of life's future generations.

These women's testimonies support what deep ecologists are describing as a "remembering of who we are." I recall David Bohm's "implicit order" which sees everything linked to the universal reservoir of life: past, present and future are all one "memory network" in a space-time continuum. Or I remember Brian Swimme's definition of us as "geological formations" as much as the rocks and the seas and the mountain ranges—a mode in the universal dynamics of evolution that is wondrous to behold, but is still only **one** manifestation of cosmic creativity among trillions. And I recall Jungian psychologist James Hollis's thought that "this little incarnation we call our life is but the vehicle for a larger journey which divinity makes through us." This perspective sees the world as an intrinsically dynamic web of relations in which there are no absolute dividing lines between the living and the nonliving, the animate and the inanimate, or the human and the non-human. Only minds within minds, a myriad of interlacing networks, to recall Bateson.

More than anything else, I conclude that the women interviewed, along with other "ecofeminist" sojourners, are finding a deep sense of belonging—of intimacy and participation—with the Earth and the entire Cosmos. **This is the shift:** we belong to a larger, greater self than our current flesh and bones configuration. Indigenous peoples have always known this intuitively; the "new science" is now telling us the same thing empirically; while Jungian psychology charts the same conclusion from the deep wells of the collective unconscious. Gebara reminds us of our relationality: everything is related to everything else and nothing is independent. We are one interconnected web with all and in all.

Shifting cosmology

If ever there was a clear-cut conclusion it is that the all-powerful, omnipotent God the Father of yesteryear is no longer a valid god-image for both the women interviewed and for those who identify with deep ecology, ecofeminist and feminist thought. Not only is this image not valid, it is considered a major obstacle—indeed, a cause—for our current ecological crisis. The essential flaw in our Judeo-Christian heritage is the belief in a monotheistic, personal male deity, creator of a universe that is clearly distinct from him. As Thomas Berry pointed out, our religious tradition has taught us that we could have direct communication from this supreme personal deity, who later appeared in human form as teacher and savior. This tradition holds that the entire human community is being led to fulfillment in a divine kingdom, a kingdom with a millennial fulfillment here on earth in historical time and a post-historical fulfillment in an eternal transcendental mode of being (heaven). Berry argues that because we see ourselves as transcendent beings, we have a hard time believing that we really belong to the earth, that we are indeed "earthlings". This, he stresses over and over again, is a deeply ingrained pathology and has led to an understanding of ourselves as having a destiny beyond that of the earth and has given us permission to use the earth as we see fit.[2]

Gebara echoes Berry's critique of Christianity's monolithic, all-powerful god-image. She argues against a personal God because if God were a person, God would be an autonomous being, which supports the patriarchal concept of God who is "above" and "over" life itself. For

Gebara, an anthropomorphic and anthropocentric God became a necessity within the psychological structure that evolved throughout the history of patriarchal culture. The need to affirm a higher power as being in ***discontinuity*** with all the powers of the cosmos, the earth, human beings, animals, plants, and even life itself appears to be of fundamental importance in maintaining the hierarchical organization of the society in which we live. She also reminds us that questions about God are really questions about ourselves. We set up pure and perfect beings to contrast them with our own experiences of impurity and imperfection. We set up powerful beings to contrast them with our own fragility and weakness.[3]

But because our understanding of ourselves is changing, because we are evolving a different anthropology of what it means to be a human being, so too are we changing our intuitions about our origins and our destiny (cosmology). In must remembered, of course, that a cosmology is both a metaphysical term dealing with theories surrounding the nature of the universe and a scientific term which addresses the origin, structure and space-time relationships of the universe. Many, but certainly not all of us humans, look for a religious meaning of life that leads us toward finding a sacred meaning in our cosmologies. As Gebara reminds us, "a cosmology has to do with our collective representations regarding the origin of the world, of the human, etc. It is larger than the sacred. The sacred comes into play as something that gives a construct of meaning to a specific group in a specific historical moment. It is we who define the Cosmos as sacred, but not everyone is comfortable with the word 'sacred'."[4]

The interviewees as well as a growing number of ecofeminists at this time in history are certainly defining the Cosmos as sacred. The older, patriarchal images to define or describe the sacred are swiftly becoming outworn vestiges of another time. The god-images of the interviewees are clearly shifting from a deity somehow outside and above the created universe, to a sense of something within yet beyond; a relationship that holds everything together. To describe this changing view of their god-images, they used words such as: Energy, Presence, Wisdom, Matrix,

Complementarity, Memory, Intuitive Space, Greater Reality, Envelopment, Fountain of life. All talked of *experiencing* this energy rather than being able to define it.

Although several used the image of goddess (Aga, Gladys), their claiming the feminine principle in Ultimate Mystery is seen as a corrective rather than a literal return to goddess worship. However, women such as those interviewed are comfortable invoking the Pachamama, Gaia, or *Madre Tierra* as root images for the deity. Many spoke of finding divinity in the natural world, of feeling part of the web of life that pulsates at the heart of the Cosmos. Silvia and Clara Luz are attracted to the Condomblé and Santaria communities because of the link with Nature of these Afro-Brazilian and Afro-Cuban religions. When they participate in their rituals, they feel a certain "coming home".

Some are clearly pantheistic or pan-en-theistic, while at least one (Graciela) still hold out for a superior being and is comfortable with parental images. I conclude that the immanent/transcendent debate reflects patriarchal dualist thinking and that the women interviewed and most ecofeminists embrace immanence as understanding that we are *part of* the earth, which is part of an ever-expanding universe. There is no "outside". I suspect many would agree with Rosemary Radford Ruether who imagines God as the font from which plants and animals well up in each generation; the matrix that sustains and renews their life-giving interdependency. Ruether argues that transcendence-immanence has been understood for too long in dualistic terms of either-or, mind-body, male-female splits. She sees transcendence not as a concept that implies a God who is a male disembodied mind outside the universe, but as a renewing divine Spirit radically free from our systems of domination, yet closer to us than we are to ourselves.[5]

The shift taking place in cosmology is nowhere more evident than in the interviewees' beliefs about death and resurrection. The majority view death and life not as separate, but as part of the same cycle. They speak of returning to that primal energy, that original goodness from which they came. Most reflected a deep peace about returning to this "matrix," to being dissolved into the Earth as a "coming home". Marcia, Alcira and Sandra Duarte have all lost parents recently and spoke of how the deaths of these loved ones have convinced them that a deep connection continues. They speak of memory—how those dearly loved are present in the memories we have of them. This seems to be the sense of "ancestrality" that several mentioned (Sandra Raquew, Silvia), which is understood as a connectedness to those who have gone before. These loved ones no longer live on individually in some other domain; they live on in the collective unconscious of the species, in our gene pool, in the very characteristics that make us kin—a certain laugh, a way of walking, a gesture. As Alcira puts it in describing her mother: "She is alive in all those kind ways she marked my life. It is based on this experience that I can say that I have felt resurrection in life. She is present in the music she liked, the food she cooked, all the advice she gave me over the years, in the garden she planted."

Gebara, the region's leading ecofeminist voice, also talks about returning to the Earth, "to a Living Body in transformation which is mortal and yet open to endless possibilities." She tells us that she prefers "for my last sigh and my last repose, the arms of the Earth—which, according to the Book of Genesis, is the place where God walks. Beyond what is imagined by reason, there is something imagined by desire, poetry, beauty."[6]

An expanding definition of the self as part of a larger whole is part and parcel of this emerging cosmology. Our body doesn't decay while our soul sours off to some eternal abode which patriarchy has told us was our "true home". No. Our very innards tell us that we share the same fate as all earthlings: we return to Earth. **This is the shift in cosmology.** Our individual ego disappears and merges again with the Great Self from which it came. We return to what Bohm called the "folding and unfolding universe," to what Bateson called "the pattern that connects," to what Berry called "the dream of the earth," to what Jung called the "collective unconscious," to what the original peoples of the earth called "the Great Spirit," to what I would call "sustaining wisdom,"[7] to what many ecofeminists would call primal energy.

Shifting epistemology

Nowhere is the shift to a post-patriarchal way of being more visible than in the way the women interviewed perceive, or "know" (epistemology). **The body and bodily experience become the *locus* for understanding, for feeling both pleasure and pain, for judging right and wrong.** The body—not in the abstract, but in our women's sexual, sensual, abused and wounded bodies—is where the interviewees construct their cosmologies and theologies, their ethics and their spiritual practices. This emphasis on the body is clearly a reaction to millennia of patriarchal oppression where women's bodies were seen as property to be used and dominated as a receptacle to reproduce the species, and to centuries of Judeo-Christian teaching where women were seen as the cause of humanity's Fall from grace and thus the font of evil, temptation and concupiscence. So much of feminist and ecofeminist insistence that we do theology from the body is an angry reaction to layers of patriarchal domination and a burning desire to cut through all the dualisms that split mind, spirit and the soul from the body. Not just the interviewees, but multitudes of women throughout Latin America are reclaiming their bodies as sacred, as a source of holiness. This emphasis is righting a long-overdue imbalance where men/mind/spirit were considered superior to women/body/materiality.

Where the women I interviewed made a major contribution to "how we know" was during the workshop with Ivone Gebara when genital embodiedness became a theological category to unmask patriarchy. All of us recognized how patriarchy has extolled the grandeur of rational thought and the insignificance of sex and the sordidness of genitality, especially female genitality. Indeed, the more the rational mind has been elevated and the spirit hailed as supreme, the more genital sex has become the object of forbidden desire, the object of lust, war and rape. It dawned on all of us during our workshop that the denial of genitality as a human attribute capable of beauty and freedom is clearly linked to an asexual image of the divine and is grounded in a dualistic understanding of life. The patriarchal God of the Bible seems to take a stand against genitality, especially feminine genitality. He exerts power over women and condemns our genitality as if it were the place of absolute transgression, of ultimate disobedience and that space where women somehow competed with Him. As a result, women have felt guilty about simply being genital and hide this guilt under the weight of sin, whether or not our genital experiences were pleasurable or whether we repressed pleasure. Retrieving our genital selves can be a major step in the process of healing and of moving beyond our current patriarchal culture, a step toward redeeming our libidos and our self-esteem.

This is a bold and new affirmation in the evolution of feminist and ecofeminist theology in Latin America and may be the most original contribution of this study. I was taken by surprise by the direction of the workshop's reflection, but now, in retrospect, I see that it is precisely this "lower" side—our menstruating, nursing, secreting woman selves—that patriarchy and patriarchal religion had to control and repress because it reminded humans of our true nature, our earthiness, our materiality.

A return to the body as the locus for our theology, ethics and spirituality does not, however, concentrate exclusively on "my" body. As eco/feminists move into a larger understanding of who we are as humans and joyfully embrace our inner and outer cosmic journeys, our sense of the borders of our own bodies fades. As the intuition of being "earthling of Earth" seeps in, as we delve into the revelation that we are clusters of energy bound for a moment in this particular body called Doris, or Fanny, or Ivone or Judy—then a sense of great communion invades our hearts—not only for those of our own species but for other members of the earth community. And for fleeting moments or for a lifetime we can enter into their pain, their pleasure, their anguish and their joy. When this communion is felt, we know we are much more than an individual ego; we are part of a 15 billion-year-old unfolding cosmogenesis.

Ethical implications

The hallmark of patriarchy is its ability to establish what is right and wrong and to punish wrongdoers. Under patriarchy, normative behavior is established by outside authorities, usually male, who decide what is orthodox and legitimate, what is allowed or forbidden. Therefore, as we move beyond patriarchy, we must evolve a new ethics. The women in my study all call for a new ethics based on the experiences of their own bodies, with all of its accumulated history, wisdom and longings. Starting from the body, then, is essential. And because ethical decisions will be made based on one's own experience, they will be contextualized, pluralistic and respectful of diversity. Such ethical decisions cannot be based exclusively on universal, unchanging law.

This said, how do we establish limits as we struggle toward a post-patriarchal ethics? What criteria can be established to govern our actions and desires? As we struggled with the question of "limits" during the workshop, we realized that we couldn't deny the heritage of the past or turn a blind eye to efforts toward justice and compassion present throughout patriarchal history. We do not pretend to be more ethical or moral than other periods of history.

An ecofeminist ethics would involve calling forth respect and responsibility from each and from all—and seeing the human in relation to the rest of the Earth community and to the unfolding universe. We are part of a greater body and therefore must take account of repercussions to the whole in making ethical decisions. This then becomes a major guideline. Emphasis is placed on those community spaces where listening to the experience and wisdom of the group becomes important to allow decisions to be made freely.

As Doris Muñoz so tellingly pointed out in her interview, the challenge coming from ecofeminism is precisely to promote a more integrated view of life, so that every decision is made with the focus of promoting more equitable relations that do not continue to crystallize domination over the weak and voiceless, including the entire life community and the

Earth itself. She says that "it is within this integrity where I believe we can pay attention to what our bodies are saying and can hold conversations with those we trust to get advice about a pending decision. Here the question of power is key. I am talking about "power with", not "power over" or outside me. If I am going to make a decision or share my deepest experiences, I'm not going to go to persons I don't even know or are going to ask me very intimate questions and perhaps "condemn" me *apriori*. No. I'm going to go to a friend or group of friends who listen to me, ask questions to help me clarify things, but in the end, it is I who make the decision, because I am the only one who knows how this decision is going to affect my history, my body. That is why the challenge is to create spaces where we women can share our power and help each other to make decisions, but not make them for the other. If we are able to return to people their power to decide according to their own conscience, this will transform ethics and give us back responsibility over our lives as adults."

Embracing a post-patriarchal ethics does not attempt to bring about an earth without evil. Both the women interviewed and ecofeminists in general are groping toward ways of living and being that are healthier for our planet and for us, but we have no blueprint. As Sandra Duarte points out: "today people are looking for meaning and not for an ethics. They are seeking those symbolic elements that will give them answers for immediate needs. Ethical questions always come later. I sense that currently we are at a moment when we need new ethical constructions—a new global ethics. We need to search for ways to build an ethics that evolves with people's aspirations." Ethical postures flow from our utopian visions; they are the concrete ways—the disciplines and practices—that we suspect will lead us toward those visions and dreams, and as such, are always derivative. Therefore, I again conclude, that with a changing sense of who we are (anthropology) and from whence we come and wither we go (cosmology), so too will our ethical practices be transformed.

It is here where we can find relevance in the life of Jesus of Nazareth and his project for a different world. Most of the women interviewed as well as Christian ecofeminists find value in the Christian experience, in the values of the Jesus movement, although they are critical of the patriarchal way these values have been communicated throughout history. No one says they are post-Christian; Jesus continues to be a major historical figure, a prophet and wisdom figure to whom we can turn for inspiration. For some, Jesus is the archetype of the good and just man, which is why he remains relevant and attractive as a human being. Moreover, Jesus was totally counter-cultural for his times. An authentic earthling, he exemplified "power within" and "power with" in an extraordinary way but in the end was felled by the same "power over" system that has all of us entrapped in its snare. I conclude, then, that Jesus will continue to be a major reference point as we grope toward a post-patriarchal time. But he will be one of several reference points.

Emerging spiritual practice

Nothing captures the shift I am documenting more than the way women are watering their evolving intuitions about who they are and what they perceive life's meaning to be. First of all, it becomes clear from the interviews that these twelve women are no longer nourished by the liturgies and worship services offered by their churches. Although some like Silvia can find a communal connection in both a Mennonite liturgy and in a Catholic Mass and Graciela continues to find community in her CEB, others (Aga, Alcira, Gladys) have simply stopped participating in the worship services of their traditions because of their patriarchal language and content.

Yet while participation in official church worship wanes, a veritable "boom" in women's rituals and celebrations is taking place all over Latin America—and most of the women interviewed are actively involved both in creating, convoking and participating in these celebrations. The hallmark of these rituals is celebrating with one's whole body—through movement and dance. And what is being celebrated? Life—their own lives, the lives of loved ones, of other women, of those suffering, the lives of their ancestors. Connection— to each other, to their own bioregion, to the seasonal cycles, to the elements, to the Earth itself and to the entire Cosmos. Dreams—their own, the community's, the planet's. Many of these rituals are inspired by indigenous cosmologies. (Alcira, Fanny, Marcia and Sandra Duarte all express their connection to these spiritualities.) The remarkable creativity present in these rituals appears to have released a bottled-up longing to get out of our heads, and celebrate wholly and freely with our entire bodies. Doris sums up what is happening: "It is my whole being that celebrates now, not just my spirit."

These women are also nurturing their spirituality through the practice of contemplation and meditation. They have moved on from traditional forms of meditation taught by Christian theology, although some still reflect on biblical passages. The great shift here is that all now turn to the natural world to find their peace, to renew their beings. Gladys climbs Mount Avila everyday. Alcira has an uncanny relationship with trees and communes with them throughout the seasons. Doris and Coca do body movement such as Tai Chi to connect with the Cosmos. Fanny gardens. Sandra Raquew paints, colors and takes photos of Nature. Without exception, all of the women interviewed speak of the natural world as the font of their spirituality. Contact with sensuality—poetry, color, music—as well as with the pain of the other, is also an essential element in this evolving spirituality.

Another source of spirituality is friendship and community—spaces for sharing heart joys and heart sorrows. Circles of (usually only) women are sprouting up everywhere and have become spaces of freedom and healing. Sandra Raquaw's experience is common: "My feminist theology collective Chimalman, is a fundamental source of sustenance for me. Together we cultivate seeds of new beliefs and values for ourselves. This is our space, the place where we can feel accepted, where we can think, share and celebrate together. The Sacred for me takes place in sharing, in sharing our experiences with others who also share their life journeys. In these moments, I know I am not alone."

However, when these circles of friendship do not exist, women on a post-patriarchal journey express deep loneliness. One of the outcomes of the workshop was the discovery that "we are not alone," "we are in good company" and are committed to form a community "a la distancia." Post-modern realists, all promised to nurture and support the circle through e-mail correspondence.

In my opinion, Clara Luz crystallizes this quiet revolution in women's spirituality taking place in the region:

> I connect with the deep in many different ways. Through strong feelings related to friendship, love, passion, joy, anger, impotence. Through those pleasurable movements of my body when I dance, when I hug someone, when I caress, when I make love. Through contact with Nature—the perfume of the flowers, the smell of the sea, the sound of the rain on my windowpane, the sound of the breeze at sunset. When I do Tai Chi, when I swim in the sea, when I meditate in my favorite corner surrounded by trees and flowers, when I can contemplate the sea or the river from afar. I also connect with the deep in the warmth of the company of my children, through the laughter and pure gaze of my granddaughter, through the love of my husband and of my parents. Through the friendship and warmth of friends, or when I hear a lovely melody or taste a rich cup of chocolate or enjoy a tasty meal; when I can extend a helping hand to someone in need, or when someone gives me a hand in tough moments; when I experience deeply the sufferings of others as a result of injustice and impotence that I want to sob with rage; when I hurt with the cry of the children and all victims of the disorders of our world; when I am able to perceive the pain of others as my own pain.

What Clara Luz describes here is also what Gebara attempts to communicate in her Preface to Lluvia para florecer, as we leave sacred space defined by patriarchy. The Sacred, she reminds us, in not "something" in itself, but a situation, a relation, a happening that takes us beyond ourselves. It is an experience of "going deep".

Relationship with liberation theology

As I write this, Doris Muñoz and I are participating in a workshop here in Santiago on gender and liberation theology with Diego Irarrazaval, one of Latin America's leading liberation theologians and the current President of the Ecumenical Association of Third World Theologians (EATWOT). Doris and I were invited to challenge liberation theology from the perspective of Latin American feminist and ecofeminist theology. (We presented the three stages of feminist theology, and then concentrated on the third phase where ecofeminism comes to center stage. I used the "genealogy" chart presented in Chapter II to explain the sources of ecofeminism.) Other sessions included talks on patriarchy and on the new masculinity. In the workshop's opening session, Irarrazaval spoke frankly about the "black holes" present in liberation theology, especially sexuality. He admitted what Finnish feminist theologian Elina Vuola found in her study—that liberation theologians have simply not taken seriously the sufferings of poor women with regard to their sexual and reproductive rights. He also talked openly about liberation theology's fear of sexuality and his own dawning realization of the link between sexuality and spirituality. Irarrazaval admits that he is quite alone in his raising the sexuality-spirituality connection, and mentions Leonardo Boff as the exception. I suspect that Irarrazaval and Boff represent one side of a growing debate within Latin American liberation theology—which is encouraging from the point of view of the region's eco/feminist theologians.

That said, however, in the workshop with the interviewees and Gebara, dialoguing with liberation theology was simply not a priority. In my original hypothesis for this research I had hoped that my work might trigger a more serious dialogue between liberation theology and emerging ecofeminist thought in Latin America. But to my surprise, there was simply no interest or energy for such a dialogue on the part of the interviewees. While all admit their origins in liberation theology, the women I gathered together simply did not see the point in debating liberation theology—either point by point, or in general.

I conclude from these two experiences (the workshop with Irarrazaval and the workshop with the interviewees), that liberation theology is not a major interlocutor vis-à-vis the road we are traveling. Liberation theology is not "the enemy," as we move into the future. Indeed, we are grateful to our liberation theologian friends for uncovering the region's structures of oppression and reflecting on them theologically. We recognize our roots here. But if José Comblin is right in his analysis, liberation theology is stagnating at this point in its development. With the fall of historical socialism, it has lost its utopian vision and has not yet found a dream (except that of "resistance") to warm our hearts and kindle our spirits, as once it did. Perhaps if liberation theologians begin to change their understanding of anthropology and cosmology, as well as learn from the wisdom of the body, they too might develop post-patriarchal yearnings. At the moment, however, most liberation theologians are "stuck" in patriarchy and the women I interviewed—whom I consider an accurate sample of what is happening to an increasing number of women leaders in Latin America—are simply not interested in the dialogue and are moving on.

Challenges to ministry

What does all this mean for me pastorally? After all, I am a Catholic missionary and a Catholic theologian who struggles daily to insist that I am not post-Christian, but only post-patriarchal! I am no psychologist, but with age have come both wisdom and grace. I perceive that our great trauma at this stage of our evolution is our narrow sense of who we are. Within patriarchy, our identity has been so limited to the individual ego that we have lost our sense of resting in the security of a much larger and grander self. My personal vocation, at this stage, is to try to convey to my small circle of influence that, indeed, we are "stardust contemplating the stars."

Because of this narrow understanding of who we are, we gage everything in terms of "power over". Where do I fit on the totem pole? Who holds the power and how can I get my share of that power? Within patriarchy, it is that "power" that gives me my sense of security and worth.

And yet, it wasn't always so. At an earlier pre-patriarchal time in our evolution, our identity was that of the tribe, the clan. We were kin to all and saw our individual selves only in relation to the larger group, which gave us our sense of belonging. As Paleolithic and Neolithic women and men, we were part of and communed deeply with the entire Earth community. The patriarchal "interlude" of the past 5,000 years has skewed that sense of kinship. But as we move toward the uncharted waters of post-patriarchal times, an expanded sense of Self is key. Cultivation of a sense of belonging to an amazing process of "folding and unfolding" is essential if we humans are to find a new yet ancient sense of security. We are not of value because of the power we hold, or because of the possessions we have. Our value, our worth, our ecstasy lies in the overwhelming realization that we form part of the "dream of the universe" that has been present from the beginning of time.

Teilhard de Chardin once said that the greatest discovery of the modern period has been the discovery of evolution. Evolution can be understood as a continual awakening, an ever more complex process of transformation, a groping toward a future horizon of possibility that was present since the beginning of the universe.

I know that simply by laying bare the aberration of patriarchy we will not move forward to create something different. The universe, the Earth, our earthling selves only evolve because of a dream, a vision, an intimation of what could be that captivates the imagination and energizes us to look for new ways of being and becoming.

And so, my ministry, my pastoral call, my vocation is to remind us of who we really are! To tell the "New Story" coming from quantum physics; to invite us to reconnect with our collective unconsciousness and to discover that in a very real way we always were—and always will be. I want to foster new relations based on "power within" and "power with," which should flow out of the realization that we belong to a greater self and that the underlying net that holds us all in one tight-woven web is relationship.

I want to convince everyone I can of the wisdom of the seed, ecofeminism's primary metaphor. The seed sprouts, grows to fruition, flowers, bears fruit, withers, dies and returns to the earth to begin the process once again. The seed will be what it is meant to be, nothing more, nothing less, enriching the entire earth community. We, like seeds, must be what we are meant to be. Can we not change our mindsets to understand ourselves as each having a unique contribution in our time— and that I will blossom forth fully only when others also sprout and bear fruit as they were meant to? This shift in consciousness would show the lie to patriarchal competition and control and move us toward celebrating complementarity and diversity.

And how shall I convince us of our grandeur? Of course through teaching and writing. But primarily through convoking and creating new rituals that celebrate who we are. I completely identify with the growing circle of madwomen, juicy crones, recycled hippies, or just weird old women who lead the dance! I am one of them.

As I conclude this dissertation, the Twin Towers, symbol of mighty U.S. capitalism, have gone up in smoke. Stock markets around the world are crashing because of revelations of corporate accounting manipulations reflecting untold greed. A U.S. bomber has just killed more than a hundred people at a wedding in Afghanistan on the pretext that they were shooting anti-artillery guns, which later turned out to be fireworks. Israel has invaded Palestine and holds Palestinian cities hostage. India and Pakistan up the ante in their threats of nuking each other. Argentina, the most developed of Latin American countries, is suddenly in ruins because of large-scale corruption. The Catholic Church is wracked by scandals of pedophilia in the United States, Italy, Ireland and here in Chile while in Africa the sexual abuse by priests of nuns has come to light. Perhaps the patriarchal constructs of centuries are beginning to fall like a pack of cards.

But perhaps not. We have been mistaken before at the tenacity of capitalism, the latest manifestation of patriarchy. But the task is to push forward with new alternatives, so than when the four horsemen of the plagues again arrive and there are collapses and depressions and famines and wars, there are also islands of possibility sprouting forth from the ashes—organic farms, ecological learning centers, post-patriarchal communities that chug away in season and out.

"Our hearts are restless until they rest in Thee"—a saying by my old archenemy St. Augustine. And yet I agree with him—except we disagree on our understanding of the "Thee". For Augustine, he would be returning to his God the Father. For Judy Ress, I will be returning to the Earth, good earthling that I am. The other day my eldest son Peter cryptically remarked that we humans are not really happy being humans and long to get back to where we came from. I recall Aga's reflection on death as that moment when "some great desire is fulfilled" and Ivone's "beyond what is imagined by reason, there is something imagined by desire, poetry, beauty."

Desire. Imagination. Utter longing. That is who we are. Or, in one of my more poetic moments, I described the whole shebang as "Surprise without End," with which I close this work, hoping that with the vision expressed herein, the people will not perish.

Surprise without end

Mary Judith Ress

The universe is full of surprises. Indeed, it is continuous creativity, surprise without end. And you and I form part of it all.

You were there and I was there when the universe burst forth some 15 billion years ago in one great flaring forth. Energy, fire, light and heat radiated in every direction creating the universe, time and space. All that one day would come into existence was present in that first flaring forth—the galaxies, stars, planets, oceans, mountains, trees, ants and elephants. Buddha, Jesus, Teresa of Avila, Montezuma, Sor Juana Inez de la Cruz, you and I—all were present in the energy of that first unimaginable first moment.

You were there and I was there during the following billions of years of fecund night when atoms joined together to become first hydrogen and then helium.

You were there and I was there when in an instant during that fecund night, the universe in another great burst of creativity birthed more than 100 billion galaxies—among them our own relatively insignificant Milky Way. Each galaxy had its own inner dynamics, each in its turn created millions and millions of stars.

You were there and I was there when some five billion years ago, in a corner of the Milky Way, our own star was born from the stardust of the explosion of a supernova. Once born, our sun demonstrated the same self-organizing principles present in the entire universe and created its own system of planets, including our own dear planet earth.

You were there and I was there when the earth mixed within its womb, minerals, gases and liquids from which was brought to birth, some four billion years later, the first tiny cell. With the passage of time, these cells learned to remember, to join together, to adapt. And in a great leap of creativity, they learned to "eat" the sun's energy! To reproduce themselves, they invented sex, and by learning to eat one another, they invented death.

You were there and I was there when, some 600 million years ago, a fantastic array of multicelular organisms was born: worms, corals, insects, crabs, starfish, sponges, spiders, vertebrates of every sort! Worms learned to crawl while other beings developed wings. Some invented teeth while others invented shells.

You were there and I was there during the following millennium when ocean waves washed up some sea plants among the rocks. These plants learned to live along the seacoasts. Little by little, some of these plants became trees and soon the continents were roaring with green life.

You were there and I was there when the sea creatures followed the plants onto the land. During the next several millennia, amphibians, reptiles and insects of all kinds inhabited the continents, including the dinosaurs.

And you were there and I was there when some 67 million years ago, a great astronomic collision changed the earth's atmosphere to such a degree that almost all the forms of animal life had to reinvent themselves or disappear. This destruction also opened new possibilities: the birds and the mammals—which were not able to develop in the presence of the dinosaurs—now flourished as a result of this so-called disaster.

You were there and I was there when the mammals, now a permanent presence on earth, some 60 million years ago began to develop emotional sensitivity—a new ability of the nervous system to feel the universe in a new way. Beauty as well as terror of the world became deeply encrusted in the mammalian psyche, including that of the human. In some rare occasions, especially among the primates, this emotional sensitivity combined with the neural ability of consciousness to be conscious of itself—which was the case of the human animal.

You were there and I was there when some four million years ago, our ancestors stood up on two feet; when some two million years ago, we began to use our hands to mold tools from the earth and to harness fire; when some 35,000 years ago, we arrived at a new level of consciousness that we expressed in dance and music, in celebrating the changing seasons of the year, in burying our loved ones who died; when, some 20,000 years ago we began a cycle of domestication of plants and animals which also domesticated us. Slowly, we abandoned our hunting and gathering lifestyle of our tribes and clans and began to settle down and grow food.

You were there and I was there when, with our food supply more secure, we began to live in villages. In this new context we were able to develop ceramics, weaving, architecture. We could build temples and perform rites to the Great Mother. Between 10,000 and 5.000 years ago, we created the structures of language, religion, cosmology and art that would define human civilization until the present time.

You were there and I was there when some 5000 years ago, we began establishing the great urban civilizations as humanity's new centers of power. Babylon, Paris, Rome, Jerusalem, Athens, Cairo, Mecca, Delhi, Teotiatlan, Cusco. These great cities were characterized by their hierarchical relationships and for their emphasis on specialization and the division of labor. An era of many transformations: rivers and seas would now be navigated and used as trade routes; forests and minerals could be exploited as natural resources. In this stage, human civilization increased in number and in wealth; we built great cathedrals, palaces and temples. To defend this wealth, we developed military force with arms that became ever more sophisticated. War became chronic. The Great Mother of Neolithic times who was so identified with agriculture was replaced by a Father God who, like the king, ruled from on high.

You were there and I was there when during the 19th and 20th centuries, we have evolved the nation state with is mystique of nationalism, progress, democratic freedoms and individual rights to private property and economic gain. When we developed tremendous power in the areas of science, technology and economics to the point where—as a species—we can control the very process of the earth itself and use it for our own good.

Chapter V / Clues for Transformation: Reflections, Conclusions...

You were there and I was there when only recently in the last few years we are discovering that the universe is not a "place", a backdrop for the stage upon which the human acts, but an evolutionary community continually birthing ever more complex life forms.

You are here and I am here when life itself is forcing us to remember what is stored in our body's memory, what our genes have always known: that nothing exists, or has existed or will exist for its own sake. Nothing exists without the rest. We are a link in a chain of DNA that is at every moment reshaping and transforming itself.

Let us remember well: **you were there and I was there** in the fireball at the beginning of the universe; then in the galaxies, then, in the planets, then in the wiggle of the worm, in the flight of the bird, in the broad-reaching branches of the Araucaria tree, in the first human who stood up on two feet and used her hands to start fire, then as a member of the tribe collecting fruit in the forest, then in the village taking part in the fertility rites to the Great Mother and then in the city dominated by the cathedral where we went to pray to God the Father.

And finally, if the earth's journey continues—and oh how we pray that it will!—**you will be there and I will be there** in those beings who will come after us who will "reach out their hands and touch the stars". We will be in those forms of life that come after us, who without a doubt will be more complex than the human species and will discover ways of being more intimately in communion than we have known. New surprises in this cosmic dance of Surprise Without End.

[1] Un published poem that I found in Madonna's notebook at the time of her death in Chile in January, 2000. The poem is entitled *Ularu,* after the aborigine sacred rock in Australia.
[2] Berry. *The Dream of the Earth*, p. 81.
[3] Gebara, *Longing for Running Water.* pp. 101, 111-112.
[4] Gebara. Letter to me, offering suggestions and corrections to original thesis text.
[5] Ruether. *Gaia and God*, pp. 252-253.
[6] Gebara. *Out of the Depths*, pp. 150-151.
[7] Mary Judith Ress, *Sustaining Wisdom: An ecofeminist renaming of Ultimate Meaning.* Unpublished manuscript.

Bibliography

Adams, Carol, ed. *Ecofeminism and the Sacred*. New York: Continuum, 1993

Aquino, Pilar. *Our Cry for Life*. Maryknoll: Orbis Books, 1990.

Bateson, Gregory. *Steps to an Ecology of Mind*. New York: Ballantine, 1972.

Berman, Morris. *The Reenchantment of the World*. New York: Bantam, 1984.

Berry, Thomas. *The Dream of the Earth*. San Francisco: Sierra Club, 1988.

_____. *The Great Work: Our way into the Future*. New York: Bell Tower, 1999.

Berry, Thomas and Brian Swimme. *The Universe Story*. HarperSanFrancisco: 1992.

Biehl, Janet. *Rethinking Ecofeminist Politics*. Boston: South end Press, 1991.

Boff, Leonardo. *Cry of the Earth. Cry of the Poor*. Maryknoll: Orbis Books, 1995.

Canadian Ecumenical Jubilee Initiative. *Sacred Earth, Sacred Community: Jubilee, Ecology and Aboriginal Peoples*. Toronto: 2000.

Capra, Fritjof. *The Web of Life*. San Francisco: Anchor, 1996.

Clifford, Anne M. *Introducing Feminist Theology*. Maryknoll: Orbis Books, 2001.

Comblin, Jose. *Called for Freedom: The Changing Context of Liberation Theology*. Maryknoll: Orbis Books, 1998.

Con-spirando: Revista Latinoamericana de ecofeminiismo, espiritualidad y teologia. Santiago, Chile: Issues 1 through current (1992-).

Colectivo Con-spirando: *Diosas y arquetipos: En memoria de Madonna Kolbenschlag*. Santiago: Con-spirando, 2000.

Daly, Mary. *Outercourse: The Be-dazzling Voyage*. HarperSanFrancisco: 1992.

Davies, Paul. *The Mind of God*. New York: Simon & Schuster, 1992.

_____. *The 5th Miracle: The Search for the Origin and Meaning of Life*. New York: Simon & Schuster. 1999.

Diamond, Irene and Gloria F. Orenstein, eds. *Reweaving the World: The Emergence of Ecofeminism.* San Francisco: Sierra Club Books, 1990.

Eisler, Riane. *Sacred Pleasure: Sex, Myth and the Politics of the Body.* New York: HarperCollins, 1995.

Ellacuria, Ignacio and Jon Sobrino, eds. *Mysterium Liberationis: Fundamental Concepts in Liberation Theology.* Maryknoll: Orbis Books, 1993.

Ellis, Marc H. and Oto Maduro, eds. *Expanding the View: Gustavo Gutierrez and the Future of Liberation Theology.* Maryknoll: Orbis Books, 1988.

Gebara, Ivone. *Longing for Running Water: Ecofeminism and Liberation.* Minneapolis: Fortress Press, 1999.

_____. *Out of the Depths: Evil and Salvation in a Feminist Perspective.* Minneapolis: Fortress Press, 2002.

Gimbutas, Marija. *The Civilization of the Goddess: The World of Old Europe*, Joan Marler, ed. HarperSanFrancisco: 1991.

Hollis, James. *The Archetypal Imagination.* Texas: A&M University Press, 2000.

Irarrazaval, Diego. *Inculturation: New Dawn of the Church in Latin America.* Maryknoll: Orbis, Books, 2000.

Johnson, Elisabeth. *She Who Is: The Mystery of God in Feminist Theological Discourse.* New York: Crossroad, 1992.

Jung, Carl. *Man and his Symbols.* New York: Doubleday & Company, 1964.

_____. *Memories, Dreams and Reflections.* Aniela Jaffe, ed.. New York: Vintage Books, 1965.

Kolbenschlag, Madonna. *Eastward Toward Eve.* HarperSanFrancisco: 1997.

Korten, David. *When Corporations Rule the World.* West Hartford: Berrett-Koehler Publications/Kumarian Press, 1996.

Latinamerica Press/Noticias Aliadas. Lima, Peru:1982 to present.

"The Legacy of Marija Gimbutas." (various authors) in *Journal of Feminist Studies of*

Religion. Vol. 12, No. 2 (Fall, 1996).

MacGillis, Miriam. "Genesis Farm links holistic living with envisioning a new world order," in *IDOC Internazionale,* Rome. (July-August, 1990).

MacKinnon, Mary Heather and Moni McIntyre, eds. *Readings in Ecology and Feminist Theology.* Kansas City: Sheed and Ward, 1995.

Macy, Joanna. *World as Lover, World as Self.* Berkley, CA.: Parallaz Press, 1981.

Maturana, Humberto and Francisco Varela. *The Tree of Knowledge.* Boston: Shambala, 1987.|

McFague, Sallie. *Models of God: Theology for an Ecological Age.* Philadelphia: Fortress Press, 1987.

_____. *The Body of God: An Ecological Theology.* Minneapolis: Fortress Press, 1993.

_____. *Super, Natural Christians.* Minneapolis: Fortress Press, 1997.

Mellor, Mary. *Feminism & Ecology.* New York: New York University Press, 1997.

Merchant, Carolyn. *The Death of Nature: Women, Ecology and the Scientific Revolution.* San Francisco: Harper and Row, 1980.

_____. *Radical Ecology: The Search for a Livable World.* New York-London: Routledge, 1992.

Mies, Maria and Vandana Shiva. *Ecofeminism.* London: Zed Books, 1993.

Nacashima Brock, Rita. *Journeys by Heart: A Christology of Erotic Power.* New York: Crossroad, 1991.

O'Murchu, Diarmuid. *Quantum Theology: Spiritual Implications of the New Physics.* New York: Crossroad, 1998.

_____. *Reclaiming Spirituality.* New York: Crossroad, 1998.

_____. *Poverty, Celibacy and Obedience: A Radical Option for Life.* New York: Crossroads, 1999.

_____. *Religion in Exile.* New York: Crossroads, 2000.

Ortega, Ofelia, ed. *Women's Visions: Theological Reflection, Celebration, Action.* Geneva: WCC Publications, 1995.

Plant, Judith, ed. *Healing the Wounds: The Promise of Ecofeminism.* Philadelphia: New Society Publishers, 1989.

Ponting, Clive. *A Green History of the World.* New York: Penguin Books, 1991

Primavesi, Anne. *From Apocalypse to Genesis: Ecology, Feminism and Christianity.* Minneapolis: Fortress Press, 1991.

Rasmussen, Larry. *Earth Community, Earth Ethics.* Maryknoll: Orbis, 1996.

Ruether, Rosemary Radford. *Gaia and God: An Ecofeminist Theology of Earth Healing.* HarperSanFrancisco: 1992.

_____. *Women and Redemption: A Theological History.* Minneapolis: Fortress Press, 1998.

_____, ed. *Women Healing Earth: Third World Women on Ecology, Feminism and Religion.* Maryknoll: Orbis Books, 1996.

Sagan, Carl. *Cosmos.* New York: Ballantine Books, 1980.

Sahtoris, Elisabet. *Gaia: The Human Journey from Chaos to Cosmos.* London and New York: Pocket Books, 1989. .

Shiva, Vandana. *Staying Alive.* London, Zed Books, 1989.

Shlain, Leonard. *The Alphabet versus the Goddess.* New York: Penguin, 1998.

Souza, Sandra Duarte. "Ecofeminist Theory, Ethics and Spirituality: An Analysis of the Discourse" (Ph.D. dissertation in Portuguese, Sao Bernardo do Campo, Universidade Metodista de Sao Paulo, Brasil, 1999).

Spretnak, Charlene. *States of Grace: The Recovery of Meaning in the Post-Modern Age.* HarperSanFrancisco: 1991.

_____. *The Resurgence of the Real: Body, Nature and Place in a Hypermodern World.* San Francisco: Addison-Wesley, 1997.

Stevens, Dr. Anthony. *Archetypes: A Natural History of the Self.* New York: Quill, 1983.

Sturgeon, Noel. *Ecofeminist Natures: Race, Gender, Feminist theory and Political Action.* New York and London: Routledge, 1997.

Swimme, Brian. *The Earth's Imagination* (8-part video series). Mill Valley, CA: Center for the Story of the Universe, 1998.

_____. *The Canticle of the Cosmos* (12-part video series). Holy Names College, 1988.

Tamayo, Juan-Jose, and Juan Bosch, eds. *Panorama de la Teología Latinoamericana.* Navarra, España: Editorial Verbo Divino, 2001.

_____. *Palabras Claves sobre Jesús de Nazaret.* Navarra, España: Editorial Verbo Divino, 1999.

Tamez, Elsa. *La Sociedad que las mujeres soñamos.* San José, Costa Rica: DEI, 2001.

"Teología con Rostro de Mujer," *Alternativas, No. 16/17.* Managua: Editorial Lascasiana, 2000.

"Teología feminista desde América Latina," *Cristianismo y Sociedad 1998, No. 135-136.* Guayaquil, Ecuador: 1998.

"Teología latinoamericana: Evaluación, Retos y Perspectivas," Alternativas, No. 18/19, Managua: Editorial Lascasiana, 2001.

Vuola, Elina. *Limits of Liberation: Praxis as Method in Latin American Liberation Theology and Feminist Theology.* Helsinki: Suomalainen Tiedeakatemia, 1997.

Williams, Dolores. *Sisters in the Wilderness: The Challenge of Womanist God-talk.* Maryknoll: Orbis, 1991.